INTERVENTION OR NEGLECT

INTERVENTION OR NEGLECT

The United States and Central America Beyond the 1980s

LINDA ROBINSON

COUNCIL ON FOREIGN RELATIONS PRESS

NEW YORK

COUNCIL ON FOREIGN RELATIONS BOOKS

If you would like more information on Council publications, please write the Council on Foreign Relations, 58 East 68th Street, New York, NY 10021, or call the Publications Office at (212) 734-0400.

Library of Congress Cataloguing-in-Publication Data

Robinson, Linda, 1960–
    Intervention or neglect : the United States and Central America beyond the 1980s / Linda Robinson.
    p.   cm.
    Includes bibliographical references and index.
    ISBN 0-87609-097-8 : $14.95
    1. Central America—Politics and government—1979– 2. United States—Foreign relations—Central America. 3. Central America—Foreign relations—United States. I. Title.
F1439.5.R6 1991
327.728073–dc20
                                91–6276
                                CIP

92 93 94 95 96 97 PB 10 9 8 7 6 5 4 3 2

Cover Design: Whit Vye

CONTENTS

FOREWORD

Intervention or Neglect grew out of a Council on Foreign Relations study group on U.S. policy in Central America—defined broadly enough to include Panama—that concluded its formal meetings in the summer of 1989. The group was directed by Susan Kaufman Purcell, at the time the Council's senior fellow for Latin America and currently vice president for Latin American affairs at the Americas Society, and was chaired by George W. Landau, president of the Americas Society. Linda Robinson, a member of the study group (and senior editor at *Foreign Affairs*) was asked to write a comprehensive overview of political, economic, and diplomatic developments in the region during the preceding decade while paying particular attention to American involvement, U.S. policy priorities during the Reagan and Bush administrations, and Washington's realistic future options. During the late summer and early fall of 1989, the author traveled twice to the area, under the Council's auspices, to conduct field research and personal interviews with some of the leading figures in Nicaragua and elsewhere.

The completion—and projected publication date—of this volume was unavoidably delayed by such seminal developments as the dramatic thaw in Soviet-American relations, the U.S. invasion of Panama, and the surprising election results in Managua. Nevertheless, both the author and the Council felt that this delay allowed for a fuller exposition of the significance of these events.

The Council wishes to express its gratitude to Rita E. Hauser, whose decision to provide a generous grant towards the funding of a series of studies on the resolution of regional conflict made possible both the original study group sessions and the subsequent commissioning of this volume.

Nicholas X. Rizopoulos

March 1991

ACKNOWLEDGEMENTS

I would like to thank all the Latin Americans, of every political stripe, as well as the many experts here in the United States, who have generously shared with me their analyses and experiences of the fascinating, if tormented, countries of Central America and Panama. Were it not for James Chace, I would not have begun this project; and without the encouragement of William Hyland, and my other colleagues at *Foreign Affairs,* I would not have completed it. Thanks to Elise, Buzz, and other friends for their understanding. The members of the Council on Foreign Relations study group and its supportive leaders George Landau and Susan Kaufman Purcell added greatly to my own knowledge. Finally, I am indebted to Peter Tarnoff, Nicholas X. Rizopoulos, Linda Wrigley, and Carol Rath for the long hours they devoted to the manuscript.

Linda Robinson
Miami

1

INTRODUCTION: CHARTING A NEW COURSE IN CENTRAL AMERICA

February 25, 1990, election night in Nicaragua, was tense, as Nicaraguans, along with thousands of international observers and journalists, awaited announcement of the results that would shape the country's future. The ten-year-old Sandinista revolution, which had survived a U.S.–backed insurgency, was now facing the test of the ballot box. Hours passed, as the Supreme Electoral Council balked at announcing its preliminary tally at 9:30 as planned; it was waiting for the go-ahead from the governing Sandinista party. Meanwhile, former U.S. President Jimmy Carter, in Nicaragua as an official observer, was involved in delicate negotiations. Having received the results of the "quick count" conducted by the United Nations, he knew the Sandinista party was going down to defeat. The fourteen-party coalition headed by Violeta Barrios de Chamorro and backed by the United States had a decisive edge, with 54.7 percent of the vote to the Sandinistas' 40.8 percent. The Sandinistas had lost a high-stakes gamble that they could win free elections and finally force the United States to end its overtly hostile policies and disband the rebel army pitted against them. But no one knew if they would concede or contest the outcome of the vote.

Once he learned the results, Carter began phoning the Sandinista party headquarters in an attempt to reach Daniel Ortega Saavedra, the Sandinista candidate and sitting president. At 11:30 p.m. Ortega invited Carter to pay him a visit. High-ranking Sandinista officials filed into the campaign house around midnight for a closed-door session; they brushed off reporters' questions, but were unable to hide their ashen faces. Outside, party supporters and lambada dancers milled around a large grandstand, waiting for the victory celebration to begin. Three hours later, the Sandinista president of the electoral coun-

1

cil announced the shocking news: the Sandinistas had been defeated. Carter had convinced Ortega that, as a young man and the leader of a strong opposition bloc in Nicaragua's legislature, he had the time to build a good future for himself as a politician. Although some of the nine leading Sandinista comandantes bitterly regretted the regional diplomatic gambit that had led them to this defeat, Ortega prevailed in his judgment that there was no alternative to conceding victory to Chamorro. Carter, in the company of Sandinista lawyer Paul Reichler, then went to see the victor.

Doña Violeta acceded to Ortega's request that she not claim final victory that night. Ortega needed some time to persuade his party's faithful to accept the totally unforeseen defeat. The comandantes had been convinced of victory by their own extensive voter surveys and, in the weeks prior to the election, waved off any suggestion that they might lose. Demonstrating an extraordinary ability to compose himself, Ortega appeared on national television early the following morning and made an eloquent concession speech. He reviewed the Sandinistas' achievements and sacrifices as Carter had urged him to do, recalling those who had given their lives to oust dictator Anastasio Somoza Debayle in 1979 and in fighting the contra rebels since 1982. Choking back tears, Ortega called for reconciliation in his conflict-torn land.

The upset victory of Chamorro in Nicaragua was just one of the momentous, and traumatic, changes of late 1989 and early 1990 that radically altered the future prospects for Central America. Once the locale of seemingly endless conflicts—and the source of acrimonious policy disputes in Washington—the region now seemed to gain a new lease on life. A few months earlier, on December 20, 1989, the United States had launched a massive invasion of Panama that toppled dictator Manuel Antonio Noriega. After two years of trying to oust him through threats, sanctions, and negotiations, the death of a U.S. serviceman had provided the pretext President Bush needed to order in the troops. On the eve of the invasion, a pro–U.S. Panamanian government was secretly sworn in on a U.S. military base located in the former Panama Canal Zone. The new president,

Guillermo Endara, had won election to the post the previous May, but Noriega had annulled the results. The vast majority of Panamanians welcomed the invasion, believing that it was the only way to rid themselves of the dictator. The turn of events in both Nicaragua and Panama altered the geopolitical chessboard of the region in a direction clearly favorable to U.S. interests, although this meant that the United States would have to bear the burden of consolidating what are admittedly fragile gains toward democratization.

For El Salvador, the net effect of events in the 1980s was more ambiguous, but it also appeared to be approaching a turning point in 1991. For ten years, Salvadorans, with massive U.S. aid, have been struggling to build a democracy while strong right- and left-wing forces waged a violent and bitter war. In November 1989, the Salvadoran guerrillas launched an all-out offensive, their largest military action since the war's inception in 1980. But they achieved no military objectives, and the population ignored their call for an insurrection. Nonetheless, the offensive demonstrated that, contrary to the belief of some on the Salvadoran Right and many U.S. officials, the guerrillas were far from defeated. In fact, the offensive was a fairly powerful signal that the guerrillas could not be defeated militarily. Five days after the beginning of the offensive, six prominent Jesuit priests were taken from their beds in Salvador's capital city and slain by U.S.–trained government soldiers, making a mockery of claims that the army had reformed. The priests' deaths put the U.S. aid commitment in jeopardy. Pressures were mounting on El Salvador to find a way out of the war or face an end to U.S. support.

All three countries are case studies in U.S. intervention. In Nicaragua, the United States opposed a revolutionary government in the face of sustained criticism from the American public, but it failed to achieve its goal until regional diplomacy became the driving force in resolving the conflict. In El Salvador, the United States undertook a long and costly effort to stave off revolution and encourage reform. Despite the massive U.S. role, however, the principal determinants of the pace and extent of change in El Salvador have been indigenous. In Panama, a domestic struggle for democracy turned into a bilateral confrontation with a former ally. The crisis came to a head primarily because of contradictions in U.S. policy and the growing salience of the drug issue.

The following chapters trace the key developments in each country, with an eye to isolating what has and has not worked in U.S. policies toward the region. The record suggests that intervention as traditionally defined—through the provision of military aid or troops—can have only limited success, primarily in forestalling worst-case outcomes. Diplomacy has been relied upon too infrequently as the means for avoiding, or ending, conflicts. Furthermore, even with the end of hostilities, the fragile peace will be preserved only if democratic practices take firm root. Without a clearly mapped-out strategy for reaching this goal, U.S. policy cannot achieve permanent success in the region. In the Nicaraguan case, the United States abstained from active support of the regional diplomatic effort instead of attempting to shape it. In Panama, diplomacy failed when the United States decided it could not, for domestic political reasons, drop the indictments against Noriega, the only concession that might have brought about his voluntary departure. In El Salvador, a concerted international diplomatic effort began only in 1990, and the United States has yet to throw its full weight behind it.

The three cases offer important lessons for dealing with the problems on the isthmus and elsewhere in Latin America. Despite great skepticism, regional actors were able to exert sufficient diplomatic pressure on parties to the Nicaraguan conflict to bring about an agreement for ending the war and holding elections. International actors, including the United Nations and a former U.S. president, played crucial roles in assuring that the agreement reached was carried out in good faith by both sides. Given these international guarantees, elections were vindicated as a means of settling the dispute over power.

In Panama, diplomacy failed, largely because of the more limited nature of the effort exerted to resolve the conflict, and because the pressure brought to bear on Noriega was insufficient. Behind-the-scenes pressure from the Soviet Union on the Sandinista government, as well as skillful Central American diplomacy, was crucial in getting the Sandinistas to agree to and comply with an election-based solution. If sufficient pressure is brought to bear on both sides of the Salvadoran conflict, not only by the United States but also by the Soviet Union, Cuba, and other international actors, diplomacy can also succeed there.

Chapter 2 of this work examines the growth of both internal opposition and armed resistance to the Sandinista government, as well as the role played by the United States in Nicaragua. Chapter 3 demonstrates how the Central American peace process set the Nicaraguan conflict on the path to resolution through elections. Chapter 4 analyzes the democratization and reform efforts in El Salvador, and Chapter 5 assesses the course of the war and the prospects for a negotiated settlement. Chapter 6 traces the development of the U.S. confrontation with Panama that culminated in the military intervention of December 1989. The concluding chapter assesses the future prospects for Central America and suggests approaches to forming a new U.S. policy for the region.

Providing security, encouraging democratization, and stimulating economic development have been and still are the basic U.S. objectives in Central America. The U.S. policy of supporting democracy-building efforts has been vindicated, but old assumptions about U.S. security interests are in need of reexamination. With the dissolution of the Soviet bloc, the Cold War rationale that undergirded U.S. policy toward the Third World lost its cogency. Although Marxist revolutionary theory still has its adherents in Latin America, other threats to regional and hemispheric security loom larger. The most serious impediment to the consolidation of democracy in the region is economic, and while the United States cannot foot the entire bill, it has a major role to play in fostering the economic basis for political stability.

The long-term prospects for stability, demilitarization, further democratization, and economic integration from Guatemala to Panama are better now than they have ever been. For the first time since the Alliance for Progress years, it is possible to envision a regionwide development policy based on real possibilities rather than wishful thinking. But realizing this vision will require continued U.S. engagement in the face of pressure to declare victory and turn away.

2

NICARAGUA: THE SANDINISTAS AND THEIR OPPONENTS

The Sandinista revolution succeeded initially because it had the support of a broad spectrum of Nicaraguan society. The story of how and why this support eroded over the course of the last decade was obscured, however, by the debate over the controversial U.S. policy of building up the contras—the armed resistance to the Sandinistas—a policy that proved to be a secondary factor in the Sandinistas' eventual defeat at the polls in February 1990. Many Nicaraguans were willing to take up arms, with U.S. backing, against the regime, and this did put pressure on the Nicaraguan government. But the Sandinistas' military and political acumen was superior to the opposition's and the execution of U.S. policy flawed. Although the contras were unable to overthrow the Sandinistas, they did become a bargaining chip in a Central American diplomatic gambit to end the Nicaraguan conflict. The Sandinistas agreed to hold free and open elections as a means of ending the costly U.S. opposition to their regime. These committed revolutionaries could not conceive that, having triumphed over the United States and the contras, they might lose at the polls. But they had discounted the indigenous opposition to their regime, of which the contra insurgency was a manifestation. In dismissing the contras as merely the tool of U.S. policymakers, they miscalculated badly.

The Sandinistas came to power as part of a coalition united by opposition to the dictator Anastasio Somoza Debayle. This coalition represented all sectors of Nicaraguan society, including the influential *Los Doce,* a group of businessmen, priests, intellectuals, and professionals, and the Broad Opposition Front comprising labor groups, businessmen, and political parties. The Sandinistas led the armed opposition, which by 1979 was receiving weapons from Cuba, Panama, Venezuela, and Costa Rica (their training camps were in Costa Rica and Cuba).

Only five thousand strong at the time of Somoza's ouster in July 1979, the Sandinistas' arms and superior organization nonetheless enabled them to set the terms of the post-Somoza political order and they emerged as the dominant force in the revolutionary junta. Beginning in 1977, the United States had tried to broker a deal for Somoza's departure, but the effort collapsed in January 1979 when both the dictator and the opposition rejected a proposal for elections. The Carter administration abandoned its efforts at this point, despite the warning of Venezuelan President Carlos Andrés Pérez that if the United States did not support the moderates and pressure Somoza more strongly, the radical Sandinistas would end up in control. The Broad Opposition Front was left in the lurch.

At the outset, many Nicaraguans supported the Sandinista-led government in the belief that it would not take the path of the Cuban or other Soviet-supported governments. On July 12, only five days before Somoza's departure, the Sandinistas had sent a letter to the Organization of American States (OAS) promising to create a pluralistic and nonaligned government and to develop a mixed economy in Nicaragua. The first junta government included businessman Alfonso Robelo Callejas and Violeta Barrios de Chamorro, widow of the slain anti-Somoza newspaper publisher, Pedro Joaquín Chamorro Cardenal.

The leaders of the Broad Opposition Front expected to wield significant influence in the new government. Historically, the Liberals of Granada and the Conservatives of León had been the main political parties in Nicaragua, although in reality they were not so much parties as umbrella organizations for a succession of feuding nonideological power seekers who had fought incessantly throughout the late nineteenth and early twentieth centuries.[1] In any event, they had been marginalized by Somoza (who coopted many Liberals). Now their leaders hoped to resume their places in the political life of the new Nicaragua, although this would certainly mean a return to parochial politics.

Nicaraguans believed that the promised agrarian reforms would be relatively painless, since Somoza's holdings far outstripped anyone else's. Other landowners whose holdings were to be expropriated would be compensated. And since Somoza had also controlled many of the country's key businesses, many Nicaraguans assumed that in the new mixed economy the proportion of state ownership would remain the same as before. The Sandinistas' mixed-economy pledge was taken as assurance that the interests of private business would be respected, although some were worried that foreign exchange and marketing controls would prove onerous.

Nicaraguans were also broadly supportive of the Sandinistas' nonalignment stance. In a country that had been subjected to numerous U.S. interventions over the past century, nonalignment was seen as a means of achieving greater political independence while maintaining close economic ties and a generally friendly relationship with the United States. The use of the term was also intended to reassure both the Carter administration and Latin Americans who were nervous about the Sandinistas' close relationship with Cuba.

But these expectations were not met. During the next four years, the Sandinistas alienated many of their non-Sandinista supporters. Personal power struggles played a part, but there were also fundamental differences over economic policy, the centralization of political power, and the Soviet-aided militarization of the country. Some prominent allies became critics; others joined the growing ranks of peasants in the armed opposition, which was actively recruiting members with the help of the United States.

ECONOMIC POLICY

The Sandinistas' handling of the economy created more opposition than any other single factor. Lacking experience in economic management, the Sandinista leaders—for the most part young middle-class students—were hampered further by their adherence to Marxist ideology. Businessmen such as Arturo José Cruz and Alfredo César Aguirre joined the government only to have their hands tied by the Sandinista directorate.

The Sandinistas kept their pledge to retain an economy of mixed state and private ownership. About 60 percent of the land in the largely agricultural economy remained in private hands;

the rest came under state or Sandinista-directed cooperative control. The manner in which land reform policies were implemented created opposition, however, especially among the peasants, who did not receive titles to land. During the first stage of the program, a million hectares were expropriated, of which about two-thirds was turned into state farms and the rest into Sandinista-managed cooperatives. The conservative peasants were not happy to have exchanged one master for another. Later on, in 1985, the government distributed land directly to five thousand individuals, especially in the north and central regions where opposition to the Sandinistas was strongest. At the same time, the government continued to alienate landowners by reneging, in 1986 and again in 1989, on promises not to expropriate more land.

According to a widely cited but still unreleased study commissioned by the Nicaraguan government, by 1989 real wages were less than 10 percent of their level in 1981, and per capita gross domestic product (GDP) was less than $300, making the country the poorest in the hemisphere. According to government estimates, the war against the contras had cost Nicaragua $1 billion in damages, blocked loans, and lost trade by early 1987. The cost of maintaining an army of seventy thousand was enormous, with the defense budget consuming half of the total government budget. Although an austerity program initiated in January 1989 resulted in a 25 percent reduction in the defense budget, the secretary general of the Planning and Budget Ministry, María Rosa Renze, could not say exactly what military cuts had been made.[2]

The Reagan administration had imposed a trade embargo in 1985, after U.S.–Nicaraguan talks broke down and Congress failed to renew U.S. aid to the contras. Many Americans considered the embargo to be the primary cause of Nicaragua's crisis, yet by this time, bilateral trade had fallen from over 50 percent to 20 percent of Nicaragua's total trade. (Over 90 percent of its imports came from the United States before the revolution.) Still, the loss of the remaining 20 percent was devastating to many businesses. The outdated Esso oil refinery, for example, which had been built in the 1950s, relied on U.S. headquarters as the only certain supplier of spare parts.[3] The air transport provided by U.S. companies had ensured that Nicaraguan fruit and sea- food exports reached their markets before spoiling; after the embargo, they went by boat. Pan American and other large airlines stopped service to Managua.

The Sandinista system of central planning and export, cur- rency, and price controls contributed greatly to the 50 percent drop in production during the 1980s. Production fell by 8 per- cent in 1988 alone, even though the contra war had wound down after the March 1988 cease-fire. Price controls resulted in short- ages of basic foodstuffs in a fertile country accustomed to feed- ing itself. The shortages and controls produced rampant inflation, which hit 33,000 percent in 1988. The hyperinflation was brought under control, at least temporarily, by massive de- valuations of the *córdoba* in January and June 1989. In an effort to stop the slide, the government budget was cut by 44 percent, and 35,000 public employees were laid off.[4]

Renze and her superior, Alejandro Martínez Cuenca, re- ceived high marks from many observers for reining in the hyper- inflation, but the problems caused by central planning were not cured, despite nearly $4 billion in direct economic aid from the Soviet bloc between 1980 and 1988. Frustrated by the San- dinistas' poor economic management, Soviet advisers urged the Nicaraguans to institute a version of perestroika in their econ- omy. Soviet economic aid to Nicaragua was cut by $75 million between 1987 and 1989. According to Comandante Henry Ruiz Hernández, a government official, the Soviets told the San- dinistas that they "could do much more" with the resources they had.[5] Nonetheless, Sandinista leaders continued to insist that the United States was principally responsible for Nicaragua's eco- nomic crisis. Even as late as 1989, Vice President Sergio Ramírez Mercado refused to admit that the Sandinistas had made any serious mistakes: "If the United States would just leave us alone, the country's problems would be cured rapidly."[6]

The Sandinistas did make an effort to foster the confidence of businessmen and rally the country to the enormous task of resuscitating the economy. The policy of *concertación*—an at- tempt to reach general agreement on the country's needs and the direction of economic policy—was introduced in 1989. It included a promise that there would be no more arbitrary expropriations. (In 1988, the largest remaining private enterprise, the profitable San Antonio sugar refinery, had been taken over by the state.) Yet, despite the country's dire economic straits, the government continued to assert its superiority in ways that were certain to alienate the private sector. In June 1989, three large coffee producers declared a production boycott to protest government policies; the government in turn announced the expropriation of their properties. "They were sabotaging the economy," said the minister of agriculture and agrarian reform, Comandante Jaime Wheelock Román. "It was an act of war."[7] Wheelock, who led one of the three Sandinista factions in the revolution—the proletarian tendency, which advocated an urban labor-led struggle—is tough, controlled, and an orthodox Marxist in economic matters. As he explained it, the imperative of maintaining control had overridden the objective of *concertación*. "If the U.S. does not end its war against us," Wheelock added, "there will be an explosion. We will expand the war to the rest of Central America. There is no other alternative!"[8] At the time, Wheelock foresaw a prolonged economic blockade by the United States. The siege mentality of the Sandinistas led them to judge all opposition by the same measure; reconciliation, even with domestic opponents, was not possible.

THE CENTRALIZATION OF POLITICAL POWER

This unyielding attitude permeated the Sandinistas' dealings with their political opponents. The Sandinista National Liberation Front (FSLN), the "vanguard of the revolution," would brook no serious challenge. In order to consolidate its power, it constructed an impressive organizational network. The FSLN had 37,500 members by 1989, and about a quarter of a million Nicaraguans were members of Sandinista popular organizations for youth, farmers, women, and so on. Party membership, which was reserved for the "vanguard," was not encouraged, but membership in the mass organizations was. Ardent FSLN supporters made up perhaps a quarter of the estimated 3.4 million population. With their zeal and impressive organizational structures, they dominated Nicaraguan society. Managua was painted in the party's colors of red and black, and every small town had its party headquarters and usually a plaque or statue commemorating the revolution. In front of the new government buildings in downtown Managua, a two-story statue of a bare-chested man raising an AK-47 machine gun to the sky was erected.

The National Directorate of the FSLN, the nine comandantes, made all the important decisions in the Sandinista government. At the pinnacle of an extremely hierarchical party structure, the directorate functioned in secret. Even intraparty rivalries (primarily between the brothers Daniel and Humberto Ortega Saavedra and Interior Minister Tomás Borge Martínez, the only living FSLN founder) were kept hidden from view.[9] A tenth man, Vice President Ramírez, was also extremely influential.[10] The noted author, who was known to be a supporter of the Sandinistas, was named in 1979 to the first junta of five that included two non-Sandinistas (Chamorro and Robelo), but it was not until later that his party membership was revealed. Thus, the Sandinistas had a 3–2 majority in the junta.

Non-Sandinista parties and politicians grew increasingly frustrated as the Sandinistas tightened their grip on power. Virgilio Godoy Reyes, leader of the Independent Liberal party, resigned his post as labor minister for the Sandinista junta government in 1984 because the Sandinistas were pushing workers into the Sandinista unions and penalizing those in other unions. Strikes were outlawed and demands for higher wages were denounced as unpatriotic. Perhaps most alienating to the average Nicaraguan town or city dweller was the creation of the Sandinista Defense Committees, which substituted for local government in many cases, dispensing ration cards as food became scarce or relaying information about government policies. But they also functioned as government-informant networks.

The national literacy campaign, one of the undisputed achievements of the revolution, also served as a vehicle for indoctrinating Nicaraguans with Sandinista ideology. Many Nicaraguans who simply wanted to be left alone were pushed into outright opposition when they were labeled unpatriotic or subversive by the government. Those who did not participate in government-organized activities were automatically suspect, and those who retained their membership in the opposition parties risked even more as the war escalated. Across the country, hundreds of members of the Independent Liberal party, which had an extensive grass-roots network, and the Council of United Trade Unions (CUS) were jailed as collaborators of the contras. Suspects were often held without charges against them. Others were tried, frequently without legal counsel, by the Popular Anti-Somocista Tribunals.

The Interior Ministry's jails became as darkly spoken of as Somoza's had been; indeed, the infamous El Chipote seemed only to have changed hands. The first prisoners were mostly Somoza's National Guardsmen, many of whom received sentences of thirty years just for being in the army. Physical torture was rare—although ex-major Pablo Emilio Salazar was literally skinned alive for his crimes—but tales of deprivation and psychological torture were common in the reports that leaked out about the security prisons.

Many Nicaraguans were deeply troubled by the Sandinistas' sour relationship with the traditional church. Archbishop Miguel Obando y Bravo had aided the Sandinistas by negotiating the release of Sandinista prisoners from Somoza's jails and by declaring the dictatorship illegitimate, but his relations with the Sandinistas progressively worsened. He was labeled an enemy of the revolution for voicing the complaints of many Nicaraguans about their lack of freedom and the Sandinistas' class-war rhetoric, and for refusing to condemn the contras. He said he could not take sides, since both sides were Nicaraguan, and he continued to denounce human rights violations as he had done in the Somoza era.[11] Although Sandinista sympathizers labeled him a spokesman for the wealthy classes, the Indian-blooded archbishop came from a peasant family in central Nicaragua. When he was elevated to cardinal in 1985, people in the crowds that lined the roads to welcome his return from the Vatican were harassed and some were imprisoned. One of these, Mauricio Membreño, youth leader of the Social Democratic party, said he spent two years in jail.

Aligned against the church hierarchy was the popular or people's church, inspired by liberation theology. In Sandinista Nicaragua it became a primary defender of the revolutionary government. Despite Vatican disapproval, two priests, the brothers Ernesto and Fernando Cardenal Martínez, became the culture and education ministers of the government and Father Miguel D'Escoto Brockmann became its foreign minister. The popular church was led by Father Uriel Molina, who had influenced many of the Sandinista leaders as youths. His liberation theology masses, held in a dramatic modern church painted with murals of Christ leading the battle against the Yankee imperialists, were frequented by visitors to Nicaragua. On one occasion, the priest encouraged Nicaraguans present to explain the benefits of the revolution to some foreign visitors, whom he invited to come around the altar to sing "We Shall Overcome."

THE MILITARIZATION OF NICARAGUA

The outgrowth of the Sandinista revolution that most intimidated Nicaraguans was the militarization of the country. Soldiers and military vehicles were ubiquitous reminders of the regime's power. The need to defend against a possible U.S. invasion—not incredible to Nicaraguans, who had swallowed a large dose of U.S. intervention over the years—as well as against the contras was the justification for this course. The fear of invasion seemed genuine even among those Sandinistas who had been educated in the United States and understood the American aversion to military intervention that was a legacy of the Vietnam War. Their ideology was defined as much by anti-Americanism as by Marxist-Leninist doctrine. The Sandinista national anthem reminded Nicaraguans that the Yankees were the "enemy of humanity."

Obligatory military service created widespread discontent, however, leading many youths to leave the country and some even to join the contras. But the army—which steadily grew to over seventy thousand troops, with a militia of some sixty thousand by 1986—was the ultimate guarantor of the Sandinistas' power. The air force expanded with the arrival of Soviet transport and attack helicopters in substantial numbers beginning in

1984. In contrast, there were ten thousand contras by the end of that year, with about five thousand operating inside the country at any one time. According to U.S. government estimates, the Sandinistas received military hardware worth $4 billion from the Soviet bloc in their first ten years in power. They built the largest army in Central American history in record time.

Even as late as 1989 the Sandinistas defended the continuing need for a vast military, although one official declared that "the contras are dead; they have been no threat to us for some time. But our plan of national defense calls for all the population to be prepared to fight."[12] This plan, which envisioned an army and militia of six hundred thousand, was confirmed in December 1987 by Defense Minister Humberto Ortega after one of his aides, Roger Miranda Bengoechea, defected to the United States. The Sandinistas saw national mobilization as their best guarantee of survival, especially since Fidel Castro had told them that they could not expect Cuba to come to their aid if they were invaded.

The presence of between 2,500 and 3,000 Cuban and other Soviet-bloc security personnel, and an equal number of civilian advisers from the Soviet bloc, was a worrisome development to many Nicaraguans. During the early 1980s, between 200 and 300 Soviet military personnel were reportedly stationed in Nicaragua, along with a similar number of civilian officials, although the numbers of the former reportedly declined to between 40 and 50 in the late 1980s.[13] These foreigners helped set up a highly efficient intelligence and police apparatus, trained Sandinistas in the use of military equipment, and even reportedly flew helicopters in combat.

The relocation policy, under which thousands of Nicaraguans were moved out of areas of contra support, also alienated many citizens. An estimated 180,000 people had been relocated by early 1985; by late 1987, another quarter of a million had been moved.[14] This policy was extremely effective in denying the contras their bases of support, particularly among the conservative hill farmers of Jinotega and Nueva Segovia provinces. The contras became totally dependent on air-dropped supplies and what they could pack in, and the depopulated areas were free-fire zones for Sandinista helicopters and troops.

The government was adept at using the war to squelch dissent. All domestic opposition to the Sandinistas was equated with support for the armed counterrevolution. This led many in the cities to resent the contras for giving the government a tool with which to deny other groups the political space they might otherwise have won from the government. Some opposition politicians were privately supportive of the contras, but they did not dare go public, since supporters and suspected supporters of the contras were dealt with harshly.

In late 1984, as the Sandinistas began a multipronged offensive, the numbers of those imprisoned as suspected collaborators escalated dramatically. According to the Nicaraguan Permanent Human Rights Commission, which had catalogued Somoza abuses and was the only domestic nongovernmental human rights group cataloguing Sandinista abuses, seven thousand Nicaraguans were arrested in 1985 and early 1986. The commission also reported six hundred cases of disappearances, torture, and habeas corpus violations. Americas Watch and the Lawyers Committee criticized the Anti-Somocista Popular Tribunals as politicized courts and deplored the high incidence of lengthy pretrial incarceration and of imprisonment without charges, as well as the frequent denial of defense counsel to the accused. Even though Sandinista policies were an effective means of controlling dissent, they created great discontent that found no outlet.

THE 1984 ELECTIONS: NO MODEL FOR THE FUTURE

As the Nicaraguans faced national elections in February 1990, opposition politicians looked back at the 1984 elections ruefully. Those who had decided then not to participate in the electoral process in order not to legitimize a Sandinista victory had forfeited an opportunity to build and expand an organizational base—and doomed the country to five more years of war.

The Democratic Coordinator, as the major opposition bloc was called, had wavered to and fro before pulling out of the race.[15] At the time, the press was censored under a state of emergency, which also restricted the right to assemble and organize. The Sandinistas owned the television stations and had closed the Catholic radio station and banished its director. Early in the campaign, a Coordinator rally in Chinandega that drew about seven thousand supporters was broken up by Sandinista militants, the so-called divine mobs, who bashed in Arturo Cruz's (Coordinator's presidential candidate) windshield.[16] Similiar groups, reportedly organized by the Interior Ministry and the Sandinista party, harassed and attacked opposition supporters elsewhere. The government claimed that these were spontaneous expressions of outrage at the *"somocista contrarevolucionarios."* The Democratic Coordinator presented nine demands for opening up the system as a condition for its participation in the elections, and Cruz made several attempts to negotiate with the Sandinistas. In September 1984, six weeks before the elections, the Sandinistas pulled out of the deal they had negotiated with Cruz under pressure from Venezuela's president, Carlos Andrés Pérez.[17]

In any case, the conservative wing of the Democratic Coordinator might well have decided not to participate even if Cruz's agreement had held up. The opposition's conservative and moderate elements, each with backers in Washington, saw the elections differently. The conservatives were more fearful than the moderates of legitimizing a Sandinista victory by their participation. But later many opposition leaders agreed that they had lost a chance to gain some influence over the government's policies, or at least a soapbox from which to denounce them.

There is no way to gauge how well the Democratic Coordinator might have done had it participated in the elections, since public opinion surveys were illegal. Although the vote count itself was fair, the electoral conditions were less than ideal. (This was underscored in 1988, when the Sandinistas agreed to make numerous changes in the system.) In any event, Daniel Ortega, the Sandinista presidential candidate, won 66.9 percent of the vote. The Conservative Democratic party's Clemente Guido won 14 percent; the Independent Liberals' Virgilio Godoy, 9.6 percent (despite his last-minute attempt to withdraw his candidacy); and the Social Christian party's Mauricio Díaz, 5.6 percent.

After the elections, the Democratic Coordinator was marginalized as a political force in the country, even though it comprised the major opposition parties. The small parties that did participate in the election became "the opposition" whenever the Sandinistas needed to acknowledge the existence of a political force other than themselves in the country, even though Godoy's party was their only staunch opponent. This nominal opposition was the group with which the Sandinistas met in order to fulfill the 1987 peace plan's requirement that the government hold talks with its domestic opponents (Cardinal Obando y Bravo was asked to serve as head of the National Reconciliation Commission). And the opposition members of the electoral council set up for the 1990 elections were selected from the parties with seats in the legislature.

The Democratic Coordinator's abstention also left it without any influence in the drafting of a new constitution. This was the task of the National Assembly, which the Sandinistas controlled with sixty-one of ninety-six seats.[18] Had it won significant representation in the National Assembly, the Democratic Coordinator might have limited the constitutional provisions for declaring a state of emergency—under which Nicaragua was governed for most of the decade. The new constitution permitted the indefinite suspension of most basic rights, including that of habeas corpus. The executive was given extensive powers, including the right to dismiss judges and appoint departmental (equivalent to state) governors. The congressional power of budget approval could be suspended under a state of emergency (which was reimposed three hours after the constitution was promulgated in January 1987).

After the elections, many of Coordinator's leaders left Nicaragua to join the contras as political directors. Alfredo César, former head of the Central Bank, went to Costa Rica to join Edén Pastora Goméz, a hero of the revolution who had been pushed aside by the Sandinistas shortly after the revolution. Pastora had begun an anti-Sandinista insurgency in 1982 with the Democratic Revolutionary Alliance (ARDE). Arturo Cruz went north to join the political opposition based in Miami. He and Alfonso Robelo Callejas, a former junta member who had his own Democratic Nicaraguan Movement, joined the political directorate of the main contra army, the Nicaraguan Democratic Front (FDN), headed by former businessman Adolfo Calero Portocarrero, in 1985. The CIA concentrated its main efforts on recruiting and organizing the FDN, which grew to be the largest of three rebel groups. Pastora resisted pressure to ally his group with the FDN; the Indian rebels did so but maintained their own structure and Atlantic Coast base.

What drove these men to join a resistance movement funded by the United States and hampered by a reputation for being a refuge for the remnants of Somoza's National Guard? They all had solid credentials as anti-Somoza, nationalist Nicaraguans. Cynics say they succumbed to bribery and pressure from the CIA. Nothing in these men's pasts, however, suggested that their politics were for sale, or that they had any desire to lead a mercenary's life. The experience of the previous five years had convinced many Nicaraguans that there was no possibility of challenging the Sandinistas' hold on power from inside the country.

THE CONTRAS

In March 1981, the Reagan administration published a white paper charging that the Sandinistas had helped transship arms to the Salvadoran guerrillas. Throughout the 1980s, critics of the administration said that this charge was inadequately documented. But in a regional summit meeting in August 1989, President Daniel Ortega finally admitted to Salvadoran president Alfredo Cristiani and the others present that the Sandinistas had indeed supplied the Salvadoran rebels. Three months later, dramatic evidence was provided when a plane flying from Nicaragua crashed in El Salvador. It carried arms, including surface-to-air missiles.

While such subversive activity was of immediate concern to the United States, it was also worried about the appearance of several thousand Soviet-bloc military personnel (some doubled as teachers) in Nicaragua. Ongoing improvements of Nicaraguan port facilities and airstrips aroused fears that the Sandinistas were planning to provide the Soviet Union with base rights and military facilities. The Soviets already had intelligence, naval, and submarine facilities in Cuba, as well as bases from which they conducted aerial reconnaissance flights off the Atlantic Coast of the United States. Construction of the Punta Huete airbase and the conversion of Corinto and El Bluff into deep-water ports would allow the Soviets to cover the Pacific Coast of the United States as well. Believing that the Sandinistas thus presented a threat to the stability of the hemisphere, President Reagan signed a National Security Decision Directive on November 17, 1981, authorizing a covert program to support the Nicaraguans who were taking up arms against the Sandinista regime.

The administration's policy aims were never clearly defined, however. Some, like Assistant Secretary of State Thomas Enders and special envoy Philip Habib, believed the object was to push the Sandinistas into negotiating a diminution of their political dominance at home and severing their ties with the Soviet military. Hard-liners like Lt. Col. Oliver North and Elliott Abrams, Enders's successor, argued that the Sandinistas would have to be overthrown because they would never agree to satisfactory concessions at the bargaining table. The administration therefore remained hobbled by internal division and external critics. Its objective became simply to guarantee a renewal of aid for the contras each year. Neither the president nor Secretary of State George Shultz nor the director of the CIA, William Casey, who fervently supported the project, intervened to resolve the internecine disputes between the pragmatists and the hard-liners at the lower levels.[19] Whenever the pragmatists tried to translate the contras' military successes into a diplomatic resolution of the crisis, the hard-liners would accuse them of selling out the resistance.

The administration's ambiguity about the aims of its contra policy meant that it could never convincingly answer questions about its strategy and the endgame it was seeking. The press and congressional critics accused the administration of duplicity with regard to overthrowing the Sandinistas. The administration initially told Congress that the contras would interdict military aid that the Sandinistas were sending to the Salvadoran guerrillas. Later it claimed that the contras would pressure the Sandinistas into opening up their political system. But only a small amount of arms traffic was intercepted by the contras; according to some U.S. officials, the main flow of weaponry entered El Salvador through the Gulf of Fonseca and from Nicaragua, rather than overland from Honduras, where the main contra force was based.[20] In any case, in the minds of the contras interdiction was never their main mission; some even reportedly sold arms to the Salvadoran guerrillas when they needed money.

If the Reagan administration was seeking a military victory, the amount of U.S. aid was insufficient to achieve that end. The Sandinistas received an average of $500 million in Soviet-bloc military aid annually. In contrast, the contras received a total of about $275 million in overt U.S. aid over the years. An initial outlay of $20 million in covert funding was authorized in late 1981, but later restrictions were placed on the use of covert funds. Covert aid from then on primarily took the form of intelligence-sharing.

More crippling than the amount of aid was the sporadic and uncertain nature of the flow. The contras received military aid from late 1981 through 1984 and from late 1986 until early 1988. From October 1984 to December 1985, all funds were halted after the mining of the port of Corinto by contras and CIA "assets" and the discovery of a CIA training manual advocating assassination, although intelligence-sharing continued to be permitted. Nonlethal aid (for food, clothing, medicine, communications, and training in communications) resumed in December 1985. In October 1986, military and nonmilitary aid once again began arriving in Honduras. (This $100-million aid package was the largest of all.) The sporadic aid flow was due to congressional and public ambivalence over the policy, which was controversial for three reasons. First, many opposed the attempt to destabilize what they saw as a legitimate government. Second, others were not convinced that vital U.S. interests were threatened by the Sandinista government. Third, the long drawn-out nature of the policy (as opposed to the later quick U.S. action in Panama) ran up against the strong public aversion to extended intervention. The Reagan administration failed to counter these objections effectively.

The U.S. management of the contra forces was also problematic. In mid-1985, control of the contras shifted from the CIA to joint National Security Council (NSC)–State Department management after Congress excluded the CIA from any role but intelligence-sharing in legislation providing $27 million in non-lethal aid to the contras. Congress mandated sole State Department control of the $27 million, but NSC staff member Oliver North had assumed many of the CIA's guidance functions and was secretly raising funds for the resistance. At various stages, the Agency for International Development (AID) and the Defense Department were also involved. The end result was bureaucratic rivalry and confusion. The CIA continued to think of the contras as "its army." The State Department was trying at the same time to remake the contras into a broad-based, essentially political, movement that would appeal to Congress (rather than to the Nicaraguans they were supposed to represent).

The original contra leaders were chosen by the CIA for their malleability, according to some accounts, to ensure that the resistance army did not take on a life of its own. Referring to the agency handlers of the contras as "a bunch of frustrated cops wanting to play cowboys and Indians," one official said that although former National Guardsmen were eventually outnumbered by other Nicaraguans, they were placed in key posts from the beginning to ensure that the CIA maintained control. Adolfo Calero's Nicaraguan Democratic Front provided the political leadership. (According to some accounts, Calero had been imposed on the FDN by the CIA.) Although Calero and Aristides Sánchez, another FDN leader, spent a great deal of time in Honduras, they were based in Miami and therefore distant from the fighting men.

The original fighting force, the September Fifteenth Legion, was made up of former National Guardsmen who had trained in Guatemala in 1980. It was commanded by Col. Ricardo Lau, who had been in Somoza's notorious Office of

National Security. In mid-1980, Col. Enrique Bermúdez Varela joined the group. A former member of the National Guard, he was seen as having the requisite military skills to lead an army. Furthermore, he had been in Washington during the revolution (as military attaché) and had not been directly involved in the brutalities committed by the National Guard in Nicaragua.

The September Fifteenth Legion and other forces gathered under the FDN umbrella, which had relocated after 1980 to Honduras with the support of Honduran armed forces chief Gustavo Alvarez Martínez and Argentinian military officers, were typified by the erratic warlord Pedro Pablo Ortiz Centeno, a former sergeant in the National Guard who took the *nom de guerre* "Suicida." His troops were fiercely loyal to him but prone to getting out of control; he himself came to loathe his higher-ups, whom he suspected of plotting to do him in—which they eventually did.[21] Two remedies to improve command and control were tried. The political leadership was changed, and efforts were made to cleanse the contra ranks of Suicida types. The first effort failed completely; the second, over time, was fairly successful.

Under State Department guidance, a new political leadership, the National Opposition Union (UNO), was formed in 1985. Calero, Sánchez, and Bermudez remained, but the political directorate of the contras became more moderate through the inclusion of Nicaraguan politicians who had left the country after the 1984 elections. These included Arturo Cruz and Alfonso Robelo and, later, Pedro Joaquín Chamorro, the son of the slain newspaper publisher. The incorporation of the exiled politicians into the contra structure convinced more U.S. congressmen that the contras were a legitimate opposition force, but it exacerbated the problems within the movement itself. The new UNO directors wanted to exert civilian control over the contra army, a move resisted by Calero, Sánchez, and Bermúdez, who did not wish to see their power diminished. The new directors were backed by State Department officials who wanted them to clean up the unsavory elements of the army. The net result of expanding the directorate was a series of power struggles, as the political leaders formed and reformed alliances among themselves.

The contra troops in the field saw the UNO in Miami as simply their liaison to the outside world, their public relations office. Their leaders were the ones who led them into battle and lived in the camps with them. Although these contras might well vote for Cruz or Robelo in a liberated Nicaragua, they could not very well be expected to follow orders transmitted from Miami. Thus, the effort to combine the political and military opposition was crippled by the manner in which it was undertaken. Cruz resigned from UNO in March 1987 after the FDN leaders successfully opposed his proposed democratic charter,[22] and Robelo left later. Chamorro was not reelected to the directorate after he failed in an overt bid to wrest power from Bermúdez.

The goal of reforming the contra army was neither misguided nor unwarranted, although middle-class Nicaraguan politicians were the wrong ones to attempt it. Those most able to choose good resistance leaders were the troops in the camps, but they did not have sufficient power to compel changes against the wishes of their FDN-CIA masters. Some changes did occur, however, after media reports of contra abuses led Congress to set aside a portion of the $100-million aid package to form the Nicaraguan Association for Human Rights, which investigated reports of abuse and trained monitors to accompany the units into the field. A military prosecutor's office was also set up to act on complaints. The severest penalty it could mete out, and to which it resorted in a number of cases, was expulsion from the movement. Those found guilty of other infractions could be temporarily withdrawn from combat. The human rights message gradually got across, even though abuses were sometimes overlooked to protect the best fighters, or because the guilty were protected by their patrons at the top levels of the movement or by their CIA liaisons. The camps were also regulated by rules that barred alcohol and strictly monitored furloughs to nearby Honduran towns.

The most significant change in the contra army came about gradually as it expanded, with peasants and ex-Sandinistas flowing into the ranks and diluting the ex-Guard and mercenary balance. Many of these former Sandinista and peasant fighters rose to field command and higher positions as they gained experience. By 1987, the majority of task force leaders were former farmers. Many of them had joined the contras rather than be forced into cooperatives; often they or a family member had been arrested on suspicion of collaboration. Eventually, men from these groups moved up to regional commands, and from there to positions in the Estado Mayor (the general command overseeing strategy, operations, logistics, etc.). They included "Denis" (Justo Meza Peralta), a farmer; "Rubén" (Oscar Sobalvarro García) and "Douglas" (Rudy Zelaya Zeledon), former Sandinista guerrillas; "Dimas" (Francisco Baldivia Chavarria), an ex-Sandinista army officer; and "Quiché" (Juan Rivas Romero), who became chief of staff. Quiché had been a sergeant in the National Guard, but according to people both inside and outside the resistance, he was one of the "good" ex-Guards. A rugged and effective leader, he commanded the respect and obedience of both the rank-and-file and the regional commanders, who were enthusiastic about his promotion and felt he truly represented them.

These changes and a developing esprit de corps within the expanding contra forces resulted in their increased effectiveness in 1986 and 1987. The contras achieved their greatest military successes of the war when they were able to cut the east-west Rama Road and hold several towns for forty-eight hours in October 1987, and to mount a coordinated attack on three towns and a Sandinista army headquarters in northern Nicaragua in December 1987. They also shot down between twenty-five and thirty helicopters with Red-eye missiles during this period, dealing a serious blow to the Sandinistas' helicopter-based strategy. Contra and U.S. sources attributed these successes to the effects of sustained aid and training in 1986–1987. U.S. government figures indicate that the contras' numbers swelled at this time to 17,000. The contras now found many willing recruits each time they visited the Nicaraguan refugee camps in Honduras.

As the contras gained the necessary qualities of an authentic guerrilla force, they naturally came to resent the heavy hands of Washington and Miami. One chronic problem, from the contra commanders' perspective, was the substantial outside intervention in decision making, which many of them felt undercut their standing with the troops. This interference extended to both operations and human rights issues. Bermúdez, the CIA, and the U.S. embassy in Tegucigalpa were the sources of a never-ending stream of instructions on personnel changes, human rights monitoring, and auditing and accounting procedures. The contra movement thus assumed many characteristics of a U.S. army division rather than a guerrilla force. Bermúdez complained that the struggle for Nicaragua, in the minds of his State Department contacts, was only in Washington: "They never understood or cared what it would take to fight the war on the ground."[23]

Some of the troops regarded Bermúdez himself as a problem. Although he held the title of commander in chief, his primary function was as a liaison between Washington/Miami and Honduras; he spent a great deal of time shuttling back and forth with a briefcase. It was probably inevitable that those who lived in the rustic mountain camps regarded as their true leaders those who lived with them rather than in Tegucigalpa and Miami. Another factor was the difference in age; Bermúdez, at fifty-six, was in charge of an army in which the median age was around twenty, and whose field commanders and general command were around thirty on average. Neither his loyalty to the original group of ex-Guard leaders nor his responsibility for executing policy directives—which may have been designed to influence the debates over aid in Washington—from Washington and the CIA enhanced his reputation. In 1988, several dissident commanders, with the backing of some on the Miami directorate, including Calero, who wanted to enhance their own powers, tried to remove Bermúdez from the general command. Bermúdez won, and "Toño," a respected commander, and a few others resigned. Bermúdez also won a seat on the directorate, consolidating his position with the help of his longstanding supporters in the CIA.

Other efforts to change the balance of power at the top of the resistance also backfired. The Bush administration took office intent upon removing the last of the worst contra leaders. One of its prime targets was Comandante Mack (José Bravo Centeno), chief of intelligence in the Estado Mayor. Mack, formerly commander of the Nicarao Command, had not only been a major in the National Guard but reportedly also Somoza's chauffeur and pimp. He was accused of torturing and killing Nicaraguans in the camps who were suspected of being Sandinista government spies. The legal office of the contra movement conducted a trial and Mack was sentenced to be expelled from the movement. But he appealed the sentence to the civilian directorate. Deputy Assistant Secretary of State Cresencio Arcos threatened to cut off U.S. aid if Mack was not removed. This strong-arm tactic caused a ruckus in the camps, however, and in March 1989, Quiché resigned as chief of staff rather than testify against Mack. Quiché, who said he was taking a seven-month leave from the army, was reportedly also frustrated by the Bush administration's decision not to try to secure more military aid from Congress, as well as by the micromanagement of the movement from Washington.[24] The directorate later granted Mack's appeal. The upshot was that the United States failed to get rid of Mack and lost an effective leader in Quiché.

These battles inside the contra movement and between the contras and Washington distracted everyone from the main battle against the Sandinistas, who were much more single-minded. The Sandinista army's capabilities had improved greatly beginning with the arrival of the first MI-25 helicopter gunships in late 1984. Thereafter the Sandinistas were able to drop quick reaction battalions into combat wherever the contras appeared. These military operations, combined with population relocation and roundups of suspected collaborators in the north, south, and central regions, led one observer to conclude that by the end of 1985 "both the Sandinistas and Reagan were headed in the direction of a military solution. The difference was that Reagan's approach was largely rhetorical, whereas the Sandinistas were well on their way to changing the facts on the ground."[25] The one opportunity for reversing this trend came with Congress's approval of $100 million in aid, including $70 million in military aid, in the summer of 1986. Indeed, as noted above, the contras were peaking militarily during this period. Then, in late November, less than two months after this aid began to flow, the Iran-contra affair broke. The revelation that some of the proceeds of arms sold to Iran to secure the release of American hostages had been funneled to accounts intended for the contras' use jeopardized the contras' prospects for future aid. Even though the contra side of the affair came to be seen as the misguided mission of zealous underlings, principally Lt. Col. Oliver North, the contra policy and the contras themselves ultimately suffered.

Thus, ironically, just as the contras became a genuine, effective insurgency, their prospects were dashed in Washington. Even though the $100 million in part provided the contra forces with new equipment, they fought throughout 1987 with the knowledge that it might be their last aid from the United States. The Sandinistas and other Central Americans also could see that U.S. policy was hanging by a thread.

During 1987, a diplomatic effort aimed at wresting control of the situation away from the crippled Reagan administration gathered steam. But even as the Sandinistas were engaging in regional diplomacy in the hope of ridding themselves of the contra threat, they pursued the war with determination. In March 1988, they made their third major incursion into Honduras with about two thousand soldiers, aiming to wipe out the main contra base in Yamales. In response, 3,200 soldiers from the U.S. Army's 82nd Airborne Division were sent to Honduras for maneuvers, although they stayed clear of the border area. This was sufficient to compel a Sandinista retreat. But the Sandinistas had signaled that if they could not bring the contras down by diplomacy, force remained an option.

President Reagan still viewed the Sandinista regime as a security threat, but his interventionist policy had collapsed. His administration was divided over how much more political capital should be invested in the Nicaragua issue. The president's domestic policy advisers saw it as a no-win morass; those still committed to the policy looked for stop-gap alternatives and began to position themselves to shift the blame for the failing policy to the Democrats in Congress. The developing crisis in Panama also began to consume an increasing amount of the time of officials responsible for U.S. policy in the region. Thus, in the last months of the Reagan administration, the initiative on Nicaragua passed to the Central Americans, who progressively supplanted the policymakers in Washington as arbiters of the Nicaraguan conflict.

3

NICARAGUA: DIPLOMACY TAKES OVER

In 1987, Central Americans seized the initiative on the Nicaraguan problem from the United States. Under the leadership of President Oscar Arias Sánchez of Costa Rica, they took the first steps in a diplomatic effort aimed at resolving conflict and promoting democracy in all the countries of the region. But Arias focused primarily on Nicaragua, hoping to supplant the Reagan administration's approach to dealing with the Sandinistas. A series of agreements negotiated by the five presidents of the region in 1987–1989 resulted in a deal that centered on trading the demobilization of the contras for the liberalization of the Sandinista regime, including the holding of elections under free and open conditions. Even though opening up their system entailed political risk, the Sandinistas, after first resisting this strategy, eventually embraced it as a way to force the United States into withdrawing its support for the contras and accepting the regime's existence. The Reagan administration was highly skeptical that diplomacy would resolve the Sandinista threat. But Congress, which had unsuccessfully pressed the administration to explore diplomatic remedies, welcomed the opportunity presented by the Central Americans' initiative to cut off military aid to the contras.

THE ESQUIPULAS ACCORD

President Arias began framing a proposal for a regional accord on democratization and conflict resolution in late 1986. His was not the first attempt to address the region's problems through negotiations, however. In 1983, Colombia, Mexico, Panama, and Venezuela (the "Contadora" group), fearing that direct U.S. intervention in Nicaragua would be the likely outcome of the contra insurgency, had begun a sustained diplomatic effort to

conclude an agreement. As they developed, the Contadora negotiations focused increasingly on regional security issues rather
than on the character of the Nicaraguan government, and although a draft treaty was produced in 1984, the process stalled,
in part because the Central American governments thought that
the Contadora mediators were trying to impose solutions on
them. The United States opposed the draft agreement because it
required no change in the nature of the Nicaraguan government
and mandated regional force reductions that would have limited
both El Salvador's capacity to wage war against its guerrilla insurgency and the U.S. military presence in the region generally.[1]

President Arias (whose country had abolished its army in
1949 and maintained only a small border guard and police force)
shared the U.S. perception of the Sandinista government as a
security threat. He also shared the Reagan administration's view
that Nicaragua would remain a threat until the Sandinista regime was liberalized. But he staunchly opposed the use of military force to achieve this goal, believing that diplomatic dialogue
and international pressure would force the Sandinistas to mod-
ify their undemocratic ways and reduce their military.

The Arias proposal, unveiled in February 1987, raised the
Sandinistas' hackles. They were no happier having their neighbors defining democracy for them than they were having the
United States doing so. But they were even more concerned that
the plan might jeopardize their hold on power. During a meeting
of the Central American foreign ministers in July 1987, it became clear that the only deal the Sandinistas would accept was
one that guaranteed them a cutoff of contra aid in exchange for a
commitment to change the governance of Nicaragua.

This tradeoff was incorporated in the accord signed by the
five Central American presidents on August 7, 1987, in Esquipulas, Guatemala. (The full text is in Appendix I.) But the
concept of simultaneity, the key to gaining the Sandinistas'
agreement, was flawed. The two processes linked in the accord—
Nicaraguan democratization and contra demobilization—required different timetables to implement. The time and effort
required to liberalize, let alone democratize, Nicaragua were
much greater than that required to neutralize the armed resist-

ance. If its funding dried up, the contra army would be effectively finished. The Sandinistas could see this, and gambled that they would not have to go the full distance toward democracy if the contras were neutralized as prescribed in the accord. In the event the bargain collapsed, the Sandinista army would still be intact to take on the contras.

The Esquipulas Accord, a slightly modified version of the Arias proposal, called for each signatory government to hold talks with its own unarmed domestic opposition, to declare amnesties, and, for those countries with armed oppositions, to "take all the necessary actions in order to achieve an effective cease-fire." It prescribed for all countries such democratizing measures as full press, party, and organizational freedoms and free elections according to the signatories' constitutional timetables. It also required all countries to deny use of their territory to insurgent groups and called on all governments, including those outside the region, to halt military, logistical, and financial aid to insurgents. In its general terms, the accord also applied to conflicts in El Salvador, Guatemala, and Honduras. Each country was to seek to resolve its own internal conflicts and to guarantee democratic freedoms. All countries were to stop assisting insurgencies, which meant not just an end to Honduran help for the contras, but also Sandinista support for Salvadoran and other rebels. In practice, however, the most movement occurred in the Nicaraguan conflict—primarily because Congress stood ready to lend a hand in halting aid to the contras.

Laboring under the overwhelming influence of their powerful northern neighbor ("the elephant up there can crush us with one movement," observed one Guatemalan official), the Central Americans had sought some assurance before their summit that the United States would not immediately set about trying to destroy their work. They received this assurance in two forms. The "Wright–Reagan plan," drafted by Speaker of the House Jim Wright and endorsed by the Reagan administration, was the first attempt by the United States in years to specify the terms for ending its opposition to the Sandinista regime. Announced on the eve of the Central American meeting, the plan called for a cease-fire in Nicaragua, with the suspension of both U.S. military aid to the contras and Soviet military aid to the Sandinistas. It set a deadline of sixty days, which coincided with the end of the fiscal year and the current contra aid program. It was understood that if the deadline was not met, the administration would be free to ask Congress for more contra aid. The hard-liners in the administration were gambling that the plan would not succeed, and that by going along with the proposal they would improve their chances of persuading Congress to renew funding for the resistance.

But the U.S. plan had a life of only forty-eight hours. Once the Esquipulas Accord was signed, Wright shifted his support from the Wright–Reagan plan to the regional accord. In the past year, other congressmen had also been meeting with Central Americans to encourage their efforts, signaling that they would support a regional accord. Even though the administration remained doubtful that diplomacy could change the Sandinistas, there was little Reagan officials could do to reverse the trend toward a negotiated solution once the Esquipulas Accord was signed.

The Sandinistas pursued the regional diplomatic gambit for a number of reasons. First, since the accord amounted to a regional repudiation of the contra policy, in which even Washington's close allies Honduras and El Salvador had joined, the Sandinistas could claim a diplomatic victory over the United States. But of greater importance to the Sandinistas was the chance that regional diplomacy might lead to the bilateral negotiations they had long sought with Washington, both as a symbol of U.S. acceptance of their regime and in order to elicit a noninterference pledge. The Wright–Reagan plan had specifically held out the possibility of bilateral diplomacy, at least in the original form drafted by Speaker Wright. The Nicaraguan ambassador to Washington, Carlos Tünnermann Bernheim, unbeknown to the administration, had held discussions with Wright during the drafting process, and he protested publicly when the White House version of the Wright–Reagan plan deleted the reference to bilateral talks. Finally, even though the Iran-contra affair seriously undermined the administration's ability to pursue its contra policy, the Sandinistas were eager to nail down the contras' demise, if not through direct negotiations with Washington, then through interlocutors who could help forestall a renewal of contra aid.

In late 1987, therefore, the Sandinistas began to take incremental steps toward compliance with the Esquipulas Accord. These proved sufficient to keep the peace process going and gave Congress the rationale for withholding military funding from the contras. In keeping with an agreement deadline, President Ortega announced on November 5 that he would conduct indirect talks with the contras on a cease-fire. Despite the efforts of Cardinal Miguel Obando y Bravo as mediator, these talks failed. At the January 1988 meeting of the Central American presidents, President Arias pressed Ortega to agree to direct talks with the contras. Congress was scheduled to vote in February on an administration proposal for renewed military aid to the contras on the grounds that the Sandinistas had not complied with the accord. Ortega agreed to the talks and on February 3, 1988, Congress voted down the administration's request for $36.25 million for six months. The small amount ($3.6 million) included for military aid damned the request. Many in the Democratic majority believed that approving military aid would provide the Sandinistas with the excuse they were seeking not to reach a cease-fire agreement with the contras or to comply with the other requirements of the Esquipulas Accord. Others argued that this would force the contras into unconditional surrender and remove any incentive for the Sandinistas to alter their rule or desist in their attempts to export their revolution. They believed that an aid cutoff should at a minimum occur simultaneously with Sandinista moves toward achieving a cease-fire, declaring an amnesty for political prisoners, and lifting the state of emergency in Nicaragua.

Faced with the loss of U.S. aid, representatives of the contras met with representatives of the Sandinistas in Sapoá, Nicaragua, and agreed on March 23 to a cease-fire. The agreement called for the contras to move, with their arms, into zones still to be negotiated and for further talks on undefined political matters. Shortly after the Sapoá cease-fire, Congress approved $47.9 million in nonlethal aid for the contras through September 1988.

The Sandinista-contra talks stalled, however, after the Sandinistas said that the delivery of the nonlethal aid to the contras in cease-fire zones inside Nicaragua could not be made by U.S. agencies but only by international organizations. The upshot of this dispute was a massive outflow of contras to their safe haven in Honduras, where they could receive aid uninhibited by this condition. By early June, the parties had agreed to an extension of the temporary cease-fire, but they accomplished nothing else and the talks broke down. Each side blamed the other. The contras said the Sandinistas were unwilling to discuss any political concessions and only wanted to talk about demobilizing the resistance. The Sandinistas charged that the contras were only interested in discussing a maximal proposal for the separation of the Sandinista party from the army and other steps the government considered nonnegotiable.

The Sandinistas had taken some steps toward liberalization, including lifting the state of siege, allowing the publication again of the opposition newspaper *La Prensa,* abolishing the popular tribunals, and pardoning 3,000 political prisoners—although this was not the complete amnesty called for by the Esquipulas Accord. According to the International Red Cross, 1,306 political prisoners remained incarcerated as of August 1989; the antigovernment Permanent Commission on Human Rights put the figure at between 5,000 and 7,000. Discussions with the opposition parties that had participated in the 1984 elections produced no significant agreement, however, and the Sandinistas retained control of the Interior Ministry, the police and the jails, the courts, and the military. The Esquipulas Accord provided no remedies for this situation, having left military and security matters for discussion in the now defunct Contadora forum and having set no deadline for their resolution. Thus, the signatories to the accord soon discovered the limits of their leverage.

When the Central American presidents met in Alajuela, Costa Rica, on the first anniversary of the Esquipulas meeting, they were stymied by the recalcitrant Sandinistas, who refused to take any further steps in liberalizing their regime, pointing out that Honduras continued to host armed Nicaraguan insurgents on its soil. The rest of 1988 was a draw, while everyone awaited the outcome of the U.S. presidential election.

Any hopes that the Bush administration would reverse the contras' fortunes were quickly dissipated. It was evident early on that the new administration did not share its predecessor's passionate attachment to the contra cause. The U.S.–based contra leaders, who had been welcomed to the White House many times by President Reagan, received a rude shock when they did not receive tickets to the inaugural ball. The slight was deliberate. Instructions were conveyed that no high-level official (above assistant secretary rank) was to have any contact with the contra leadership.

Less than a month after President Bush's inauguration, the five Central American presidents met at Costa del Sol in El Salvador. After two days of discussion on February 13–14, they reached agreement on a stunningly concrete plan. Nicaragua stole the show by announcing that it would hold elections for president by February 25, 1990—earlier than constitutionally required. Although the Costa del Sol Accord reaffirmed the commitments made in the Esquipulas Accord, its specific provisions boiled down to a narrower deal: in exchange for measures to guarantee that the Sandinistas would hold free and fair elections in February 1990, the presidents committed themselves "to formulate, within a period of no more than 90 days, a joint plan for the voluntary demobilization, repatriation or relocation in Nicaragua and in third countries of Nicaraguan resistance members and their families." (The full text is in Appendix II.)

In response to the signing of this accord, the Bush administration opened negotiations with Congress over contra aid. The new secretary of state, James Baker, met secretly with congressional leaders in April. This initiative resulted in an unusual cooperative arrangement, under which it was agreed that nonlethal assistance would be provided to the contras only as dictated by the course of the Central American peace process. If the Central Americans agreed on a demobilization plan, the aid could be converted to help relocate or repatriate the contras. In November 1989, the congressional leadership (and the intelligence and foreign affairs committees of both houses) would advise the administration of its opinion as to whether the aid should be continued. By this agreement, the administration secured $50 million in aid and a commitment from Congress, albeit a conditional one, that it would continue funding the resistance until the February 1990 elections in Nicaragua. Having agreed to nonmilitary aid only, the administration then began to insist in discussions with the Soviet Union that Soviet military aid to the Sandinistas should also stop. In May, Mikhail Gorbachev told President Bush in a letter that military deliveries were discontinued at the end of 1988. The Soviet foreign minister later qualified the Soviet position, saying replacement materiel would still be provided. Nonetheless, the gesture signaled the Soviets' willingness to contribute to a nonmilitary resolution to the conflict within the Esquipulas framework.

Under the Bush administration, State Department officials began to cut the U.S.–based contra leaders and Enrique Bermúdez out of the policymaking loop, as they sought to encourage contra cooperation with the regional diplomatic efforts. Bermúdez was furious with the administration's failure to support the resistance more aggressively and he accused it of inconstancy and even hypocrisy, and of failing to take the Sandinista threat seriously.[2] He believed—as did Adolfo Calero and others—that U.S. officials were dealing directly with contra field commanders in the expectation that they would be more pliable. But even though the field commanders could see that U.S. aid might be ending, they refused to concede that this would finish their struggle. Comandante Franklyn had become chief of staff in early 1989 after Quiché's resignation. The twenty-nine-year-old Franklyn, elevated from the Jorge Salazar Regional Command, had played a leading role in the Rama Road attack of 1987. He and other commanders increasingly downplayed the importance of U.S. backing to their troops: *"Con ayuda, sin ayuda la lucha continua"* ("with aid, without aid the fight continues").[3]

During the summer of 1989, each regional command of the contra army sent a task force into Nicaragua. Their stated mission, during this awkward hiatus before the February 1990 elections, was to maintain a presence to protect their supporters and demonstrate to their countrymen that they were still a force; they would also try to instill confidence in the peasants, who were afraid of Sandinista retribution if they voted for the opposition. When asked whether contra troops were observing the condition tied to U.S. aid, that they not engage in offensive actions, Franklyn replied, "The line is very hard to draw. We have to protect ourselves. And if we set an ambush and they walk into it and begin shooting, who is the offensive party?"[4] He thought that several thousand fighters, at least, would stay with the resistance even if all U.S. aid ended. Another comandante in charge of logistics confirmed Franklyn's estimate, adding that the guerrillas had arms caches buried inside Nicaragua and were conserving ammunition and their precious anti-aircraft missiles.[5] Throughout 1989, the contras continued to infiltrate Nicaragua in preparation for carrying on their fight—as an autonomous resistance that would go on without the aid (or the shackles) of its erstwhile patron.

TELA: TRYING TO FORCE DEMOBILIZATION

The Central American presidents met once again at Tela, Honduras, on August 5–7, 1989, to set a date for the demobilization of the contras. The accord that issued from this meeting called for the creation, within thirty days, of an International Commission of Support and Verification (CIAV) and urged the Nicaraguan resistance to "accept the execution of the present plan" within ninety days after the formation of the commission, that is, by December 5. (The full text is in Appendix III.) Composed of representatives of the United Nations and the Organization of American States, CIAV was charged with sending a monitoring force to receive the contras' arms and verify the dismantling of the camps and to oversee the repatriation of the rebels and ensure their continued safety within Nicaragua.

It soon became clear that the December 5 deadline was unlikely to be met. After November 30, U.S. congressional leaders would decide whether to restrict aid to the contras for use in their demobilization, repatriation, or relocation. Anticipating this possibility, the contras stepped up their infiltration of Nicaragua in the fall. The Sandinistas cried foul, and on November 1 terminated the cease-fire that had been in effect since March 1988. Congress in turn condemned this announcement and the congressional leadership rejected President Ortega's plea for restricting U.S. aid to the contras.

The seeds of this outcome were planted in setting the demolization date as December 5. The contras' prior public position was that they would respect the outcome of fair elections in Nicaragua. Had the Tela Accord set the date of the February elections as the deadline for demobilizing the contras, they would have been hard pressed to refuse to demobilize if the Sandinistas won in a clean contest. But the Sandinistas convinced the other presidents at Tela that they should not be expected to hold elections while the contras remained intact as a fighting force. So the Tela Accord created a gray area between December 5 and February 25. President Arias acknowledged soon after the accord was signed that the demobilization was unlikely to occur on schedule, and announced his support for the continuation of U.S. nonlethal aid until February 3.[6] Once the date, December 5, was established in the accord, however, the Sandinistas had justification for balking at fulfilling their own requirements if demobilization did not occur by then. Even though President Ortega reiterated the Sandinistas' intention to hold elections on schedule, the fear that their position might change was palpable once the cease-fire was called off.

The Tela Accord also raised the sensitive problem of finding homes for contras who did not want to go back to Nicaragua. CIAV was asked to "carry out negotiations for the reception by third countries of those who do not wish to be repatriated and give them . . . assistance." But no Central American country would be a willing host for large numbers of contras. Honduras and Costa Rica, in particular, were worried that the tens of thousands of Nicaraguans already in their territories would become a permanent burden. After the accord was signed, Washington encouraged the contra field commanders to negotiate with CIAV. The contras were willing to explore the options that the Tela process offered for those who wished to return to Nicaragua or otherwise abandon the armed struggle. But they insisted that the demobilization called for at Tela was voluntary, a reading supported by all but the Sandinistas. There was little chance that the United States would forcibly disarm the contras, however, and the Hondurans and CIAV shied away from suggestions that they do so.

PREPARATIONS FOR THE ELECTIONS

By late 1989, it was clear that demobilization of the contras depended on the implementation of the commitment to elections that the Sandinistas had made at Costa del Sol the previous February. They had promised that the process would be fair and free and open to international observers. They had pledged to revise Nicaraguan electoral law, taking account of opposition complaints. The electoral law was first revised and approved by the Sandinista-dominated National Assembly in April 1989 without input from the opposition. Then, on the eve of the Tela summit in August, President Ortega sat down with representatives of all the opposition parties, including those that had not participated in the 1984 elections. After a marathon meeting, the opposition gained several major concessions from the government; in return it joined the government in a call for the contras' demobilization.

The Sandinistas agreed to suspend conscription for military service until after the elections; to grant the opposition parties a half-hour of free television airtime daily; to repeal a Somoza-era law that permitted the detention of individuals for up to six months without charges; to move registration dates from weekdays to Sundays; and to move up the date for the inauguration of the newly elected president from the January 1991 date set in the constitution to April 25, 1990. The Sandinistas also made a number of other commitments, including ones aimed at ensuring opposition access to registration lists and voter tally sheets. Although not all the opposition's concerns were addressed, these concessions went a long way toward establishing rules that would permit an open contest.

At Costa del Sol in February, the Sandinistas had also promised to invite international observers to observe the entire electoral process from August 25 through the elections, giving them access to the whole country. This international contingent, comprising representatives of the OAS and the United Nations, as well as a group headed by former U.S. President Jimmy Carter, had the task of detecting flaws in the electoral process and putting pressure on the Supreme Electoral Tribunal to correct any irregularities. Some opposition rallies were broken up or prevented from convening, but Elliot Richardson, the head of the UN delegation, reported that voter registration had gone smoothly, with 90 percent of eligible Nicaraguans registering.[7]

THE CONTENDERS

As widely expected, the Sandinistas put Daniel Ortega and Sergio Ramírez up for reelection as president and vice president, respectively, although their candidacies were not announced until the registering of candidates had begun. Ortega, who in the early years of the Sandinista government often appeared ill at ease or retiring in public appearances, had become a fairly forceful speaker. The Sandinistas projected an image of youth and strength, and to their supporters at least, were the embodiment of Nicaraguan nationalism. Their rhetoric was strident, however, and they fueled the polarization of Nicaraguan society in small ways, as, for example, by denouncing citizens holding passports as traitors eager to jump ship. They had increased the distribution of land in recent years in order to win wider support, but they were forced to acknowledge that the state of the economy was their Achilles' heel. Even though the rampant inflation had been tamed and was down from 33,000 to 1,700 percent, the Sandinistas could provide few tangible improvements or even quick fixes to appeal to the voters. President Ortega may have canceled the cease-fire in November in order to rekindle the war issue and draw attention away from the economy.

The main opposition was a bloc of fourteen of the twenty-one opposition parties that came together in the summer of 1989 in the UNO, although many of them had cooperated for years. The first challenge UNO faced was to agree on a platform that its diverse membership, which ranged from the National Conservative party on the right to the anti-Sandinista Communist party on the left, would support. The core of the opposition, however, was centrist, and these parties had worked together since the 1984 campaign—a fact that was overlooked by those who predicted the imminent collapse of the coalition.

UNO agreed on a platform on August 24, 1989, in which its primary goals were given as peace and reconciliation, political pluralism, and a social market economy. It promised an end to the military draft, a drastic reduction in military spending, and a general amnesty. Reaffirming the right to private property, UNO promised that beneficiaries of agrarian reform would receive ownership titles (not simply use titles) to their land. It pledged the separation of the police from the armed forces, "which do not belong to any political party."

The next test for UNO was the selection of presidential and vice presidential candidates. Given the intense rivalries—among the parties as well as among individuals—and with no party or individual dominant, the coalition decided early on that the most successful strategy would be to go outside the parties and pick a unifying figure as its presidential candidate. In any case, there were no well-known, charismatic opposition politicians, in part because the parties were weak, but also because the Sandinistas for the past ten years had occupied nearly all of the prominent official positions in Nicaragua. The search for a candidate centered fairly quickly on Violeta Barrios de Chamorro, widow of Pedro Joaquín Chamorro, Sr., whose murder in January 1978 sparked the nationwide uprising that had brought down Somoza. He had been a leader of the anti-Somoza opposition, using his newspaper, *La Prensa,* to crusade against the dictator's corruption and depredations. For this reason, Doña Violeta had been asked to serve on the first revolutionary junta, although she resigned less than a year later, citing health reasons. She indicated later that disagreement with the Sandinistas' rule had also influenced her decision.

Although her political standing was indisputably anchored in her marriage, Chamorro did not shrink from the role that being a martyr's widow thrust upon her. The Chamorros are a prominent family in a country where family ties have always dominated politics. In a 1986 interview, Doña Violeta forcefully

defended the anti-Sandinista position as being Nicaraguan, nationalist, and democratic in character, a claim the internal opposition had been struggling to convey over the din of constant
Sandinista charges that they were pro–U.S. lackeys who secretly
hoped for a contra victory to bring back Somoza-style rule. She
did not denounce the contras, but she did say that "the fight is
here, inside Nicaragua." Her son had just gone to Costa Rica to
join the exile dissidents and the contras. When asked if she
thought he should come back, she shrugged and said, "He's a
grown man; it's his own decision."[8] All of her children had made
their own decisions. One daughter, Claudia, a Sandinista, had
served as ambassador to Costa Rica; her other son was editor of
Barricada, the official Sandinista newspaper, which attacked her
regularly. At that moment, only her daughter Cristiana, then the
editorial page editor of *La Prensa,* sided with her.

Like most of the opposition, Doña Violeta laid the blame for
the state of the country on the Sandinistas rather than on the
United States or the contras. She criticized the Sandinistas for
thinking they owned the revolution. The majority of the population resented their extension of control over every aspect of their
lives, she said, and blamed their mismanagement for the daily
hardships they faced. She cited the increasing shortages, the
breakdown of the transportation system, and declining incomes,
and pointed out that living standards were lower than before the
revolution, a fact documented in a 1989 confidential study by
foreign economists that had been commissioned by the Sandinista government. But popular discontent was not confined to
economic matters, she emphasized; Nicaraguans had hoped for
more freedom and less political polarization after the revolution
but had been disappointed on both counts.[9]

In May 1989, Chamorro made many of the same criticisms
during a visit to the United States, and charged that the Sandinistas had not kept promises they had made under the Esquipulas Accord. The FSLN had maintained control of the
Supreme Electoral Council, had not reconvened the all-party
dialogue, and had not issued a general amnesty. But even
though the Sandinistas controlled access to television and the
flow of newsprint, Chamorro thought the opposition might be

able to win. At the time, however, she said it was "premature" to speak of potential candidates. Nonetheless, the media attention she received during this visit caused some grumbling among opposition politicians at home.

A public opinion poll conducted the previous month for a new Nicaraguan opposition weekly, *La Cronica,* had shown her to be just a tenth of a percentage point behind Daniel Ortega when respondents were asked to say whom they would like to see as president. The poll also indicated that 36.2 percent of the respondents thought the opposition should lead the government; 29.6 percent preferred the FSLN; and 25 percent were undecided.[10] Two later polls conducted by a Costa Rican firm and a Venezuelan institute agreed with this early sounding, showing the Chamorro-led opposition ahead of the Sandinistas, 37 to 30 percent and 41 to 33 percent, respectively.[11] But these polls giving the edge to Chamorro were given far less coverage, or weight, in the U.S. media than surveys showing margins of 25 percent or more in favor of Ortega.

One of Chamorro's principal rivals for the nomination was Enrique Bolaños Geyer, who had headed the Superior Council of Private Enterprise (COSEP) for several years and was influential in the opposition coalition's decision not to run in the 1984 elections. Although a well-known and forceful figure, Bolaños was considered to be too conservative to unite all the parties in UNO; his nomination would likely have caused the leftist parties and possibly even the Independent Liberal party (PLI) to leave the coalition. The other name most frequently mentioned was that of PLI President Virgilio Godoy; he was an intelligent, able politician, but his somber demeanor and extremely dry wit led many to consider him lacking in charisma. Like Doña Violeta, he had trod that delicate line between the anti-Sandinista and pro–U.S. contra stances that the Sandinistas did their best to erase. He was frequently critical of the United States and had served in the junta government as labor minister, so he was immune from attacks on his patriotism and for lack of support for the revolution. UNO ruled out the possibility of an exile returning to run at the top of the ticket, since this would have been not only unfair to those politicians who had struggled to keep alive whatever base they could, but would also have opened the coalition up to the charge that it was simply the front for the contras, who would reimpose a Somoza-style dictatorship.

By June, Pedro Joaquín Chamorro was contemplating a return to Nicaragua from Miami to help his mother campaign. He put in a call to his sister Cristiana, who reported that against the advice of her doctors (Doña Violeta suffers from a serious case of osteoporosis), their mother was enthusiastic about the idea of running for president and would do so if UNO asked her to be its candidate. In early September, UNO selected a Chamorro–Godoy ticket after two days of voting.

THE ELECTORAL CONDITIONS

With its candidates selected, the opposition turned its attention to more serious hurdles. The Sandinistas had a number of advantages over UNO, including that of the incumbency. Their resources, after ten years in power, were significantly greater than those of all the opposition parties combined. The opposition's access to television remained constrained. Even though UNO had access to radio stations with powerful frequencies—the most important means of communicating with rural and poor Nicaraguans—television was important in urban areas where the Sandinistas had the most support. Even though UNO comprised fourteen parties, it received the same amount of free airtime— thirty minutes daily—as the other, tiny opposition parties outside of UNO. Furthermore, the signal of the television station on which the opposition was granted airtime did not extend far beyond Managua in its range. Originally, the opposition had hoped to lease a television station from the Sandinistas, or at least have one transferred to an independent entity. President Arias supported this idea, but the Sandinistas would not agree to it. Finally, free airtime was provided only until December 2, as specified in the electoral regulations; between December 3 and February 25, the opposition had to buy airtime at rates set by the electoral tribunal. This meant that the opposition required substantial funds to continue disseminating its message in the two-and-a-half months prior to the elections. The Sandinistas purchased advertising time, too, but since they were in power, their candidates received coverage daily in news programs. UNO rallies, on the other hand, were not considered to be news events—except for one rally, where two UNO leaders scuffled. For days afterward, Sandinista television news replayed the footage, edited to create the impression that Godoy's spokesman was repeatedly punching Chamorro's campaign chief.

Another problem for the opposition was the composition of the Supreme Electoral Council, which was somewhat weighted in favor of the Sandinistas. Costa Rican officials, among others, had hoped that this could be rectified, but the Sandinistas, who were legally entitled to two of the tribunal's five seats, based on the results of the 1984 elections, steadfastly refused to change its makeup. The allotment of the remaining three seats was the subject of even greater dispute. The one that created the most contention was that reserved for a "notable citizen," which went to Rodolfo Sandino Argüello, dean of the law school of the University of Central America. He had been a member of the Somoza-appointed electoral tribunal, but the opposition claimed he was nonetheless sympathetic to the Sandinistas. Of the other two seats, one went to anti-Sandinista businessman Guillermo Selva, a member of Godoy's party; the other to Aman Sandino Muñoz of the non-UNO Democratic Conservative party. The Democratic Conservatives had finished second in the 1984 elections, which justified Sandino Muñoz's selection to the tribunal, but according to UNO, his party cooperated with the Sandinistas to such an extent that it would be misleading to characterize it as part of the opposition. The composition of the council was a matter of serious concern, since it was not only responsible for the vote count but also had the crucial task of appointing all provincial electoral councils, as well as the local electoral bodies. Furthermore, it was charged with monitoring the adherence of all parties to the electoral law, regulating the use of television in the campaign, and bringing disciplinary action against offending parties. During the campaign, the council ruled that the pro-Sandinista newspaper *El Nuevo Diario* had been unfairly linking UNO with Somoza's National Guard, but it did not have the means to enforce any disciplinary measures and the practice continued.

Finally, the Sandinistas had the means to control or pressure a large segment of the population. The lowering of the voting age to sixteen meant that all seventy thousand members of the military could vote. The young soldiers had been intensively indoctrinated in the course of their military training, as had the students in the public schools. The opposition worried that these young people, who were only six years old at the time of the Sandinista victory, might not see any alternative to the continuation of the regime. But it was also possible that older family members or the general mood of discontent at the state of the country would sway them in the other direction. State employees, who made up about 10 percent of the voting population, might be swayed by the fear that involvement in any opposition activity would jeopardize their employment. The Sandinistas also had the means to intimidate the electorate through pervasive surveillance by military and Interior Ministry security personnel and the denial of ration cards and other essential state services.

If the opposition was to surmount these obstacles, it would have to campaign vigorously, recruit over four thousand poll watchers, and ensure a large turnout against any attempts at intimidation. This required funds that the cash-strapped parties did not have. The offices of most of these parties—in stark contrast to the large new quarters of the Sandinistas, who also occupied modern government office buildings—were tiny, dark, and ill-equipped. Manpower was also a problem. The Independent Liberal party, for example, which was one of the best-organized, had several hundred members in jail for being suspected contra collaborators. Years of intimidation and past experiences of imprisonment had left many Nicaraguans on the outside fearful of active organizing.

The congressionally funded National Endowment for Democracy (NED) had already sent $3.5 million in 1989 to opposition groups in Nicaragua, when the Bush administration asked Congress to approve $9 million more to help alleviate the opposition's financial woes. The NED's charter prohibited it from backing political campaigns anywhere, however, and a dispute erupted over whether the NED would be backing democracy or a specific party, UNO, in the Nicaraguan elections. The opposition coalition was deemed to be the "democratic" force in the country, and it was the NED's mission, after all, to encourage the spread of democracy. But those opposed argued that direct NED aid would amount to a U.S. attempt to prejudice the outcome of the Nicaraguan elections. The Bush administration stopped pushing for NED funds out of fear that the endowment would be compromised. Nonetheless, the *New York Times* editorialized in favor of the proposed NED aid, pointing out that aiding campaigns was a common practice of the European foundations—such as the Friedrich Nauman and Konrad Adenauer *Stiftungs*—to which the NED is often compared. International party organizations (such as the Socialist International and the Christian Democratic International) often supported campaigns of member parties. Proponents also argued that such aid was not prohibited by Nicaraguan law, and was justified by the fact that the opposition's resources were much smaller than the Sandinistas'.

On October 17, the Senate approved the Bush administration's request for $9 million to be channeled by the NED for use by the opposition. Half of the proposed aid would go to the Supreme Electoral Council as dictated by Nicaraguan law. The remaining half was to be used for such activities as voter registration and education conducted by parties but not for the campaigns of individual candidates. To win congressional support for this measure, the administration had promised publicly that it would not provide covert aid to Nicaraguans. UNO campaign manager Antonio Lacayo estimated that the coalition would receive $2 to 3 million for voter education and other purposes consistent with the NED charter. The remainder of the $9 million not allocated to the Supreme Electoral Council was earmarked for the costs of sending the OAS delegation to Nicaragua and for other organizations, including a UNO-linked voter-education institute. About $400,000 was allocated to Carter's observer delegation. After so much debate, however, the aid to the opposition proved to be a mixed blessing. UNO sorely needed the money but was widely criticized for accepting official

U.S. help. To make matters worse, the assistance arrived too late to be of much use. Due to U.S. bureaucratic delays, the first funds were not sent to Nicaragua until late December, and the Nicaraguan Central Bank did not begin to release them until late January—only a month before the election. The Sandinistas used the fact that the assistance came from the United States to attack the nationalist credentials of the members of the opposition, who they alleged were simply the tools of Washington.

The initial efforts of the opposition in the summer of 1989 to organize public gatherings did not bode well for the future. At a UNO rally held in León in June, a group of Sandinistas rushed the opposition crowd. The UNO-affiliated Social Democratic party (PSD) held an indoor rally in Boaco in July, which went off without incident, although one local party member had been arrested earlier after he went door-to-door to encourage residents to attend. Party member Alfredo César, a former director of the contra resistance, had returned to Nicaragua in June. He was among several exiles to come back to help the opposition campaign. UNO had decided to downplay the role of such returnees, but at Boaco César was greeted with enthusiasm. He and Guillermo Potoy, party president, gave the keynote speeches in a theater crammed with Nicaraguans despite the sweltering heat. Those inside, along with those outside clustered around the front door, numbered close to two thousand, although the FSLN newspaper subsequently reported only five hundred people turned out to hear the *"somocista contrarevolucionario."* A few Interior Ministry police Jeep vehicles were parked at the perimeter of the activity, but no attempt was made to interfere with the rally, and no Sandinista bands appeared.

The same weekend, however, UNO was denied permission to hold an outdoor rally in the northern town of Ocotal. Various reasons were given for the denial, including a claim that no request for permission to hold the rally—parties were required to seek permission for such rallies until August 25, when voter registration drives were to begin—had been made. Another was that the Sandinistas themselves had already planned an activity in the town square, although no rally took place at all. Peasants, unaware that the UNO meeting had been canceled, were barred from entering the town's center by police and official vehicles. In November, a UNO rally in Masatepe ended in violence and one brutal death as militants of both sides fought while the Sandinista police stood by. The incident received international attention, and subsequent rallies were closely monitored by both police and international observers, preventing a recurrence of such violence.

Another, less publicized form of intimidation of the opposition continued, however, primarily in remote areas. UNO supporters were threatened or bribed to drop their candidacies or poll-watching duties. On election day, numerous polling sites found that insufficient ballots had been allotted to them. About thirty other polling places opened late or not at all because local officials said there was contra activity nearby.

The Sandinista campaign was extremely well organized and suffered from no lack of funds. Campaign chief Comandante Bayardo Arce Castaño mobilized and coordinated the grassroots and mass organizations of the party in order to turn out thousands more at each rally than the opposition was able to muster. Heavy use was made of government vehicles to transport people to rallies, and state workers were monitored to ensure they attended. Arce said the vehicles were rented, with money (some $7 million) donated by foreigners, including the West German Green party.[12] But he denied a report that the Mexican ruling party had given the Sandinistas $10 million. The Sandinistas made use of a superb sound system, catchy tunes, and slick advertising and gave away baseball equipment, knapsacks, and trinkets at their rallies. Their efforts convinced many onlookers that with such advantages they were certain to win.

The Sandinistas also released 1,900 prisoners, contras, and former members of the National Guard, in the final phase of the campaign. They promised to build 7,000 new homes annually and distribute land to 34,000 more families. Their slogan, "Todo Será Mejor" ("Everything Will Be Better"), seemed to admit that their record was less than compelling, but they claimed that their polling data showed that Nicaraguans held the United States, not the Sandinistas, responsible for the collapsed economy and the ongoing war. Furthermore, they argued, the United States would be forced to change its policies after their electoral victory. The contras would be disbanded and the painful economic embargo lifted once the Sandinistas were thus legitimized, although Vice Foreign Minister Víctor Hugo Tinoco said they expected neither aid from nor a rapid rapprochement with the United States.[13] But other countries and multilateral institutions would be free of U.S. pressure and would resume their lending to Nicaragua.

Both sides cited polls showing they were going to win. Most diplomats and other analysts, taking the huge turnout at Sandinista rallies at face value, believed the Sandinistas' polls. But the vote was not even close: UNO won by a 14 percent margin, 54.7 to 40.8 percent. UNO won fifty-two seats in the National Assembly to the Sandinistas' thirty-seven. Only one other party, led by a former Sandinista, gained a seat in the legislature. UNO did not win enough seats to be able to revise the constitution, as it had hoped to do, but with the strong executive powers built into the government, it was assured of the leading governing role.

By Central American standards, the voting process, which was closely scrutinized, was as fair as any had ever been. Layers of safeguards prevented any irregularity from significantly affecting the outcome. If the vote had been extremely close, however, these safeguards might not have been sufficient, since international observers were present at only a fraction of the polling sites. There was also a problem with the supposedly indelible ink used, which was found to be removable with household bleach. But UNO managed to have poll watchers at the majority of the polling places. To prevent fraud, the poll watchers from all parties at each site signed every ballot and were present when the ballots were counted. Observers were also given copies of the tally sheets to safeguard the count at this stage. Most important was the quick count conducted by the United Nations, which yielded a reliable projection of the results three-and-a-half hours after the polls had closed. And because Carter had developed a good rapport with both sides, he was able to help smooth the way for acceptance of the results by the Sandinistas.

Most foreigners following the election were shocked by the Sandinista defeat, leading many to wonder how they could have misread Nicaraguan sentiment so badly. Because the contra policy had been the center of the bitter debate over Nicaragua in the United States, it was widely assumed that this was true in Nicaragua as well. But the Nicaraguan elections were a referendum on the Sandinistas, not the contras. The widely divergent opinion poll results indicated that many voters were wary of stating their intention to vote for the opposition. According to one Nicaraguan pollster, Nicaraguans, even the peasants, knew which polling firms had been hired by each side. This said, what accounts for the Sandinista upset? In the immediate aftermath of the elections, some Sandinista officials speculated that many Nicaraguans doubted that U.S. pressure on the country would cease so long as the Sandinistas were in power. But this explanation of a cowed electorate is insufficient. It overlooks a central factor: the widespread discontent with Sandinista policies. On the main issues of the war and the economy, the vote indicated a lack of confidence in the Sandinista promises of a brighter future. Before the election, many peasants could be heard to say, "We're dying of hunger."

A Soviet analyst concludes that the Sandinistas' own errors contributed substantially to their defeat:

> The backlash against the Sandinistas was largely justified. Their thoughtless economic administration and their suffocation of the market hit the economy hard. Ousted from political offices, the private sector was unwilling to give a helping hand to the floundering Sandinistas. On the contrary, in a huff, many politically indifferent entrepreneurs joined the opposition and called fire and brimstone upon the heads of the most ideologically committed. Blunders in the agricultural and cooperative sector only fueled the dissatisfaction. . . . The defeat may become a useful reminder for any government to listen to the people, even the opposition, and be democratic and quick to respond.[14]

Voters could also see that an UNO government was likely to receive substantial U.S. assistance, and with the Sandinistas out of power, the contra war would probably end. The UNO platform promised an end to the military draft, a drastic reduction in the size of the army, and a complete amnesty—all of which the Sandinistas had refused to promise, even if the contra war ended.

After helping to convince the Sandinistas to concede defeat on election night, Carter worked on subsequent days to facilitate transition talks between the two sides. He departed after hosting a meeting of UNO campaign chief Antonio Lacayo and Defense Minister Humberto Ortega, who had been designated the heads of their respective transition teams. The most volatile issues they faced involved control of the security forces, the disposition of property confiscated in the Sandinista revolution, the disbanding of the contras, and guarantees to both sides that there would be no retribution for acts perpetrated during the previous ten years.

During the campaign, President Ortega had pledged to turn over all power to the new government, but Interior Minister Tomás Borge seemed to contradict this when he announced that the revolutionary armed forces would never obey the "insane" orders of a Chamorro government. In the delicate talks that followed the election, the Sandinistas sought to maintain the "integrity" of the forces they had built. Borge was replaced with a Chamorro coalition member, but Humberto Ortega was retained as the Sandinista army chief of staff. Borge's feared secret police was absorbed into the military's intelligence unit. The "integrity" of the Sandinista army was guaranteed above all by a Sandinista decree implemented just before Chamorro's inauguration. The measure handed over sweeping powers that had belonged to the defense minister to the chief of staff. This meant that, even though Chamorro announced the military would be cut in half by the end of 1990, Humberto Ortega would be in charge of selecting those to be dismissed. Chamorro did not want a head-on confrontation with the army, but many conservatives in her coalition criticized her decision to leave so much power in Sandinista hands. The government could not be sure of the army's loyalty, and even with its numbers reduced to 28,000 troops, it would be a formidable potential threat.

To resolve the inflammatory property issue, the UNO government-elect proposed the creation of a tribunal to hear appeals for reclaiming houses or land. At the same time, it promised not to evict any peasants from land they had been given by the Sandinista government, and proposed to offer instead compensation to the former owners in the form of long-term government bonds.

Chamorro joined Ortega's call for immediate demobilization of the contra rebels, who wished to remain armed and in place until the actual transfer of power and until the promised changes in the Sandinista army occurred. Nicaraguan, Honduran, and U.S. emissaries tried to persuade the contras that warfare was no longer the path to change in Nicaragua. Newly elected Honduran President Rafael Callejas announced that he wanted the contras out of Honduras "as soon as possible," and sent his foreign minister to Nicaragua to discuss this issue.

The contras, however, were deeply skeptical that the Sandinistas would actually cede control of the army to the new government. Contra leader Israel Galeano (Comandante Franklyn) was worried that the Sandinistas—even if they gave up the top positions in the government—might continue to wage war against the contras and their supporters: "Chamorro may take office," he said, "but assuming real power is another thing." A month after the elections, he claimed that the rural areas of the northern and central provinces were being bombarded and the Sandinistas were handing out arms to supporters, a development also reported by the foreign press.[15] Even though most outsiders believed that the contras were a source of continuing trouble, the contras themselves remained convinced that their guns were their only real guarantee of safety. In the hinterlands of Nicaragua, where few reporters or observers venture for long, few are held accountable for their acts. This is where the process of reconciliation will be the most difficult. Many rebels told me that they would keep their arms since they did not believe that a real transfer of power would take place in the rural hinterlands. The peasants of these areas are the contras' friends and family members. To them, the UNO government is remote and the Sandinista police and military power very real. The gulf in perception between rural and urban Nicaraguans presents an enormous challenge to the new government.

In a remarkably smooth process supervised by the United Nations and the OAS, the contra forces were demobilized by June 1990 and the weapons turned in were dumped in the Gulf of Fonseca—an ironic gesture since many of the arms sent to the Salvadoran guerrillas crossed that body of water. The ex-rebels were given food and civilian clothing, and promised land and farming implements. The process got bogged down, however, and by the fall of 1990 the government still had not found land for them.

Along with the United States and other intermediaries, the Chamorro government must address the concerns of rural Nicaraguans so that the contras do not become an obstacle in the transition process. The demilitarization and reconciliation efforts, if they are to succeed, will require continuing international scrutiny—of the sort that ensured the election's fairness—to guarantee that hostilities in fact cease throughout Nicaragua.

The degree of pragmatism and the desire for reconciliation exhibited by both the Sandinista and UNO leadership in the weeks after the election seemed almost miraculous. Daniel Ortega pledged to defend the revolution's achievements, but he said the Sandinistas would do so by constitutional means. The meaning of his rallying cry, "We will continue to govern from below," became clear in the months ahead. After Chamorro decided against the mass firing of government workers, the Sandinista union called strikes in May and July, paralyzing the new government and forcing it to backtrack on its political and economic program. The specter of the Sandinistas as a disloyal opposition loomed.

In addition to their labor weapon, the Sandinistas remained the strongest single party, with 40 percent of the seats in the National Assembly. This put pressure on the UNO coalition to stay together in order to retain its legislative majority. The problems of keeping the coalition together were immediately apparent, however: not only did the UNO parties span a wide spectrum of ideologies, but Chamorro relied far more on her personal advisers than on her coalition partners. The differences among coalition leaders were as much personal as political. Chamorro's vice president, Virgilio Godoy, for example, who leads the strong Independent Liberal party and is a forceful and ambitious politician, subordinated his own interests to the larger goals of the coalition. But he is unlikely to be happy in a supporting role for long. The danger that factionalism might undermine the new government became obvious in the first six months of its existence. Godoy was not permitted to have an office or a staff, so he continued to work out of his party headquarters. Aside from his political reasons for maintaining a separate identity, there were very real ideological disagreements between his camp and Chamorro's. Godoy did not believe Chamorro seriously challenged the Sandinistas' determination to keep their power base in the military. He also thought it was necessary to take firm action against the Sandinistas' use of their labor confederation to frustrate the government's program to stop inflation, privatize badly run state companies, and implement free market policies. These were policies that many who voted for the government advocated, and Godoy and others believed Chamorro had let them down by forming a tacit alliance with the Sandinistas. The president's advisers countered that the best way to keep the Sandinistas from wreaking havoc was to pursue conciliatory policies; in any case, the government's tools for curbing the Sandinistas' remaining powers were limited. If it provoked a confrontation, it might lose.

The problems of factionalism are nothing new in Nicaragua. Its political parties have historically been unable to form lasting, coherent bases of power. Throughout fifty-two years of dictatorship, the Somoza clan successfully coopted most of the Liberal party, as well as the business elites. The main opposition, the Conservative party, was fragmented and weak. Both of these parties remain splintered today, although some of their leaders are attempting to reunite them. But a two-party system is not a realistic outcome for Nicaragua. The Chamorro clan may be able to unify the Conservatives, but one of the president's key allies, Alfredo César, has his own Social Democratic party and an eye on the presidency. The Sandinistas themselves are in serious disarray and may split if internal party elections fail to establish the dominance of either the hard-line or moderate tendency. The best hope for Nicaragua is that four or five blocs will coalesce, and that, over time, the electorate will show which of these have lasting appeal.

Such a process of democratic competition could lead to a more stable political future for Nicaragua, but only if Chamorro, Godoy, and the Sandinista comandantes refrain from the behind-the-scenes maneuvering characteristic of the Somoza years and fight their political battles in the appropriate legislative and judicial venues instead. The government should carry out its promise to introduce constitutional reforms to give those branches more power. Many non-Sandinista Nicaraguans faulted the Sandinistas for the obstructionist tactics they used against Chamorro in her first months in power, but they were also unhappy that Chamorro was so much more accommodating to her adversaries than to her own coalition partners. Her actions led Godoy to retaliate by criticizing Chamorro, when he should have been organizing the coalition's legislators to press the conservatives' interests. "What Nicaragua needs," said Andrés Zuñiga, the leader of a small party in UNO, "is to overcome the personalist, factionalized politics that has plagued it since time immemorial. A process of political education and institution building is our real task."[16] It is up to its leaders to initiate this process if Nicaragua is to become a truly democratic society.

4

EL SALVADOR: THE DUARTE ERA AND THE ADVENT OF ARENA

For almost a decade, El Salvador has been trapped in a civil war that has taken the lives of some 75,000 of its 5 million citizens. During the 1970s, moderate Salvadoran leftists were radicalized when their demands for reform of the country's stratified economic and political systems were met with severe repression. Many joined the ranks of the Soviet-supported Marxist insurgency, which was buoyed by the success of the 1979 revolution in Nicaragua. The Left has fought with grim determination to transform El Salvador, but the guardians of the old order have fought with equal ferocity to stave off change. Since 1981, the United States has provided massive aid to the Salvadoran government, both to promote reform and to help defeat the insurgents. By 1990, some important changes had occurred that gave impetus to efforts to end the war. But bringing the region's most intractable conflict to a close will require a bold effort by the government to demonstrate a commitment to reform that many doubt it has.

The debate over the degree of political change in El Salvador resembles one over whether the glass is half-empty or half-full. The election of José Napoleón Duarte as president of El Salvador in 1984 was the culmination of an arduous transition from military to civilian government that began after a group of reformist military officers overthrew Gen. Carlos Humberto Romero in 1979. Another milestone on the democratic path was passed in mid-1989 as Duarte completed his term and transferred power to his elected civilian successor. Considering this tiny, densely populated country's severe problems, such achievements may seem small, especially when stacked up against the remaining obstacles to progress; on the other hand, they look enormous when viewed in the context of the decade-long war and the extreme resistance that has been overcome.

In 1979, revolution or military dictatorship appeared the most likely alternatives for El Salvador; now, neither does. After five elections generally judged by the international community to have been fair, a new habit of respecting the results of elections has taken hold. This acceptance of the rules of the democratic game is neither universal nor irreversible, but each step makes it harder to reverse. Of course, elections are not all there is to institutionalizing democracy. Salvadorans still have major decisions to make about the power of guns and money. But however excruciatingly slow the pace, change is occurring.[1] To understand the situation in El Salvador today, one must take account of the 1979–1984 transition period and the 1984–1989 Duarte term.

THE REFORM JUNTA, 1979–1984

The 1979 revolution in Nicaragua galvanized both the U.S. government and the Salvadoran Left: both believed that El Salvador was also ripe for revolution. El Salvador's Romero dictatorship was discredited. Unwilling to meet the growing demands for change, it had resorted to repressive measures. But these measures had failed to stifle the demands for reform. Unlike the Nicaraguan National Guard, however, the Salvadoran army did not collapse. Instead, a group of Young Turks staged a coup with the cooperation of some of their senior officers. This coup, in October 1979, marked the beginning of the military's split from its traditional allies, the wealthy landowners, at whose expense the reform junta declared land, banking, and commerce reforms. But the new government was riven with conflict. Its military members were divided between moderate and radical reformers, and its cabinet members included leftist leaders Guillermo Ungo and Salvador Samayoa and others who later joined the guerrillas. Pressuring the junta from the outside was a massive worker- and peasant-based movement organized by the Left. According to junta member Gen. Jaime Abdul Gutiérrez, "there was not a single institution that had not been infiltrated [by the Left] and was not against the government. . . . They had infiltrated everything and could easily paralyze the country."[2]

Less than three months after the coup, the junta dissolved and was replaced by a military–Christian Democratic junta. After it too dissolved, in December 1980, military officers offered José Napoleón Duarte, a Christian Democrat, the presidency of the junta, despite their fears of the left-of-center politician. Against the wishes of many in his party, Duarte, the former mayor of the capital city, accepted. After he and Ungo had been defrauded of their 1972 victory in presidential elections, and he had been beaten up by soldiers, Duarte went into exile in Venezuela. But in 1980 he decided that reform might be possible if he worked with the new military government. His participation was the junta's only remaining hope for a centrist coalition; without him, the alternative was a return to the old military-landowner alliance. Of his much criticized decision to accept the presidency, Duarte later said, "The killing in El Salvador was going on and on. I could not stop it as yet, but I had to work toward that day, one step at a time."[3] His reputation had already suffered as a result of his decision to stay with the junta after the March 1980 assassination of Archbishop Oscar Arnulfo Romero, presumably by right-wing extremists, which had brought the country to the brink of insurrection. Most of Duarte's leftist colleagues, including the left wing of his own party, subsequently formed the Democratic Revolutionary Front (FDR), which allied itself with the guerrillas.

The United States' dilemma was similar to Duarte's and, like Duarte, it chose to support what it saw as the lesser of evils. A military government, even a violent one, was preferable to a victorious Marxist revolution, especially when that government promised a transition to elected civilian rule. In the last months of 1980, the guerrilla groups, prodded by Cuban leader Fidel Castro, united in the Farabundo Martí National Liberation Front (FMLN). The Carter administration, which had halted its minimal aid to the junta after the December 1980 killing of four U.S. religious women by National Guardsmen, reversed itself in January 1981 after the FMLN launched a general offensive. The incoming Reagan administration, fearing that the Duarte-led junta would not be able to survive the guerrillas' offensive, decided to step up support for the junta, which managed to hold off the FMLN. In 1982, elections for a constitutional assembly were held, the first step in the transition to democracy. The Christian Democrats' failure to win a majority meant that right-wingers itching to force Duarte out could do so. With U.S. backing, the junta rebuffed a bid for the junta's presidency by the right-wing Roberto D'Aubuisson, a retired army major who was president of the constitutional assembly. An independent, the moderate conservative Alvaro Magaña, was chosen instead to lead the junta until the presidential elections scheduled for 1984.

The military-dominated junta saw elections and political and economic reform as the key to legitimate government, but it was either unwilling or unable to call a halt to the repressive measures that were being employed to staunch the war. Hundreds of corpses turned up every month. Military, security, and paramilitary forces—paramilitary "death squads" had cropped up after the 1979 coup—did most of the killings. The coup by reformist officers had convinced many in the wealthy class that the military had abandoned them as the protectors of their privilege, so they looked elsewhere for protection. Landowners funded some of these death squads to fight the expropriation of their lands, which had been mandated by the 1979 coup-makers.

The Maximiliano Hernández Martínez Anti-Communist Brigade (named for the general who put down a 1932 uprising by killing at least ten thousand peasants) and other such groups claimed responsibility for many of the deaths, which peaked at about eight hundred a month in the early 1980s. This shadowy group claimed to have executed five leaders of the FDR in November 1980 and warned "the priests who have an affinity for the terrorist Marxist bands that they will have the same fate if they insist in their sermons on poisoning the minds of Salvadoran youth." In his last sermon before he was killed, Archbishop Romero had appealed to the security forces: "No soldier is obliged to obey an order contrary to the law of God. . . . It is high time you recovered your consciences and obeyed your consciences rather than a sinful order. . . . I order you in the name of God, stop the repression!"[4]

A few intrepid reporters traced the subterranean linkages of the ultraright to the military,[5] although very little has been proven in the courts of law. Roberto D'Aubuisson was accused of being the "intellectual author" of Romero's death, which he denied. He had headed a military intelligence service specializing in political surveillance until he was cashiered after the 1979 coup, taking the agency's files with him. D'Aubuisson's extreme anticommunist rhetoric and his verbal attacks on individuals are a matter of public record, as is his plan to assassinate a U.S. ambassador. He took credit for masterminding the November 1980 killing of the FDR leaders. Therefore, many find plausible the reports that he formed death squads to systematically torture and eliminate political enemies.

The levels of abuse correlate closely with the rise and fall of the war's intensity. In 1980 and 1981, the threat was of insurrection, with the cities as the main battlefield. The Right's reaction resulted in the deaths of a majority of the nearly ten thousand who died in 1980. After the failure of the 1981 general offensive, the FMLN concentrated on building its guerrilla armies and securing sanctuary. When the Left next attempted national mobilization (combined with significant military actions) in 1983 and 1984, its adherents again met with widespread repression. Thus, far from being unpredictable or continuous, right-wing abuses escalated only when the threat of insurrection arose.

The U.S. government came under heavy criticism for supporting a government that was suspected of indiscriminate violence in its war against the guerrillas. After Vice President Bush went to El Salvador in December 1983 to protest the high levels of torture, kidnapping, and murder by military and paramilitary units, the high command transferred some of the suspect officers. After Bush's visit, abuses began to decline, although the decline probably resulted from the fact that the repression had accomplished its objective. The urban insurrection was quelled in 1984, and the war moved to the countryside as the rebels found refuge in the northern and eastern parts of the country.

THE DUARTE PRESIDENCY, 1984–1989

The 1984 elections brought Duarte to the presidency in a vote generally deemed fair despite protestations of fraud by his chief rival, D'Aubuisson. That this was the Christian Democrats' moment was underscored the following year when they won with an eleven-seat margin (30–19) over D'Aubuisson's Nationalist Republican Alliance party (ARENA) in legislative elections. An agrarian reform program was initiated after the 1979 coup and elections took place on schedule, but Duarte failed to subordinate the military and get the justice system to function. With the extreme Right and the guerrillas stoking the fires of violence, this was perhaps the most reform that could have been expected.

Duarte came to office with an overwhelming agenda: to keep the country on a democratic path, to fight the war while looking for a way to end it, and to pursue reform and keep the war-torn economy afloat. He managed the first two objectives by maintaining the tripartite alliance with the military and the United States that had formed during the junta period. Critics faulted Duarte for not "taming the military" as he had vowed to do, but the military was the ultimate guarantor of his survival in office. Time and again, Duarte ran up against obstacles to political and economic reform.

During 1983 and 1984, the military sustained heavy losses as a result of guerrilla attacks on the San Miguel and El Paraíso brigades in the east and north. This compelled the chief U.S. adviser to the Salvadoran military, Col. Joseph Stringham, to warn the military: "Look, this is not my country, but you guys better get serious about this thing or you are not going to have to worry about me complaining to you much anymore."[6] The army did get serious, revising its general objectives and force structure in line with the 1982 Woerner Report. This report had been drawn up, at Duarte's request, by Salvadoran officers and a U.S. task force led by Gen. Fred Woerner. Beginning in 1983, U.S. military aid exceeded $100 million annually for training and arms and to increase the army's size. The army's capabilities improved from 1984 on, although at a cost of over $1 billion by 1990. Fearful of being drawn into another Vietnam, Congress limited the number of U.S. military advisers to El Salvador to fifty-five.

The formation of elite rapid-reaction battalions and the aerial bombing and artillery attacks of a better-equipped military were responsible for much of the gain, but the Salvadoran army also adopted programs to rebuild the country's infrastructure. The record of the "National Plan" of 1983, which served primarily to introduce the military to the idea of a political-military strategy of "winning hearts and minds," was mixed. It was nonetheless later expanded into a nationwide program known as the "United to Reconstruct Plan" (UPR). Col. René Emilio Ponce, now the defense minister, was one of the leading promoters of the program. "In this type of war," he said, "we need the support of the civilian population . . . so the UPR objectives include economic recovery, reactivating agriculture and local commerce, self-defense campaigns, and refinancing agricultural production."[7] According to Ponce, by 1986 nine hundred projects, from building or rebuilding schools, bridges, and roads, to installing or repairing water or electric service, had been undertaken. Critics of the program said the scope was too broad, preventing the military from permanently securing the UPR areas. It did its hearts-and-minds work and moved on, and the FMLN came right back in.

Nonetheless, the military's adoption of this approach was a welcome part of its broader acceptance of democratic civilian rule. President Duarte cited the military's professionalization and support for democracy and reform as the "most difficult but most important achievement" of his presidency. "How they are changed from serving dictatorship for fifty years to serving democracy now," he remarked in August 1986. "Obviously there remain many problems, but the change in their . . . minds is very important."[8] To some, however, this strategy was just camouflage: the military still ran the country. Ponce said that the military's primary role was "to clean [out the] guerrillas and keep them out, and organize civil defense." He acknowledged, however, that the government should have carried out the work on the country's infrastructure. "But it didn't," he said, "so we did. The politicians were fighting, and the army [was] the only institution capable of taking the initiative."[9]

President Duarte had campaigned on a promise to bring peace to the country, but neither side in the conflict was prepared to make concessions of any significance. He did initiate a dialogue with the FMLN, overcoming a taboo against talking to the guerrillas. It became politically disadvantageous for any sector, including the military, to declare itself opposed to the idea of a negotiated peace. The Catholic church played a key mediating role, and several meetings were held both in and out of the country between 1984 and 1986. But the conflict was not ripe for resolution; both sides were seeking military advantage. Both the civilian government and the military insisted on adherence to the constitution, and rejected the guerrillas' demands for a share of power in the government. For their part, the FMLN and the FDR refused to participate in what they saw as a sham democracy. They had abstained from all elections beginning with the 1982 constitutional assembly vote. "Legality is not the same as legitimacy," noted the leading intellectual of the Left, Father Ignacio Ellacuría, rector of the Jesuit University of Central America in San Salvador.[10] Duarte had raised Salvadorans' hopes for an end to the war, so his failure to achieve more progress toward that end cost him in political terms.

Far more costly to Duarte, and to the Christian Democrats, was the worsening state of the economy throughout his tenure. The cost of the war, falling commodity prices on the world market, drought, and a devastating earthquake all conspired against the government. But to this was added the incompetence and corruption of officials and Duarte's animosity toward the private sector. Reform measures were undercut by widespread inefficiency, graft, and favoritism in the agrarian reform institute, in the banking system, and in INCAFE, the national coffee marketing institute.

The cost of economic sabotage and war damage amounted to about two-thirds of the $2.8 billion in U.S. economic aid El Salvador had received by 1989, the bulk of which went to offset balance-of-payments deficits. Coffee production in 1989 was nearly one-third that of 1979. Revenues had slumped drastically with the falling coffee prices, and fell further after the international coffee pricing agreement collapsed in 1989. Yet even when prices were up, coffee growers charged that INCAFE paid them prices too low to make reinvesting economically practical. A director of INCAFE had decamped with millions of dollars. The coffee-grower cooperatives formed under the agrarian reform program were less productive than the plantations had been under private owners, partly because of a lack of credit and expertise. The new owners were saddled with enormous debts, while the former owners raged because only 10 percent of them had been compensated for the loss of their property. In another case of mismanagement, the foreign relief aid provided to the government for the construction of housing after the 1986 earthquake was squandered and very few new homes were built.

The lack of improvement in El Salvador's system of justice was Duarte's most glaring failure. How could justice be said to exist when no military officer had been convicted in a civilian Salvadoran court for human rights abuses? Despite the $10-million U.S.–funded Administration of Justice program, very little judicial reform was achieved. The U.S. ambassador, William G. Walker, admitted in early 1989 that "until the justice system is turned around and performing better, one can't really claim that El Salvador [has] a democratic system."[11] The outgoing Supreme Court president, Francisco José "Chachi" Guerrero (who was later assassinated by the FMLN), proposed in June 1989 that any detentions not reported to the courts within twenty-four hours be investigated. The proposal, while welcomed, implied that abuse of the right of habeas corpus and the mistreatment of detainees were still problems.

Under Salvadoran law, evidence of wrongdoing against the security forces can only be introduced in court by the forces themselves or by an investigating judge. In May 1988, a judge was assassinated after he refused to grant amnesty to former officers allegedly running a kidnap-for-profit ring. Many other cases involving security forces never made it to court. The military, which views an accusation against one of its own as an attack on the institution as a whole, resists the notion of civilian prosecution. The Special Investigative Unit set up under the U.S. program to deal with abuse of the law by the military is staffed by military personnel who remain on the military payroll and on active duty.[12] Loyalty in the officer corps is strong, especially among officers who trained together in the same class or *tanda* at the military academy. The commitment to constitutional government in El Salvador is gradually evolving into a greater regard for law in general, contributing to a lower level of human rights abuses. But the process has been slow. Preventing abuses has proven far easier than prosecuting past abuses. "What has been established is a tacit pact with the military which basically assumes that we will forget the past and that certain measures will be taken to keep the situation under control and within certain bounds in the future," said one analyst in El Salvador.[13] Most of the cases of the early 1980s were closed under a 1987 amnesty for guerrillas and soldiers—as called for in the 1987 Esquipulas Accord. The case of Archbishop Romero was exempted, but then effectively closed after the Supreme Court ruled that a request for extradition of a key witness from the United States had been improperly made. The court threw out the extradition request and ruled that the available testimony was too old, and contradictory, in December 1988.

Considering the ongoing war, it is amazing that El Salvador managed to maintain a barely positive rate of economic growth during the second half of the 1980s, although the population growth rate exceeded it. This is a testament not just to U.S. largesse but also to the tenacious, hard-working Salvadorans, who did not give up on their country. Their spirit was also evident in their commitment to electoral democracy. Between 1982 and 1989, the turnout in five elections ranged between 40 and 80 percent. Elections alone do not make a democracy, of course, but even in war zones Salvadorans have been intent on exercising their right to vote.

In terms of political freedoms, El Salvador traversed a great distance during the 1980s. In the early years of the decade, demonstrations were violently crushed and the media were controlled by conservatives. By the end of the decade, protest marches by groups known to be linked to the FMLN occurred without incident. A centrist newspaper, *El Mundo,* appeared and television news became much bolder in its reporting. Although the society's deep cleavages remain, progress is demonstrated daily in such events as a televised debate between the feared right-winger D'Aubuisson and one of his nemeses, leftist politician Guillermo Ungo.

The improving climate for freedom of the press and association, the declining numbers of human rights abuses (from eight hundred a month in the early 1980s to twenty a month by 1988), and the Esquipulas Accord, which called for democratization and a negotiated end to war throughout the region, led to the return of some of the democratic leftists who had joined forces briefly with the armed Left. Among these were Ungo and Rubén Zamora, who had participated in the 1979 reform junta government. They returned to El Salvador in late 1987, acknowledging the existence of a political space in which they could operate and that they wished to try to widen. Zamora described practicing politics in El Salvador as "like being in a dark room: you run into some objects and you can move them, and there are others, like a piano, that you have to go around."[14]

Upon their return, Ungo and Zamora linked their parties, the National Revolutionary Movement and the Social Christian Movement, with a third, the Social Democratic party, to form the Democratic Convergence. This coalition ran Ungo and Reni Roldán, secretary general of the Social Democratic party, for president and vice president, respectively, in the March 1989 elections. Wearing bulletproof vests as they campaigned, the returned exiles were vivid testimony to the mixed track record of the democratic project. They did test the democratic waters, while sandbagging the walls around the Convergence offices and prudently staying clear of more radical groups who were also pushing the boundaries of the permissible. But Ungo and Zamora refused calls by President Duarte and others that they end their alliance with the FMLN guerrillas to show that they rejected violent revolution in favor of peaceful political change through elections.

The Democratic Convergence polled only 3.8 percent of the vote in the elections, in part because of the confusing signals of its ally, the FMLN. After months of denouncing the upcoming vote, in January 1989 the FMLN suddenly offered to participate in the elections if they were postponed from March to September 1989. When its terms were rejected, the FMLN once again called for its supporters to boycott the elections. It later modified its stand and asked its supporters either to nullify their ballots or vote for the Convergence if they wished to participate. This equivocal endorsement of the Convergence probably diminished the number of votes it received. Before and during the elections, the FMLN conducted a campaign of sabotage, blacking out areas of the country and calling for a national transportation stoppage. One of the largest labor federations, UNTS (National Unity of Salvadoran Workers), also called on its members to boycott the elections.

The Democratic Convergence politicians, meanwhile, defended their continued alliance with the FMLN on the grounds that they were the only available channel for negotiating with the guerrillas—even though the FMLN had held direct talks with the government. These politicians are unlikely to sever their alliance with the FMLN formally, although they have been distancing themselves from the guerrillas' hard-line positions. But as long as their ties to the guerrillas remain, they will gain few supporters from the middle of the political spectrum. Despite this handicap, Ungo and Zamora have cast their lots with those working to change the political system from within. If they persevere—and survive—they may become the basis of a significant democratic left in El Salvador. For now, they are still moving around in a dark room.

THE ARENA GOVERNMENT

Many observers feared that the fragile gains made in El Salvador would be jeopardized by the coming to power of ARENA, the right-wing Nationalist Republican Alliance, in mid-1989. But in fact it has proved a far more moderate government than expected, illustrating the extent to which U.S. public perceptions have not kept pace with Salvadoran change. ARENA was founded as an antireform party in 1981 with the backing of wealthy Salvadorans angry over the expropriation of their land. In a country where bodyguards and weapons are commonplace, ARENA's image is a particularly militaristic one. As ARENA's Alfredo Cristiani put on the blue-and-white presidential sash in June 1989, many in the United States feared a return in short order to the bloody repressive practices of the early 1980s. The party's president-for-life, Roberto D'Aubuisson, had been denied a U.S. visa because he had reportedly plotted the death of U.S. ambassador Thomas Pickering. Allegations about D'Aubuisson's paramilitary activities remain unproven in the courts of law, but his televised denunciations of Salvadorans in the early 1980s were often followed by their disappearance or death.

ARENA won the presidency in fair elections, building on the impressive gains it had made in 1988 when it won control of the National Assembly, as well as a majority of the country's municipalities. It was aided by the dismal governing record and campaign performance of the Christian Democrats. Strong U.S. support for the Christian Democratic party (PDC) could not compensate for the party's mistakes of governance, which were compounded when a long-simmering battle for Duarte's mantle split the party. Julio Rey Prendes refused to support the PDC candidate, his rival, Fidel Chávez Mena. Duarte, suffering from terminal stomach cancer, tried to stave off the split by suggesting his adviser, Abraham Rodríguez, one of El Salvador's wise men, as a compromise candidate. But Chávez Mena and Rey Prendes were both determined to be candidates, and the rupture proved irreparable. Rey Prendes formed his own party, ran for president, and then negotiated a role in the ARENA government. Because of these problems, the future of the PDC is cloudy. Rey Prendes took many of its political operatives with him, so it must rebuild its base; to do so, it must find a message that voters want to hear. During the electoral campaign, the PDC drew dark pictures of what would happen if ARENA won, but the voters were not rallied by the "They're Worse Than We Are" theme of the PDC campaign.

ARENA did not win simply as a result of protest votes against the PDC. Contrary to predictions, it won on the first ballot, with almost 54 percent of the vote. Its strong showing was due in part to the savvy and well-funded organization it had built after it turned its energies to winning power by electoral means. But it was also the result of two overlooked or downplayed factors: the appeal of its message to a large number of Salvadoran voters, and the changes that have occurred within the party since its founding days, which broadened its base. (These factors also suggest that ARENA's rule may turn out to be very different than anticipated.)

It is difficult for people in the United States to understand how ARENA, "the party of the death squads," won the presidency. Some observers tried to explain its win with the "two-ARENA theory," which holds that the party put on a moderate face to win elections, duping the Salvadoran voters into believing that it was something it was not. It was for this reason, the theory goes, that ARENA picked a moderate businessman as its candidate. (Cristiani joined the party in 1984 and became its president in 1986 when D'Aubuisson relinquished the post.) Although it was true that Cristiani's candidacy would be well received in the United States, it was also true that D'Aubuisson was not much of a liability within El Salvador. When D'Aubuisson ran for legislative office in 1988, Duarte revived the accusations of his complicity in the death of Archbishop Romero and initiated extradition proceedings against an accused accomplice, but D'Aubuisson and twenty-nine other *areneros* won deputies' seats nonetheless. In fact, D'Aubuisson, a recognized, crowd-rousing figure and an experienced campaigner, was a key asset in ARENA's 1989 presidential campaign. Most analysts and reporters do not like to confront the fact of D'Aubuisson's popularity, and what it says about a significant portion of Salvadoran society.

Cristiani and D'Aubuisson are a study in contrasts: the former is an even-tempered coffee millionaire who is married to one of the so-called oligarch's daughters (whose sister is married to the former defense minister, Gen. Carlos Vides Casanova). During a campaign visit to the countryside, a U.S. diplomat who was present put a little dirt on Cristiani's suit, suggesting to the shocked candidate that he should try to blend in more. D'Aubuisson, on the other hand, is a volatile ex-military man with a reputation for hard drinking and womanizing. In the United States, such a reputation can be a political liability, but it contributes to D'Aubuisson's popularity in El Salvador. Furthermore, since D'Aubuisson is not a member of the elite, the common man, with whom he mixes easily, identifies with him. Cristiani's style is reserved, D'Aubuisson's inflammatory. But for all their differences, both men are hard-core anticommunists. The violence associated with D'Aubuisson has not made him anathema to a great number of Salvadorans. Violence is endemic in war-torn El Salvador, a country of extremes, where the political spectrum is wide. The conservative end includes not only the minority elite but also members of the petite bourgeoisie and peasants. Many in the latter sectors who joined the armed Left did so only after a family member was killed or because they lived in zones controlled by the guerrillas rather than out of communist convictions. In a surprising, but little noticed, finding of an extensive survey conducted in 1988, the FMLN was named by Salvadorans more often than any other group as "the sector that violates human rights the most in the country now."[15] The poll, conducted under Catholic church auspices, was part of the National Debate, an effort to convene representatives of all sectors of the population to air proposals and seek a consensus on how to solve the country's problems.

It was no contradiction in Salvadoran terms to vote for a D'Aubuisson and to also respond favorably to the image of efficiency and prosperity projected by a party made up of businessmen like Cristiani, particularly after the mismanagement of the PDC administration. "Most people don't know what a free market means," observed Cristiani, "but [they] see that I'm a successful businessman and hope that I will be able to do the same for them."[16] He might have added that the electorate hoped that a wealthy politician would be less corrupt than others.

Among ARENA officials, moderate is a relative term; they are all conservatives who share the same basic objectives. Armando Calderón Sol, president of the party, is often called the "new man" of ARENA. As the mayor of San Salvador, he led a drive against tax evasion and undertook other populist initiatives. He, and most others in the party, also applaud the increasing "professionalization" of—that is, declining human rights abuses by—the military, but they also see the need for strong action against the "terrorism" of the FMLN. They are all acutely aware, in the face of the deaths of several prominent conservatives, that they could be next. The key difference between ARENA's "moderates" and "hard-liners" is in the tactics that they countenance in the war against communism. Even though during the campaign Cristiani advocated a law-and-order approach, it was presumed that D'Aubuisson would resurrect the paramilitary squads. Although Cristiani opposed the use of violence against civilians, many feared that he would not have sufficient power to prevent it. This, in turn, led to a debate about which man wielded more power in the ARENA government.

In order to allay fears that Cristiani would be a mere figurehead, the candidate announced during his campaign that D'Aubuisson would not be given a cabinet position. "He's a member of the party and an important voice, but he won't be part of the administration."[17] But this did not change the fact that the major is a powerful force in the party and therefore has influence in the Casa Presidencial. Cristiani has not repudiated D'Aubuisson, without whose support he would not be president. As a deputy, D'Aubuisson also has a power base in the legislature, so he has a formal means of exercising influence over government policy. The U.S. embassy in San Salvador, reversing its prior ostracism of D'Aubuisson, invited him to its Fourth of July celebrations in 1989. Yet some U.S. officials worried that he would take this and Vice President Quayle's visit with him in February 1989 as encouragement for his own presidential aspirations. At a July 1989 press conference, he accused Duarte, who was suffering from cancer, of corruption and asserted, "I have already defeated him, and if he is cured of AIDS [sic] and runs in another election, I will defeat him again."[18]

Even though D'Aubuisson wields sufficient power to undercut initiatives he disagrees with, the evidence suggests that Cristiani's policies have at least his provisional endorsement. He knows that ARENA's flexibility helped it gain and hold political power and that a party that endorses indiscriminate violence cannot expect to become the majority party. Furthermore, the ARENA hard-liners realize that such violence could jeopardize U.S. aid—although many, remembering that even in the worst days of the early 1980s Congress did not cut off assistance, believe the United States' tolerance level is quite high. But even if the hard-liners are willing to give policies of restraint a chance to work, the ARENA leadership still has to worry about the extremists on the right. One of the most radical, and vocal, right-wingers is Orlando de Sola, a scion of the landowning class who, with others, founded ARENA in 1981. But he is not now an ARENA member; his bid to run for a legislative seat on the ARENA ticket was rejected in 1986 because he was seen as too conservative. Criticizing Cristiani, De Sola claimed that "people didn't vote for his kind of moderation. Basically, people voted for D'Aubuisson, not for Fredy's kind of sissy politics."[19] In "The Limits of Democracy," an essay he wrote for a Salvadoran newspaper, he complained that "the executors of U.S. foreign policy espouse democracy as if it were a panacea or cure-all. . . . What we need in El Salvador is to defend our Republic, severely limiting the delinquents and punishing their abuses without clemency, be they of the majority or the minority. There is no place for moderates in war."[20]

It is such views that stirred fears of what an ARENA victory would bring. But the ARENA government set out on a different course, and the U.S. Congress expressed its willingness to take Cristiani at his word and give him a chance.[21] The government's policies, although conservative, were not reactionary or repressive. On such issues as negotiating with the guerrillas, improving the economy, reforming the military, and upholding human rights, the incoming ARENA government indicated a willingness to adapt to current realities rather than to seek to return to the past. ARENA's increasing flexibility was most visibly demonstrated by its willingness to hold talks with the guerrillas. This stands in stark contrast to its earlier opposition to Duarte's dialogue with the guerrillas. But it was politically astute: The National Debate public opinion survey referred to earlier had revealed a large majority in El Salvador solidly in favor of a negotiated settlement of the war and continued reforms. ARENA's pro-negotiation stand was also intended to defuse criticism in the United States. In his inaugural speech, Cristiani announced that he intended to appoint a commission to talk directly with the FMLN. Its goal would be to produce a draft proposal for an overall solution that would be submitted for approval "to the highest political organizations." Opposition leaders said the proposal's lack of substance showed that the government had no intention of negotiating an end to the war.

The government replied that proposals should only be made in secret to prevent grandstanding. It also sought a joint commitment not to break off negotiations unilaterally.

The ARENA government has not reversed economic reform wholesale, although it was sharply critical of its predecessor's economic policies. Cristiani proposed a "national rescue plan" aimed at reducing the state sector and stimulating export-led growth. In his inaugural speech, he promised to promote "the effectiveness of agrarian reform," encourage the "progressive liberation" of the economy, and foster "social promotion." But whether a purely market-based strategy can cure this highly stratified society's serious economic ills, during a war no less, remains doubtful.

The most politically sensitive economic issue is the program of agrarian reform that was initiated in the 1970s and continued by Duarte. Given the history of ARENA's founding and the fact that many of its leaders had lost land as a result of the reform program, many assumed that the party would dismantle the program. But the party would lose the popular base it had been building if the peasants ended up without land and unemployed or underemployed. Cristiani denied from the outset that he intended to reverse the reforms, and most ARENA members supported the idea of trying to make the program work through the application of free market principles. The notion of "reforming the reforms" is not without merit, given the dismal performance of the economy under Duarte. If Cristiani can encourage greater productivity and reduce corruption, these achievements alone could ensure ARENA's reelection.

A fourth of the rural population had received land under the reform program, but few of the country's cooperatives on good land have been productive; some attribute this to the war, others to their politicized management. To those worried about ARENA's intentions, retired Colonel Sigifredo Ochoa Pérez, who now runs the hydroelectric company, says, "It is a fantasy to think we could return to the past. What we want to do is correct the errors of the Christian Democratic government, in the economic area principally. These socialist, communitarian ideas are not national ones, they are exogenous. . . . They were imposed on us, including on the [Duarte] government."[22] The government proposes to give land titles to individual peasants who are members of state-run cooperatives, allowing them to leave the cooperatives or sell their land if they wish. Whether the peasants will choose to keep or sell their land depends in large measure on whether they are able to obtain the necessary credit from the banks to keep on farming. It is still possible, however, that the courts will return a substantial amount of property to its former owners. Several disputed expropriations were overturned by the courts in 1989.

The ARENA government plans an overall liberalization of an economy it says is burdened by state intervention, arguing that under the Christian Democrats, government control simply replaced the control once exercised by the small moneyed class, and with less productive results. While ARENA did not abolish the national coffee marketing institution, for example, it did end its monopoly status so coffee producers could shop around for the best price. (The effects of this policy could not be evaluated due to the collapse of the international coffee market agreement for 1990, which caused world prices to plummet.) The government also plans to privatize the banks, charging that the Duarte government had extended credit to friends who were often bad risks. As of June 1989, 40 percent of bank loans were nonperforming. However, ARENA bank officials said that the banks' weak balance sheets would prevent the government from carrying out its plan for several years. Finally, the new government opposes subsidies of all sorts and, in an attempt to spur production, lifted price controls on utilities and hundreds of consumer goods. This means, however, that the poor will bear the brunt of higher prices.

In advocating free market policies, Cristiani points to Chile's export-led economic revival as a model for economic reform in El Salvador. He believes, as do many experts, that the long-term solution for his country's economic problems lies in nonagricultural sectors. El Salvador is the most densely populated country in the hemisphere, and there is not enough agricultural land to provide jobs for the 50 percent of the work force that is under- or unemployed. Yet if Cristiani's strict free market approach appears to be benefiting only the wealthy, ARENA may suffer for it in the 1991 legislative elections. Political pressures may therefore force the government to adopt some redistributive welfare measures while still reducing the state's role in productive activities. In any case, Cristiani will not find it easy to implement radical changes. He has his hands full managing the disastrous fiscal and monetary situation he inherited. The government budget deficit in FY 1989 was $460 million, despite U.S. aid and credits in the same amount, and foreign reserves were nearly depleted. The continuation of the war in any case makes the process of reform extremely difficult. Cristiani recognized this in his speech marking his first year in office by naming his second year "The Year of Peace." Negotiating an end to the war is a prerequisite for economic growth.

Christopher Dodd, chairman of the Western Hemisphere subcommittee of the Senate Foreign Relations Committee, visited El Salvador in June 1989. He expressed confidence in Cristiani as a moderate who can end the war. The primary criterion that will be used to judge the Cristiani government in the U.S. Congress, absent a peace treaty, will be the security forces' record on human rights. Here there were some hopeful signs. In Cristiani's first year in office, the level of tension rose considerably, but the number of abuses attributed to the Right did not increase dramatically. Many observers had believed that ARENA and the military would implement a "total war" against the guerrillas, without regard for human rights. But this did not occur. The same domestic and foreign pressures that had operated on the Christian Democratic government remained in place. When Vice President Quayle visited San Salvador in February 1989, and again in June, he clearly expressed the Bush administration's desire that there be no increase in human rights violations, and he emphasized that this was the administration's own position and not simply a requirement imposed by the Democratic majority in Congress. Acknowledging the U.S. concern in his inaugural address, President Cristiani pledged to seek "increasingly efficient administration of justice, and greater respect for human rights." But he also reassured the military that these objectives would not be pursued to the detriment of the military itself or its prosecution of the war—thus raising the question of what would happen when the FMLN escalated the war.

In a marked change from past rhetoric, a number of ARENA and military officials voice the opinion that respect for human rights will produce concrete benefits, beyond assuring U.S. aid. They use the term "professionalization of the armed forces" to mean both improving respect for human rights and prosecuting the war more effectively. They see these as complementary objectives that will also serve to increase popular support for the military. They believe that a citizenry that trusts the military is more likely to provide crucial intelligence. Improving human intelligence capabilities is a key element of the strategy propounded by Sigifredo Ochoa, who denies that he favors the "total war" strategy that is often associated with his name. Therefore, he says, "Cristiani must be hard with any who commit massacres. Massacres are not the way to win the war; it is necessary to win the hearts of the people."[23]

Although Cristiani has repeatedly voiced his commitment to military reform, he warns that "criticizing the army aloud makes them less willing to make changes. They feel besieged, antagonistic."[24] Duarte's strident rhetoric raised the military's hackles, and as a result he did not have much influence over military affairs. But it remains to be seen whether Cristiani's approach will be any more successful. The Salvadoran military, like the military elsewhere in Latin America, continues to see itself as an autonomous institution rather than one subordinate to civilian authority. "You cannot destroy this mentality," Cristiani argues. "You've got to work with it. The task is to find the right group within the armed forces. Some of them are not the right kind of people, the guys who wear dark glasses even in dark rooms. You have to find someone who is a leader in that group who can give them a sense of what their territory is, the mission of defending the country, and give them the esteem they are entitled to."[25]

Cristiani has sought out such leaders, albeit with some wavering. He named Gen. Rafael Humberto Larios as defense minister in June 1989. Colonel Ponce was named chief of staff. Larios is viewed as a moderate, nonpolitical officer who, together with the heir-apparent Ponce, stands as a professional role model. Gen. Juan Rafael Bustillo, the powerful head of the air force, made an unsuccessful bid for the top post with the support of some ARENA hard-liners and was retired in 1990. But hard-liners, including the two deputy defense ministers, were placed in positions of power. Officers in important posts—some of whom are close associates of D'Aubuisson—are resistant to the "new thinking" of professionalization, although Colonel Ponce retired some of them when he became defense minister in September 1990. Furthermore, the growth of the officer corps in response to the needs of a 55,000-man military has resulted in intense competition for promotion to higher posts. Thus Ponce's job requires balancing the demands of his peers against those of junior officers, and reformists versus hard-liners. Disappointed younger officers and hard-liners are potential coup-makers.

In the crucial area of punishing abuses by the military, Cristiani fell down. "The army's way of punishing their own officers for what they believe are war acts, not violations of human rights," Cristiani acknowledged, "has been simply to send them out to some embassy in a different country."[26] He conceded the disastrous state of the judicial system and pledged to take steps to create an independent body to investigate the security forces. "We are going to move [the Special Investigative Unit] under the jurisdiction of the attorney general, and employees will be paid by the attorney general. . . . We have talked to the high command of the armed forces and they have accepted that they are going to lose that committee to the attorney general."[27] Although this step would increase the chances that charges will be brought against wrongdoers, the intimidation of judges continues to be a problem.

As a candidate, Cristiani declined to make specific promises regarding human rights cases, noting the harsh criticism that Duarte incurred after he failed to keep his. But he did pledge to make public the results of the investigation of the September 1988 killing of ten peasants who were in army custody near San Sebastian—the worst case in years. A major and a lieutenant were among those arrested, raising the possibility that an officer might be convicted of human rights abuses in a civilian court for the first time ever. In the summer of 1990, a judge dismissed charges against all but the major. Cristiani's hope "that the San

Sebastian case is a breakthrough . . . that the army officers start to get the message that they are not above the law"[28] remained unrealized as 1990 drew to a close.

By 1990 it became clear that the Bush administration was prepared to put greater and more visible pressure on El Salvador's government and military to address human rights problems and move toward a negotiated end to the war—in stark contrast to the Reagan administration's policies. A late 1988 State Department report had candidly stated: "The process of change in El Salvador remains incomplete. . . . The present situation remains too imperfect to qualify El Salvador as an institutionalized democracy capable of ensuring respect for the human and civil rights of all its citizens."[29] What was not yet clear was whether the pressure Bush officials were willing to employ would be sufficient to the task.

The major test on the human rights issue would be Cristiani's handling of the worst crime since the 1980 assassination of the archbishop. On November 16, 1989, in the midst of the largest guerrilla offensive since the war began, six Jesuit priests were taken from their beds and brutally murdered by government soldiers. One of the murdered priests was the brilliant Ignacio Ellacuría, rector of the University of Central America in San Salvador. The university's vice rector was also killed. All six had been critical of human rights abuses and were prominent left-leaning intellectuals. Ellacuría was a major influence on the rebel leaders (he had taught some of them in their university days), criticizing their more violent tactics and prodding them to moderate their negotiating position. In the months before his death, he had expressed support for Cristiani's moderate positions and would certainly have been a key figure in any serious negotiations between the two sides. But the extreme Right had denounced him for years as a fellow-traveler of the guerrillas. Were the black days of the early 1980s returning with a vengeance? As he wept at the priests' funeral, Cristiani must have realized that if he could not bring their killers to justice, the worst scenario predicted for his government might come true. He had to succeed where Duarte had failed and bring the military to justice or watch his American backing crumble away.

5

EL SALVADOR: THE WAR AND THE FMLN

At the end of 1989 El Salvador's war entered a new phase, drawing renewed U.S. attention to the problems of this beleaguered country. On November 11, the guerrillas unleashed their most savage offensive since 1981, targeting the capital and other major cities. Five days into the three-week offensive, Father Ellacuría and the other priests were murdered. Together with the guerrilla offensive, this atrocity, which produced an international outcry, served to disprove in the starkest terms the claims of the Reagan administration that its Salvadoran policy had produced a success story. The political reforms outlined in the previous chapter were not inconsequential, and both the reforms, in their basic outline, and the practice of regular, free elections have been embraced by the new right-wing government. But the November events demonstrated that both sides were still inclined to resort to violence when it served their interests.

Nonetheless, the very fact that the guerrillas decided to throw all their forces into a general offensive suggests that they were uncertain about their future war-making capacity and thought they needed to take dramatic action to reverse their declining fortunes. They had achieved very little militarily in recent years, as the effectiveness of the Salvadoran government forces improved, and they had lost much of the support they once commanded in international social democratic circles. Increasingly, foreign leaders were urging them to end their war and seek power through the electoral process. The massive upheaval in the Soviet bloc threatened their supply of war materiel; and the electoral defeat of their Sandinista allies further diminished their prospects for external assistance in the future.

Senator Dodd and other onlookers worried that these factors might increase the confidence of the Salvadoran army in its ability to win the war militarily, prolonging the struggle against the guerrillas. In the early 1980s, many observers believed that the Salvadoran armed forces were too brutal and inefficient to wage a successful counterinsurgency war. Over the course of the decade, the armed forces increased nearly fivefold, from 12,000 to 56,000, and although change came far more slowly than had been hoped, there were discernible improvements in the military's conduct of the war. The army held off the guerrillas, even though it required massive U.S. aid to do so.

Defeating the insurgents was another matter, however. By the end of the decade, few on the government side spoke of a military victory. Even the military leaders had come to understand that the Salvadoran struggle was primarily a political one. Therefore, President Cristiani agreed after the November guerrilla offensive to seek renewed negotiations, and the United Nations agreed to mediate talks that began in May 1990. Cristiani's ability to persuade the hard-liners to accept a negotiated solution to the war will certainly be tested, but his leverage may be increased by U.S. pressure. A consensus is growing in Congress—born out of frustration at the Salvadoran military's return to the brutal tactics it had used liberally in the early 1980s, as evidenced by the slayings of the Jesuit priests—for some restrictions on U.S. aid.

THE FMLN

The Faribundo Martí National Liberation Front is a formidable military force, with a well-organized logistical and political support network. The FMLN's strategy has at different times aimed at paralyzing the government through strikes, destroying infrastructure, crippling economic production, and encouraging mass insurrection, as well as occasionally attacking military garrisons. The guerrillas hoped that this strategy would force the collapse of the government, or failing that, produce a negotiated settlement on terms favorable to them.

At the end of 1988, the U.S. embassy estimated that the FMLN had between six and seven thousand fighters, down from between seven and eight thousand in early 1987. The front is composed of five armies, of which the two largest are the Popular Liberation Forces (FPL) and the People's Revolutionary Army (ERP), followed by the Armed Forces of National Resistance (FARN), with its large urban organizations. Each army has its own mass organizations of workers, students, and peasants, and although they all operate throughout the country, each has a regional stronghold. The armies have also organized popular militias of part-time fighters in recent years. The FMLN component armies closely coordinate their military and political actions, although personal and doctrinal differences persist. In addition to its guerrilla forces, the FMLN can count on the backing of an estimated fifty thousand committed supporters. Perhaps as much as 10 percent of the population of the countryside could be called FMLN sympathizers. The FMLN has "ample support to wage a guerrilla war," observes James LeMoyne, who reported on El Salvador from 1982 to 1988. "But the rebels cannot win a fair election. They have never had the support of the majority and so far have failed to increase their popularity significantly."[1]

The general command of the FMLN is composed of five comandantes, each representing one of the organization's constituent armies. It directs military activities and works closely with its Political-Diplomatic Commission (CPD) to formulate policy and communicate it internationally. Each of the five armies and the civilian Democratic Revolutionary Front (FDR) has representatives on the CPD, which has its headquarters in Mexico City (until 1983 they were in Managua, where they maintain a political office) and an office in Washington, D.C.[2] Although the leaders of the FDR have returned to political work inside El Salvador, they and their parties remain allied with the FMLN.[3]

Many of the FMLN's leaders joined the armed struggle after working in popular organizations; the repression of the 1970s convinced them that the reformist avenue would not succeed in El Salvador.[4] The oldest guerrilla army, the Popular Liberation Forces (FPL), was formed in 1969 by Salvador Cayetano Carpio, who split with the Communist party over the issue of launching an armed struggle. Another faction of the Communist party led by Joaquín Villalobos, an economics student at the National University of San Salvador, formed the People's Revolutionary Army (ERP) soon afterward. In 1975, a faction of the ERP led by Ernesto Jovel broke away to form the Armed Forces of National Resistance (FARN), and another schism in 1976 produced the tiny Trotskyite Central American Revolutionary Workers' party.[5] Finally, in 1979, the Communist party decided to join the armed struggle, forming the Armed Forces of Liberation (FAL) under the leadership of Shafik Handal.

Spurred on by the Sandinista victory in Nicaragua and Fidel Castro's counsel, four of the Salvadoran armies formed a front in December 1979. The ERP was excluded because of friction between it and FARN.[6] The five armies united by the end of 1980, but another famous rupture occurred in 1983 within the FPL, which resulted in the death of Carpio. The founder of the armed struggle—and an egomaniac—Carpio reportedly chafed at his diminishing power. He also opposed the FMLN's new strategic emphasis on unity among the five armies, on alliance with other antigovernment sectors, and on dialogue with the government over its previous focus on military operations. In April 1983, he had his rival FPL comandante, "Ana María" (Melida Anaya Montes), killed and then killed himself when his role was discovered. The new strategy was officially approved in the Seventh Revolutionary Council of the FMLN held in Managua soon thereafter.

Although the five comandantes do not acknowledge rank among themselves, Carpio's death left Villalobos, the ERP's founder, *primus inter pares*. He had the most military experience of the five, even though he was the youngest (he was then thirty), and he is regarded by many as the FMLN's chief military strategist. Since 1983, the leaders of the guerrilla armies have maintained an impressive degree of unity, avoiding major public schisms; yet in 1989, signs of division over strategy emerged. This time it appeared to include those in the lower ranks who were dissatisfied with the emphasis on political over military tactics.

The Carter administration cut off aid to the new Sandinista government in Nicaragua in 1979 when it discovered that the Sandinistas were sending the FMLN weapons. But the Salvadoran guerrillas have reportedly also obtained weapons from the contras and on the international market, as well as by capturing them from Salvadoran soldiers. They manufacture bombs, mortars, and mines themselves. Ransom monies paid to the FMLN in the 1970s for kidnap victims, which was then invested, laid the foundation for the organization's substantial monetary resources. The FMLN also receives aid from friendly countries and levies a war tax on the areas under its control. Large farms or plantations pay $12,000 a year; smaller ones, $6,000.[7] By 1989, it became apparent that the FMLN was receiving a substantial infusion of Soviet-made arms. Many troops were carrying AK-47 machine guns, rather than U.S. M-16s. Soviet-made Dragonov sniper rifles for use in assassinations and surface-to-air missiles for shooting down the government's helicopters also began turning up in rebel inventories.

THE SALVADORAN ARMED FORCES

The expansion of the Salvadoran armed forces since 1979 has been funded from the Salvadoran budget, with U.S. assistance for training and equipment. The United States provided $2.1 billion in military aid between 1981 and 1990, representing about a third of total U.S. assistance to El Salvador during this period. The other two-thirds, economic aid, was for institution-building and development aimed at removing the causes of the war and for balance-of-payments support. Congress also limited the number of U.S. military advisers to fifty-five.

Of the 56,000 men under arms, only 20 to 30 percent are assigned to full-time combat. Most of the remaining troops guard fixed installations—military garrisons or economic assets such as coffee plantations and bridges—or carry out administrative and other support tasks. Some infrastructure is guarded by security forces under the direction of the state telephone and hydroelectric corporations. Thus, while the armed forces outnumber the guerrillas on paper by eight to one (close to the ten to one ratio thought necessary for defeating an insurgency), the actual ratio of combat troops to guerrillas is much smaller.

There have been reports of forced recruitment of soldiers (on the guerrilla side as well), although in a country where over half the population is under- or unemployed, some join the military readily. Conspicuously missing from the ranks, however, are the sons of the upper class.

THE BATTLEFIELD RECORD

After the government and right-wing forces crushed the 1980 general offensive and quelled the massive urban protest movement centered in the capital, San Salvador, the guerrillas moved into the countryside and began attacking military and economic targets there. In the mid-1980s, the armed forces countered this guerrilla move with the effective use of airpower and bombing. U.S.–supplied helicopters ferried troops quickly to the sites of guerrilla attacks, and slowly the military began countering its image as a "9-to-5" army. The military remained very conservative in the deployment of its resources, however, particularly of helicopters and other aircraft for which it had no assurance of rapid replacement if they were lost.

After the March 1987 attack on the El Paraíso garrison, in which sixty-nine Salvadoran troops and one U.S. adviser lost their lives, the frequency and success of guerrilla attacks on major military installations declined. In 1988 and early 1989, the level of small-scale military attacks increased, but the FMLN temporarily took over only one installation, San Francisco Javier in Usulután.

In 1988, according to Salvadoran armed forces statistics (obtained by the U.S. embassy), small-scale "harassments" and incidents of sabotage by the rebels increased by 28 and 50 percent, respectively, over the preceding year, while larger attacks and ambushes declined by 12 and 14 percent. These attacks did not pose a serious military threat. Sabotage and mining operations served as reminders of the guerrillas' presence but alienated the population. The statistics also indicated that the guerrillas lost a thousand men on average in both 1987 and 1988—about twice that of the military—losses that were compensated for to some degree by new recruits, many of them teenaged offspring of guerrillas.[8]

Although the guerrillas gained no ground in recent years, they remained entrenched in their strongholds in the north and east, controlling about a third of the country. The military conducted periodic campaigns in their strongholds, largely to keep them on the defensive, and the infrequency of major guerrilla attacks indicated that this objective was being met. But most military operations to clear areas of the rebels' presence proved only temporarily successful. In 1989, the military directed operations against the guerrillas in the Guazapa volcano area near the capital; after an earlier clearing operation in 1985–1986, the FMLN had moved back in and established a strong presence there. The military "cannot control every point of territory," said Defense Minister Larios, but he added that "the guerrillas do not control any area of the country" (by which he meant that the military can move into any area it chooses).[9]

Despite Larios's assessment, the "Four Colonels' Report"—a detailed critique of the military's performance by four U.S. lieutenant colonels on leave at the Kennedy School of Government at Harvard—concluded that "as of April 1988, a tough, resourceful opponent remains in the field, reduced in strength but showing no inclination to give up. Although Americans no longer fear a sudden Salvadoran collapse, a U.S. investment approaching $3 billion [now over $4 billion], along with substantial advice and training, has produced not success but a seemingly interminable war of attrition."[10] Although some U.S. officials criticized the report for the authors' reliance on outdated data from the mid-1980s, others defended its conclusions, particularly those relating to U.S. policy. The colonels concluded that the United States had given insufficient attention to developing a counterinsurgency doctrine, and that the quality of U.S. military personnel assigned to El Salvador—not a "prestige" post—had often been poor.

Nonetheless, the colonels thought that the military had the ability to stabilize the country (despite a continuing overreliance on heavy artillery and helicopters). The problem lay in winning the "other war" (the allegiance of the Salvadorans), and here the missing ingredient was an effective civilian government. And even though the Salvadoran military became more sophisticated in its counterinsurgency strategy and more respectful of human rights, instances of brutality undermined its progress.

The government's attempt to win over the "hearts and minds" of the people through a program of building and rebuilding the country's infrastructure illustrates the difficulty of development work in wartime. Through the "Municipalities in Action" program it distributed funds directly to local governments for infrastructure projects of their own choosing. In response, the FMLN called on all mayors to resign or face execution. Eight mayors were killed in late 1988, and a wave of resignations followed. By January 1989, 100 of 262 municipalities were without mayors.[11] The guerrillas justified this strategy on the grounds that the mayors, by participating in the military's counterinsurgency program, were enemies of the revolution. The local governments were not only responsible for the infrastructure projects but also for civil defense and for providing intelligence to the armed forces. "A mayor is . . . apparently a civilian but plays a military role," said Comandante Fermán Cienfuegos. "Mayors are . . . paid *colones* for their information and are responsible for murders, so they deserve the death penalty."[12]

The counterinsurgency strategy in El Salvador aims at strengthening civilian government. Yet, when civilians are ineffective or intimidated, the military tends to assume responsibility for counterinsurgency programs. This problem is compounded by the restriction against the use of U.S. Agency for International Development funds in the conflict zones to avoid any possible criticism that the agency is participating in counterinsurgency. Few AID personnel get out into the field, therefore, and are often unaware that schools and medical clinics built with AID funds cannot operate because teachers and supplies do not reach them. The ARENA government hopes to solve this problem by establishing greater control over the implementation of development programs.

Another factor affecting the counterinsurgency effort is the lack of adequate intelligence. "Intelligence-gathering" in El Salvador has often meant the torture and targeting of innocent people, which alienates rather than cultivates potential informants. ARENA's leaders are aware that they must improve the government's intelligence-gathering capabilities in order to wage a discriminate war and also reduce casualties due to infiltration, which by many accounts is extensive. "We need to organize people," points out Col. Sigifredo Ochoa, "not as an armed paramilitary organization, but rather to obtain good intelligence. . . . We do not want a scorched earth policy, but a war of intelligence."[13] To ensure that such informant networks are recruited and used without violence or coercion, however, requires watchfulness on the part of Salvadoran and U.S. officials and the media.

There is near universal agreement on the necessity of improving the military's ability to interdict the arms flows to the guerrillas. Defense Minister Larios argues that if the arms flow was stopped, the "logical consequence" would be an end to the war. That might be an overstatement, but if the guerrillas were limited to weapons they could capture from the Salvadoran armed forces, the level of the conflict would obviously decrease. According to U.S. officials, most of the arms traffic comes by sea from Nicaragua (although some also comes across the Honduran border).[14] It is therefore surprising that U.S. Customs and the Coast Guard have not shared their expertise in the interdiction of contraband with El Salvador.

The largest FMLN cache ever unearthed was found in May 1989 in San Salvador. The National Police confiscated over three hundred AK-47 machine guns of North Korean and East German make, more than a quarter of a million rounds of ammunition from Cuban Loading Factory 13, dated 1988, as well as grenades and grenade launchers.[15] The guerrillas have claimed that they buy many of their AK-47s from the Nicaraguan resistance and the Honduran military. But the U.S. government counters that the AK-47s supplied to the Nicaraguan rebels are of Chinese manufacture, while the AK-47s found in El Salvador are of Soviet make. Daniel Ortega admitted at the Central American summit at Tela in August 1989 that the Sandinistas had been supplying and facilitating transit of arms to the Salvadoran rebels, and promised to end this assistance. But on November 25, after the FMLN had begun its offensive, a plane from Nicaragua crashed in eastern El Salvador and was found to be carrying a cargo of Soviet-made surface-to-air missiles. Other deliveries of this potent weapon had been made successfully—a sure sign that FMLN was intent upon escalating the war.

Finally, there is the issue of FMLN sanctuaries in the disputed border zone with Honduras and in the refugee camps. The FMLN has a secure area in Honduran territory along the Salvadoran border, and controls the Salvadoran refugee camps there, enforcing strict discipline. The existence of FMLN sanctuaries on Honduran soil creates frictions between the neighboring countries, particularly when the Salvadorans pursue the guerrillas across the border. In 1989, some Honduran soldiers were killed on their own soil when Salvadoran soldiers mistook them for FMLN troops.

Thousands of refugees who fled to Honduras in the late 1970s and early 1980s have been returning to El Salvador, to camps in the north-central region that was their home. In 1987, international organizations led a caravan of returning Salvadorans, most of whom settled in Las Vueltas, a rebel stronghold. Most of the returning refugees settled in camps administered by international humanitarian organizations that are off limits to the Salvadoran military. The military charges that the refugees in these camps are rebel sympathizers; the international organizations in turn say that the refugees are in danger of harassment or repression by the military. Whether the refugees want to be part of the FMLN structure or not, the guerrillas do enter the camps in El Salvador to recruit, receive food, or simply to rest in a secure place. The international organizations, intent on carrying out their humanitarian mission, avert their eyes from the use that the FMLN makes of these camps. President Cristiani broached the question of refugee policy with UN officials, since the United Nations provides most of the funding for the camps. "We should not treat refugees coming back . . . as people who have to be placed in a refugee camp, and then have to live from donations," he argues. "As Salvadorans they have the right to come back, but we should

promote their incorporation into normal life. Why have a refugee camp of Salvadorans in Salvador? That doesn't make much
sense, except obviously that the FMLN uses them as a base of
operations. We say: why not use some of the government-owned
farms [outside the conflict zones] that are not being worked,
settle them there and give them a plot of land."[16]

In light of the ARENA government's conviction that the
refugees are rebel sympathizers, and the fact that these people
were driven into exile in the first place by an earlier government's
indiscriminate bombing of suspected rebel strongholds, it is
highly unlikely that the donor organizations will cede administrative responsibility of the camps to the Salvadoran government. Nonetheless, the government also has the right to
determine what happens on its sovereign territory. A compromise is possible: the government could agree to allow the international organizations to administer the camps, reserving for itself
the right to determine their location. The refugees would be free
to decide if they wished to move to the camps or remain in their
home territories.

The ARENA government may yet make some headway
against this refugee problem, and thus reclaim more of the
country from the guerrillas. If it does not seek a compromise,
however, it will only compound its troubles on the rural front.
But the war will not be won or lost in the countryside. Urban
insurrection has always been a crucial component of the FMLN
endgame. In recent years, the guerrillas rebuilt their network in
the cities and in 1988 launched an urban campaign, culminating
in the 1989 offensive. This is now the critical front of the war.

THE URBAN FRONT

The urban activity of the FMLN falls into three general catego-
ries: attacks by urban commandos on military targets, attacks on
high-profile civilians, and nonviolent strikes and other protests.
Beginning in November 1988, the FMLN launched attacks in
San Salvador in successive months against the headquarters of
the National Guard, the army's Estado Mayor, the Treasury
Police, the National Police, the Navy Command, and the Casa

Presidencial. During this period, the FMLN forces also attacked guard posts and garrisons around the country. Most of the attacks caused minimal damage and few casualties, although thirty-five people—mostly civilians—were wounded in the December attack on the Estado Mayor. Defective weapons undermined the effectiveness of several operations. In May 1989, after an attack on a bus in which eight civilians were killed, the FMLN issued an apology but also warned civilians to stay clear of military and security facilities. While not military successes, these attacks signaled an escalation in the war and raised the level of tension among the populace.

The FMLN also stepped up its assaults on high-profile civilians associated with the government or conservative circles. This was a risky strategy, since the attacks invited retaliation in kind from the Right. Observers worried that it might trigger a repetition of the widespread bloodshed in the cities of the early 1980s. In January 1989, the house of former Defense Minister Carlos Vides Casanova's mother was attacked. Shortly thereafter, on February 16, a former top FMLN commander, "Miguel Castellanos" (Napoleón Romero García), who had defected from the FPL four years earlier, was killed.[17] On March 15, Francisco Peccorini Letona, a conservative Jesuit intellectual, was murdered.[18] The editorial director of the conservative journal *Analisis*, Carlos Ernesto Mendoza, lost his arm in a April 5 bomb attack on his house while he was having lunch with his family. (The New University of San Salvador, which published the journal, subsequently stopped its publication.) On April 12, Attorney General Roberto García Alvarado was killed by what a fellow ARENA member described as a "sophisticated, brutal explosive device affixed to the roof of his car directly above him."[19] In the same month, the home of Vice President and Interior Minister Francisco Merino, a close D'Aubuisson associate, was also bombed. Merino was in the United States at the time, but a child in the house was wounded.

Most of these killings were not widely reported in the United States. But on June 9, 1989, Antonio Rodríguez Porth, the cabinet-ranked minister of the presidency and a top ARENA intellectual, was machine-gunned, along with his bodyguard.

This killing did receive the attention of the media, and some U.S. congressmen began to focus on the pattern of assassinations in El Salvador, which suggested that there was a campaign to strike at the brains of the Right. The timing was not fortuitous for the guerrillas, because Congress was in the process of debating renewal of both military and police aid to the Salvadoran government. The FMLN denied responsibility for the death of Rodríguez Porth, but in October, President Cristiani announced that ballistic tests showed that the weapon used was the same one that had been used on Castellanos, whom the FMLN had acknowledged killing.

On June 30, the head of the Institute of International Relations, ARENA party leader Edgar Chacón, was shot while driving in San Salvador with his wife. Although Cristiani subsequently rejected the idea, Chacón had proposed that ARENA form its own defense patrols, prompting critics to charge that a new death-squad network was being created. On July 19, another director of Chacón's institute was shot and wounded. Col. Roberto Armando Rivera, the chief of the fire department, was assassinated on June 26. The FMLN later said that Rivera qualified as a military target since the former head of the national military academy was performing covert intelligence functions.

The FMLN's stated policy is to claim responsibility for any assassinations or other actions it commits. In practice, however, it has not always issued such acknowledgments. Furthermore, the international press has focused overwhelmingly on the extensive brutality of the Right (only in June 1990 did Americas Watch finally publish a report devoted to abuses by the FMLN). But during a weekend meeting in July 1989 with a small group of U.S. citizens, including former Senator Dick Clark and Rep. Michael Barnes, high-level FMLN members took responsibility for the recent wave of killings, except for the murder of Rodríguez Porth. In the cases of Edgar Chacón and Roberto García, these admissions appeared to be inadvertent. When asked if he thought the attorney general's assassination—for which the FMLN had not yet taken responsibility—was an error, FARN commander Fermán Cienfuegos hesitated and then nodded; the other guerrillas looked askance at him for having divulged the truth after four months of denials.[20]

The FMLN leaders were extraordinarily candid in discussing the pros and cons of political assassination. The guerrilla delegation expressed ambivalence over the net effect of the policy, acknowledging its high political costs to their image, both internationally and among some sectors of Salvadoran society. They admitted that several of the assassinations in the previous months had been mistakes, that they should not have responded to purely political adversaries, such as Peccorini, with violence or attacked the homes or the relatives of officials. But they emphasized the military utility of assassination; as one member, Salvador Samayoa, put it, assassination is justified "if the civilian performs some military role, even if a covert one."[21] Cienfuegos held out the the possibility of suspending the executions but said the costs of doing so would have to be considered. "We are reflecting on the consequences. This line can become a tactical mistake, we can lose friends." But, at the time, Cienfuegos limited himself to a narrower self-criticism. "Not having acknowledged [responsibility for] these actions at the opportune moment created confusion," he said, "and it must be admitted that an error was committed in not claiming them."[22]

When asked whether their self-criticism for specific attacks meant that the FMLN leaders had changed their minds after issuing the orders or were having a problem with cadres acting without orders, Comandante Luisa (Mercedes del Carmen Letona) explained that the high command set general policy only; it was up to the regional commands to decide upon specific actions to be carried out by urban commandos. But henceforth, she said, the general command would clarify who and what constituted legitimate targets, and would approve "political actions" proposed by the regional commanders (as opposed to "military actions," which could be authorized at lower levels). Despite this procedure, the possibility remains that the urban units will choose to go their own way; if they do, there is little the general command can do to stop them. Communication in the cities is difficult and dangerous. As Comandante Luisa acknowledged, "While we can have strict control in the rural areas, it is simply not possible for us to approve each of, say, two hundred actions in the urban areas."[23] Nonetheless, targeting of the highest-level officials has probably always been approved by the general command.

Samayoa and other members denied that the FMLN was deliberately trying to provoke the Right to initiate repressive measures and thus destabilize the country.[24] Nonetheless, the increasing urban action blurred the already hazy line between combatant and noncombatant and made increased violence in the streets almost inevitable. Asked whether the popular organizations were not more vulnerable as a result, Cienfuegos replied, "Opposition of whatever sort in the streets has provoked repression. This time [the popular organizations] are preparing to defend themselves."[25]

The Duarte government and its security forces generally responded with restraint as civilian demonstrations began to mount once again in 1987. In September 1988, for example, the police looked on as demonstrators organized by the Movement for Bread, Land, Liberty, and Work wound through the central district of the capital. Some of the demonstrators—mostly young boys with their faces covered—toted barely concealed arms; others carried iron poles wrapped in bunting. The week before, a civilian and a policeman had been killed in a confrontation at the National University, but this protest against the Duarte and Reagan policies disbanded without incident.

After the ARENA government took office in June 1989, however, the mood grew more hostile. The military public relations office took out full-page advertisements in the daily papers showing a photograph of arms and ammunition, with a caption in which UNTS, a labor union, and the teachers' union were equated with the FMLN. The arms were said to have been found in the labor union's office. The military and ARENA were trying to publicize the fact that the unions and other mass organizations were performing military functions for the FMLN. The unstated implication was that these groups' members would be treated as if they were combatants. Just as the FMLN considered civilians performing military roles as legitimate targets, so did the Salvadoran military. It is this absence of a clear line between combatants and noncombatants that makes guerrilla war so "dirty," and El Salvador's particularly so.

When asked how he would deal with various kinds of subversion, President Cristiani said that he would try to stop the FMLN's urban campaign with tougher laws, at the same time respecting human rights. A package of reforms of the penal code was introduced in the legislature at the end of June 1989 at the request of the executive branch that increased the prison sentences for a variety of terrorist or violent acts. The legislation carries penalties of ten to twenty years for crimes against "the life, personal integrity or liberty" of current or former officials, retired military men, or foreigners accredited to work in El Salvador, as well as for transportation stoppages and the contamination of water or food supplies. If death or serious injury results from such acts, the penalty increases to twenty-five to thirty years. A more general provision carries the same penalty for destructive acts "with the aim of provoking or maintaining a state of terror" or "serious perturbation of the public peace or . . . international relations."[26] Some analysts believe that this last provision might be used to prosecute international human rights organizations lobbying against human rights abuses by government forces.

The broad language of some of the penal code revisions stirred fears of an indiscriminate crackdown. Article 400-B, which called for a term of five to ten years' imprisonment for such acts of voluntary collaboration as providing "information about people . . . installations or buildings . . . that could be significant for terrorist activities" or giving material aid to the guerrillas, created the most concern. Journalists worried that press freedoms would be restricted, but Cristiani assured Ambassador Walker and visiting U.S. Senator Terry Sanford that the law would not be used to restrict the press.

In May 1989, Samayoa predicted that the expected ARENA victory would lead to unrest. "We can just wait for this to happen," he said, elaborating a scenario in which the government would eventually fall as a result of its repressive policies and the deepening economic and political crises in El Salvador.[27] Rubén Zamora also predicted that the Cristiani government would lead the country into chaos after six months or so. The hard-liners then would either win control of the policymaking process or begin conducting their own extracurricular policy.[28] Samayoa believed that the United States would recoil at the mounting violence and pressure the government, which would find itself squeezed between the Salvadoran Right and the United States. Eventually, the United States would either withdraw aid or force the government to negotiate with the FMLN, or there would be a coup by the extremists; any of these scenarios would ultimately leave the FMLN the winner.

Yet none of these scenarios materialized. Instead, almost exactly six months after the ARENA government took office—on November 11—the FMLN launched a massive offensive that clearly had been planned well in advance. The guerrillas took over many neighborhoods of the capital and other major cities, forcing the government forces to engage in block-by-block fighting. As the scope of the offensive became apparent, the government resorted to bombing and the use of aerial artillery at the cost of hundreds of civilian casualties. The guerrillas withdrew after about a week, only to reappear in the wealthy neighborhoods of San Salvador—as if to dare the government to bomb its own supporters. They also took over the former Sheraton Hotel, trapping a dozen U.S. Green Berets inside. The guerrillas slipped away from the hotel during the night, however, after FMLN spokesmen repeatedly denied rebel intent to hold U.S. hostages.

The FMLN had taken a risky gamble. In bringing the war so brazenly to the cities, the rebels had demonstrated their strength. And yet, so long as the United States maintained its support for the Salvadoran government, the FMLN could not expect to win a military victory. In fact, the guerrillas did not succeed in overrunning any military targets. As many as a thousand people died, however, and thousands more were wounded. No insurrection occurred. An FMLN spokesman said that the offensive's objective was to press the government to make concessions in negotiations, but the rebels did not inflict sufficient damage to extract any immediate diplomatic gains. Indeed, the government hardened its position.

Members of the popular organizations who had taken up arms alongside the rebels were now exposed to prosecution or repression from a government that had been charging all along that they were tantamount to rebel soldiers. The assassination of prominent conservatives resumed with the murder of former Supreme Court President Francisco José Guerrero on November 28. Nonetheless, the guerrillas' offensive had not brought the country to the crossroads Samayoa, Zamora, and others had predicted. But it did demonstrate that, while both sides could continue inflicting damage, neither could win the war by military means. Gradually, the lesson was being driven home; if they wanted to end the war, both the military and the FMLN would have to make concessions. Both could resort to violence to improve their bargaining positions somewhat. But other, more important external pressures were growing on both parties to negotiate an end to the war.

THE DIPLOMATIC FRONT

The most concerted guerrilla offensive of the war made some observers more optimistic about the chances for such an outcome. The offensive and the killing of the Jesuits focused an unprecedented degree of international attention on El Salvador, and the violent actions of both sides were roundly condemned. The Jesuits' case was the proximate cause of greater pressure on the Salvadoran government. More important was the diminishing geopolitical rationale for supporting the Salvadoran war effort. Revolutionary regimes and communism were in retreat around the world, so why could not El Salvador resolve its conflict by negotiation, as other countries had? For its part, the FMLN was faced with certain international realities that made its long-term outlook uncertain. The Soviet Union under Gorbachev has signaled that it will not commit itself to support another revolutionary regime in the hemisphere. The Sandinistas' electoral defeat diminished their ability to aid the FMLN. And even if Cuban leader Fidel Castro remains committed to helping the FMLN, he will find it much more difficult logistically without the Sandinistas functioning as a bridge.

Finally, the FMLN's failure to spark a popular uprising in November showed it had little appeal at home at a time when its ideology and image were being discredited abroad. The Salvadoran war seemed to the world to be an anachronism.

Even so, the FMLN's offensive showed that the rebels were not disposed simply to wait for the government's best offer. Negotiations would be arduous and lengthy. Furthermore, the FMLN was not without friends. The Cuban foreign minister, in pointing out that the United States was still arming the Angolan rebels as well as the Salvadoran government, implied that Cuba would not halt its aid to the FMLN until the United States agreed to a collective pact.[29] As for a U.S.–Soviet security pact being negotiated over the Central Americans' heads, Comandante Cienfuegos asserted, "The two superpowers can make the decision but we are not going to follow it." He suggested that "the U.S. is the one that needs to change, to accept socialist systems in Latin America. That it has not been willing to do so is shown by its intervention in Nicaragua, in Panama in violation of the treaties, in the Cuba blockade and its military bases in Honduras."[30]

A rebel document captured in 1988 reveals that even as recently as two years ago the FMLN believed time was on its side: "In dialogue as such we must have as our central objective keeping the enemy tied at the table with a view to his strategic weakening and the building of a political umbrella against [foreign] intervention. . . . Dialogue is one of the forms of conspiratorial struggle and we must maintain it."[31] In early 1989, just after this document was captured, Joaquín Villalobos published an article spelling out the FMLN's vision for El Salvador as a pluralistic state, where private enterprise would be permitted (within limits) and in which there would be an important role for the Catholic church.[32] Villalobos and Leonel González, leader of another of the FMLN armies, the FPL, had made a tour of European and Latin American democracies and of Cuba in the latter half of 1988, and the trip apparently convinced them that the FMLN had to moderate its positions. Presidents Oscar Arias Sánchez and Carlos Andrés Pérez had urged them to lay down their weapons and incorporate themselves into the political process. Although some were wary of such advice—as Samayoa said, "Arias thinks that elections will solve everything; he thinks every country can be like Costa Rica"[33]—the FMLN decided it was in its interest to adopt a more conciliatory stance. "It is always better to have war and a negotiating table than only to have war," commented Villalobos at the end of the tour.[34]

The shift in the FMLN's thinking was apparent in a watershed proposal it made on January 23, 1989. The FMLN would participate in the presidential elections then scheduled for March (by backing its FDR allies in the Democratic Convergence) if they were postponed until September. It pledged to accept the outcome of the vote if the government guaranteed that the military would withdraw to its barracks during the voting process and that there would be a halt in the assassination, abduction, and repression of its supporters. This amounted to an offer to join the political system as then constituted in El Salvador, a landmark declaration. This was such a radical shift from the FMLN's previous stand that many doubted the proposal had been made in good faith. The FMLN had earlier demanded, in exchange for ending its armed struggle, a share of power in a coalition or transition government, and the integration of its armed forces with the army. Whether or not the new proposal was sincere, it set a precedent from which it will be difficult for the FMLN to back away. Henceforth, the FMLN will be under pressure to frame its negotiating proposals in terms of the conditions under which it would be willing to participate in elections under the system of government already in existence.

The proposal foundered on the issue of postponing the elections, however. The Duarte government, caught off guard, rejected the proposal without considering whether the guerrillas might be trapped into abiding by their own words. If the guerrillas were cynically banking on the government's rejection, they were on the mark. Neither the president nor the ARENA-controlled assembly would take the gamble that the rebels might win and, in the end, the elections went forward as planned, in March.

The January proposal did lead to a meeting in February in Oaxtepec, Mexico, where the FMLN and the Salvadoran political parties seriously discussed terms for ending the war for the first time. The FMLN spelled out its conditions: trial and punishment for those responsible for "massacres, irrational and unjustifiable political crimes, such as the assassination of Monseñor Romero, the four churchwomen, [and] the FDR leaders"; a reduction of the armed forces to the 1978 level of 12,000 troops; and the dissolution of the National Police, National Guard, and Treasury Police and the creation of a single professional body for public security under the civilian Ministry of the Interior. The FMLN promised to end its armed struggle and enter into political life of El Salvador if these demands were met. The central issue here, the transformation of the army and security forces, represented a significant departure from earlier FMLN negotiating positions. (The guerrillas' previous demand for a share of power and the incorporation of their armies into the constituted military force of the country would have given them a power base from which to take over the government and radically transform the political and economic system.) The timetable for implementing the transformation was open to discussion, according to Salvador Samayoa, who acknowledged that the army would only reduce its forces as the FMLN laid down its arms.[35] Defense Minister Larios said in June 1989 that the military would have no objection to reducing its forces after the threat from the guerrillas had ended, because "there would be no need for such a large army."[36]

The demand that the perpetrators of human rights abuses be prosecuted would perhaps be the most difficult to meet, since the officers of the military and security forces protect one another. Yet there was a growing acknowledgment by some members of the military hierarchy, if not the hard-liners, that weeding out a few bad individuals would not threaten the institution of the military. Retirement or dismissal of these individuals was possible, but prosecution would be far more difficult. Most such cases were effectively closed by the 1987 amnesty that followed on the Esquipulas Accord. The amnesty could be repealed, of course, but the practice in most Latin American countries (except in Argentina, whose military lost a war) has been to try to forget the past. A purge, therefore, may be the most that can be expected. The military is also likely to strongly resist putting security forces under civilian control, at least while insurgency is a major threat to stability. Cristiani, however, has recently endorsed the idea.

After Cristiani's decisive victory in March, signs of division within the FMLN surfaced. Some members of FARN, believing that ARENA would isolate itself by embarking on reactionary policies, wanted to pull back from the moderate stance set out in February. A new set of proposals was released in April, reportedly without the agreement of the full FMLN leadership, which called on the Cristiani government to declare itself transitional and hold new elections, and for the cutoff of U.S. military aid and the withdrawal of U.S. advisers.

When Cristiani proposed in June 1989 that the FMLN enter into a dialogue with a governmental commission—a move indicating his independence from the extreme Right—the FMLN categorically rejected the idea of negotiations. They thought that Cristiani's proposal was simply a tactic to win greater international support. But in mid-September, in an about-face, the FMLN announced that it would accept the president's terms and meet with his commission, without preconditions, outside of El Salvador. (The rebels had been widely criticized for their intransigence in the face of Cristiani's unexpected moderation.) On September 13 and 14, the two sides held preliminary talks and agreed to convene negotiations that would be held on a monthly basis, beginning on October 16 and 17 in Costa Rica.

Just before the September talks, the FMLN released a new negotiating proposal in which it attempted to bridge the gap between its February and April positions. This proposal included a wide range of political and economic, as well as military, demands but left the manner of meeting them open to negotiation. It asked the government to appoint a new Supreme Court and a new attorney general; to prosecute the killers of Archbishop Romero and "all persons" involved in the death squads; to preserve land reform and freeze prices for basic goods; to force the armed forces to reform themselves; to undertake unspecified constitutional reforms; and to advance the date of the legislative and municipal elections scheduled for 1991. In return, the FMLN would agree to a cease-fire. It did not specify at what point it would permanently lay down its arms, however. At the October talks in San José, Costa Rica, the government proposed an immediate cessation of hostilities and demobilization of the FMLN in January 1990, without offering any concessions to gain the guerrillas' agreement. There were some indications that the government might have been willing to meet some of the FMLN's latest demands, but it was not about to make significant concessions except in return for an agreement for a permanent cease-fire. The FMLN negotiators hardly expected all of their demands to be met, but so long as the ARENA government was unwilling to meet any of them, the guerrillas would continue to fight. Both sides were deeply suspicious that the other's primary motive was to *appear* willing to negotiate without actually intending to do so.

As proof that neither side was abandoning violence, even as the two sides were meeting in October, a daughter of a senior military commander was killed, and the Estado Mayor was attacked. The Right responded with attacks on a union headquarters in San Salvador, in which eleven people died, and on an organization of relatives of "disappeared" Salvadorans. A bomb was thrown into the house of Rubén Zamora. The cycle continued as the brother of a retired colonel was killed and another colonel's home was bombed. The FMLN, accusing the government and the army of complicity in the union attack, said it would boycott the November talks. Cristiani denied these charges and condemned the bombings, calling for the talks to go forward. Then came the massive guerrilla assault on the capital and other major cities across the country on November 11. Its scope showed that even as the rebel representatives had been meeting with the government, the FMLN was preparing its largest military action since the 1981 offensive. The FMLN gained little militarily and lost international credibility.

The FMLN's image slipped another notch when a plane that had taken off from Nicaragua crashed in Salvadoran territory on November 25 and was found to be loaded with SA-7 antiaircraft missiles destined for use by the FMLN. In response to this stark evidence of the existence of the long-alleged arms pipeline, Cristiani broke off relations with the Sandinista government in Nicaragua. Other shipments had reportedly reached rebel hands, raising the possibility that the guerrillas would begin shooting down helicopters, which were a mainstay of the government's war strategy.

The biggest indirect benefit the guerrillas gained in the offensive was a result of the killing of the Jesuit priests by members of the Salvadoran army. Provoked by the rebel offensive, the Right had responded with a heinous act that damaged Cristiani's credibility as a moderating force and raised the specter of a cutoff in U.S. aid. Father Ellacuría had great influence with rebel leaders. Sympathetic to the causes for which they fought, he had nonetheless criticized the rebels in recent years for their brutal tactics and argued that the time was ripe for development of a "third force" that would seek to achieve those goals by nonviolent means. His influence was clearly visible in the evolving moderation of the FMLN's negotiating proposals, although several hard-line rebel leaders disagreed with his suggestion that they contest the 1991 local elections, as settling for too little in return for ending their war.

Ellacuría had accepted Cristiani's invitation to serve on a panel set up to investigate the October union office bombing, signaling his belief that the president's moderation was genuine. (He had been meeting with Cristiani to offer advice on moving the negotiating process forward.) His death meant the loss of a uniquely well-positioned interlocutor. The Right, however, had long viewed him as the guerrillas' top agent within the country, and had subjected him to threats for some time. It had castigated him for publishing articles by FMLN leaders in his journal, *Estudios Centroamericanos (ECA)*, even as they criticized the human rights and polling work of the other murdered priests as contributing to the FMLN's cause.

The priests' slaying set off a campaign to cut U.S. aid to El Salvador. On November 20, the U.S. House of Representatives turned down a proposal to withhold 30 percent of the $85 million in military aid pledged to the Salvadoran government, on the grounds that the government forces' complicity in the murders had not been established. But the speaker of the House formed a task force to monitor the Salvadoran investigation, in an attempt to assure that the killers would be discovered. Just before Congress reconvened in January 1990, President Cristiani announced that six soldiers and one colonel would be charged with the murders. This announcement not only demonstrated Cristiani's intention to pursue the case, it was particularly significant because the colonel, Guillermo Benavides, was a member of the class of officers currently dominating the top army positions. In the past, officers from the same class had fiercely protected each other against any attempt to prosecute them for human rights abuses. With the arrest of Benavides, this traditional solidarity appeared to have been breached. The arrests were only the first step in a long process, however, and under Salvadoran law gaining a conviction is an extremely arduous process. Furthermore, many onlookers shared the concern expressed by Rep. Joe Moakley, the congressional task force chairman, that the investigation would not probe the issue of whether higher officers participated in the planning or the coverup of the murders.

It became clear during 1990 that a consensus was developing in the United States for a significant aid cut. Progress on the Jesuits' case was certain to be an issue upon which U.S. aid for FY 1991 would be conditioned, but so was the larger issue of progress toward a negotiated settlement of the war. For the first time, the U.S. administration seemed to agree that it was time to get tough with the Salvadoran government. Many congressmen were frustrated that after years of hard-won reform efforts and $4 billion in U.S. aid, an atrocity reminiscent of those committed in the early 1980s could still occur and perhaps go unpunished. The pursuit of justice in this particular case could also help negotiations to end the war, since failure to prosecute those accused of human rights abuses has long been a sticking point for the rebels. The Bush administration indicated that it was prepared to seek bipartisan agreement on a 30 percent cut in the $85 million in military aid for FY 1991 if the Salvadoran government failed to move further. In June, the House of Representatives passed an amendment for a 50 percent cut. And the final legislation sequestered half of the aid, which could be released if the guerrillas launched a major offensive. Such a bipartisan agreement would initiate an unprecedented test of U.S. leverage and, given the current stalemate in El Salvador, might provide the push needed to get both sides to negotiate seriously to end the conflict.

In October, just before the Senate was due to vote on Senator Dodd's proposal to sequester 50 percent of FY 1991 military aid (matching the House-approved measure), President Cristiani arrived in Washington to lobby against the proposal. He conceded the stiff odds he faced, however, by saying that the aid restrictions would be acceptable if they were tied to the FMLN's agreement to a cease-fire. Supporters of the Dodd amendment felt that this would undercut the monthly face-to-face negotiations between Cristiani's government and the FMLN, which had been occurring since May 1990 under the auspices of UN mediator Alvaro de Soto. But a number of other congressmen feared that the FMLN would stall at the bargaining table while waiting to see if the aid cut would improve its prospects. Indeed, at the August talks, the guerrillas had hardened their position, calling for dissolution of the army rather than just troop reductions. Clearly, what was needed was some imaginative diplomacy and orchestrated pressures to make the most of the aid cut that seemed imminent.

For years the U.S. embassy in El Salvador seems to have been caught in a defensive attitude, as if the aid the United States provided required it to apologize for the failings of the recipient government. In El Salvador's polarized climate, this bunker mentality is understandable, but it gives the public impression that the United States is wedded to whatever Salvadoran government is in office. Bush officials in Washington, however, have been much more vocal and clear in enunciating their support for a negotiated solution than their predecessors in the Reagan administration. In testimony to Congress in February 1990, the chief of the U.S. Southern Command, Gen. Maxwell Thurman, said he thought that the Salvadoran armed forces could not defeat the FMLN and that negotiations were the only way to end the fighting.

The November offensive covered both sides in blood, but the correlation of forces was unchanged by the fighting: neither side can prevail militarily. At the bargaining table, both sides have moderated their positions in principle, but their willingness to make concessions remains untested. What will it take to break the logjam? A 50 percent cut in U.S. support for the government put pressure on it to make concessions, but the cut should be combined with efforts to prevent the guerrillas from hardening their stand. The current stalemate on the battlefield is in fact a necessary condition to convince both sides that negotiation is the only path to peace. But it is not a sufficient condition: added to it must be strong U.S. pressure for reasonable concessions from the government—a purge of suspected killers from the army, for example—in exchange for an internationally monitored demobilization of the guerrillas. The U.S. goal should be to get the Salvadoran government to make the FMLN an offer it cannot refuse. Diplomacy went a long way toward resolving Nicaragua's conflict, and similar tactics are now called for if U.S. policy is to succeed in El Salvador.

Foreign observers of El Salvador tend to be much more pessimistic about this benighted country than Salvadorans themselves. This is in large part a reaction to the tendency of many U.S. officials to gloss over El Salvador's serious problems. The Salvadorans' own views may be a better barometer, and few of them believe their war is endless. Father Ellacuría, who possessed one of the keenest minds in the country, believed (even though he was quite aware of death threats against him) that El Salvador had reached a promising juncture. Several months before his death, he published an article in which he posed the question: "Will Cristiani represent an increasingly firm and consolidated moderation and economic and political modernization of the right, which will reach peace through negotiations . . . or will he be nothing more than a front for the return of an oligarchy which will harden the war and the repressions? . . . [T]he first possibility is more likely, which is certainly better for the popular majority, and therefore for the whole country."[37]

6

PANAMA AND THE UNITED STATES: FROM SYMBIOSIS TO FESTERING CRISIS

In December 1989, after two years of simmering crisis and U.S. policy failures, the Bush administration sent an invasion force to Panama to topple its erstwhile ally, Gen. Manuel Antonio Noriega, from power. Two years of frustration and the growing salience of the drug trade as a domestic political issue had brought the Republican administration to the point of ordering the largest U.S. military operation since the Vietnam War. This was a risky undertaking: high U.S. casualties would not be acceptable to the American public, and even a successful invasion would damage relations with Latin America, which was acutely sensitive to any display of U.S. interventionism.

The struggle in Panama was different from those in El Salvador and Nicaragua, where the existence of leftist insurgencies added an East-West dimension to the conflict. Communism was not the issue in Panama, which had no insurgency. The problem was a corrupt dictator who could not be removed by a disaffected population. This familiar Latin American problem was overlaid by another element, what Panamanians called "narco-militarism." The dictator's alliance with drug traffickers brought him international condemnation, even as it made his grip on Panama more tenacious.

The United States was drawn into the battle against General Noriega by the growing prominence of the drug issue, which had assumed at least equal status with communism as a security threat in Latin America. But the Panamanian crisis was a self-inflicted wound for the United States. Manuel Noriega had been steadfastly supported by the U.S. government, even as suspicions about him grew. When it finally decided that he had become a liability, Noriega had grown so strong that only the most drastic measures would dislodge him.

Even so, the United States' opposition to Noriega was a far less contentious issue domestically than its opposition to communists in Nicaragua and El Salvador—not least because on the questions of drugs and the future of the Panama Canal, the stakes were clearer to Americans. Although a debate arose over appropriate ways of intervening in Panama, mirroring the debate on the proper use of U.S. power in Nicaragua and El Salvador, the history of the Panamanian case nonetheless suggests that Americans are more prepared to accept the direct use of U.S. military force to fight drug trafficking in Latin America than to fight communism there. The military intervention in Panama was immediately successful—another factor that made the action more acceptable than the lengthy, although less overt, U.S. interventions in Nicaragua and El Salvador.

A CRISIS IN THE MAKING

In 1964, riots broke out in Panama over U.S. control of the Panama Canal, prompting Lyndon Johnson to open negotiations to revise the 1903 treaty that gave the United States control over the canal and the Canal Zone "in perpetuity." Thirteen years later, the United States and Panama signed treaties that provided for the gradual transfer of the canal to Panamanian sovereignty.[1] Although the 1977 treaties removed one source of instability in Panama, they brought into focus another potential one—the nature of the government itself. Panama was ruled by the charismatic populist Omar Torrijos Herrera. Whatever his attributes, the United States was not about to turn over control of the canal to a dictator. President Jimmy Carter and General Torrijos therefore reached a tacit understanding that Torrijos would permit the evolution of representative government in Panama. Key congressmen supported the treaties on the understanding that the promised democratic transition would occur.

But there were numerous obstacles to the implantation of democracy in Panama. First was the dominance of the United States and the Panamanian military in Panamanian life. Since

Panama's secession from Colombia in 1903—which was encouraged by the U.S. government for the purpose of gaining the right to build an isthmian canal—a symbiotic relationship had existed between Panama and the United States. Through its control of the canal, the United States assumed the role of senior partner in this relationship, and thereby extended its control over many aspects of Panamanian life. The U.S. dollar (the *balboa*) circulated as the Panamanian currency. The Panamanian National Guard was formed to work closely with the United States in defending the canal, and the U.S. Southern Command, which is responsible for all U.S. military activities in Central and South America, was headquartered in Panama. The U.S. military bases in the Canal Zone, established to provide protection for the canal, also served as a platform for projecting force in the region. The close U.S.–Panamanian military relations in turn bolstered the domestic power base of the Panamanian military. Furthermore, Panamanian politics have traditionally been characterized by collaboration rather than conflict. The service- and trade-based economy accounts for this to a great extent. The financial services sector, the commercial business of the free trade zone in the port city of Colon, and the canal formed the basis for the rapid economic development of the 1970s.[2] The merchant class had no interest in setting itself against the military, which controlled the ports and transit routes. Furthermore, under Torrijos, state-promoted growth created numerous ties between government and business.

The sudden death of Torrijos in a plane crash in July 1981 jeopardized the transition to democracy (elections were planned for 1984), which, even had he survived, was not assured. Torrijos had stepped down in 1978, turning over nominal power to his Democratic Revolutionary party (PRD). An alliance of business interests and the powerful National Guard, the PRD was not the ideal vehicle for a transition to democracy. In 1982, the four top National Guard officers agreed on a plan for rotating command of the Guard among themselves, with each outgoing commander taking up a position of power within the PRD. The scheme broke down when intelligence chief Manuel Noriega became commander in 1983. He reneged on the agreement that would have made his predecessor, Gen. Rubén Darío Paredes, the PRD's presidential candidate in 1984. Nicolás Ardito Barletta, whom Noriega believed he could control, ran instead on the PRD's ticket. Barletta won in a close race (Noriega's chief of staff later said he helped fix the vote count to ensure his victory). Combining all police, immigration, and National Guard forces into the new Panamanian Defense Forces (PDF), Noriega began to consolidate his power over business and the government, including the Panama Treaty Affairs Executive Directorate (DEPAT), which was responsible for the Panamanian side of canal affairs. This visible acquisition of power by Noriega, who was considered to be an extremely helpful ally and source of intelligence by many in the Reagan administration, was not opposed in any concerted way by the U.S. government. From 1983 on, Noriega was the de facto ruler of Panama. Instead of protesting the general's power grab, which might have forced him to back off at this early stage in the consolidation of his rule, the United States quietly permitted Torrijos's promised democratic transition to be derailed.

Although it was not then common public knowledge, the fact that the country's main businesses included drug trafficking, arms smuggling, and illicit trade of all sorts was an even more ominous development. The growth of this trade was facilitated by the same factors that had made Panama an important center for legal, financial, and commercial businesses in the Western Hemisphere during the 1970s. In 1970, legislation was passed permitting the establishment of tax-free, secret bank accounts, and easing the requirements for ship registry and the incorporation of businesses and dummy companies. Well before Noriega's rise to power, some Panamanian officials (including Torrijos's brother) had become involved in this illicit trade.[3]

As intelligence chief of the PDF under Torrijos, Noriega had detailed knowledge of all the subterranean dealings in Panama, which he used to amass power and wealth for himself. The U.S. government began to receive reports during the 1970s of the corruption and drug dealing of the Panamanian military. Not only did the United States choose not to expose those involved, it actively blocked U.S. prosecutors' efforts to bring charges against Noriega in 1979. For two decades, the United States found one pressing reason or another to overlook PDF corruption—for intelligence reasons, for getting the canal treaties passed, or for sustaining the contras, whom Noriega was helping.[4] During the 1988 U.S. presidential campaign, this issue caused George Bush some difficulty. A former U.S. ambassador to Panama, Everett Ellis Briggs, said that he had been convinced of Noriega's involvement in illegal activities during his tour there in the mid-1980s, and had reported this to Washington. When asked why the reports had not been acted upon by the Reagan administration, the vice president responded that the United States did not have hard proof of Noriega's complicity. (Briggs concurred with this statement.)

The United States was forced into open confrontation with Noriega in February 1988, however, when he was indicted by two U.S. federal grand juries in Florida. Noriega was charged with assisting in the transshipment of drugs from Colombia to the United States; laundering drug profits in Panama-based banks in return for a payoff; providing security for the transfer of funds; permitting the establishment of cocaine processing plants in Panama; and selling ether and acetone to the drug cartel. During the course of the year, detailed information about Noriega's dealings became public as a result of hearings held by the Senate Foreign Relations Subcommittee on Narcotics and Terrorism and the indictments handed down by the Florida grand juries.[5] The star witness in these hearings was a former Panamanian official, José Blandón, who testified about various illicit activities of Noriega and the PDF. In September 1989, the Bush administration finally corroborated some of these charges and said that Noriega had accumulated between $200 and $300 million from his role in drug trafficking, and had given safe haven to Colombian drug barons after the 1984 killing of Colombian justice minister Rodrigo Lara Bonilla spurred a crackdown against them.

It was apparent from these indictments and congressional hearings that the United States had known of Noriega's dealing for a number of years yet had chosen to look the other way. The question was why it had done so. One reason was that Noriega was useful to the United States. He helped the Nicaraguan contras financially, granted landing rights for their resupply flights, and provided training for some Costa Rica–based rebels. And although it was well known that he traded intelligence with Cuba as well as the United States, this made him both a useful source of information and a channel for communications. He also cooperated with the U.S. Drug Enforcement Administration, aiding in the occasional capture or arrest of traffickers, even as he was in league with them. On the other hand, he possessed an intimate knowledge of U.S. military and intelligence operations, which meant that he was in a position to compromise U.S. interests. Those who had dealt with Noriega knew how formidable an adversary he could be, which explained, in part at least, why the U.S. government was reluctant to take him on.

The Reagan administration was also leery of Arnulfo Arias Madrid, the leading opposition politician, whose antimilitary stance—were he to come to power—might jeopardize U.S. interests in Panama. Arias had been denied the presidency after winning elections in 1941 and 1951, and ousted in a coup in 1968 after winning once more. He was the apparent winner again in 1984, but Barletta, the PDF-backed candidate, was installed instead. Secretary of State George Shultz attended Barletta's inauguration, lending a stamp of legitimacy to the new Panamanian government. Barletta fell from power, however, after he sought an investigation in late 1985 into the brutal killing of Hugo Spadafora, a Torrijos supporter who had been about to accuse Noriega of drug trafficking. Rumors were circulating that the PDF had killed Spadafora, causing a scandal in the normally peaceful country. Barletta was locked in a room by Noriega's henchmen until he submitted his resignation. He was replaced by his first vice president, Eric Arturo Delvalle. The United States condemned Barletta's ouster—its first public sign of dissatisfaction with Noriega—but took no further action.

THE CRISIS ERUPTS

The United States was dragged into opposition to Noriega by degrees, and only after widespread unrest erupted in Panama.

The Panamanians' growing discontent with corruption and the PDF's dominance over the political life of their country burst into the open in June 1987 after Col. Roberto Díaz Herrera, the PDF's second-in-command and Torrijos's cousin, accused Noriega of corruption, the rigging of the 1984 elections, the murder of Spadafora, and even of planning the crash that killed Torrijos. Díaz Herrera was motivated by revenge: Noriega had retired him, denying him his turn in the top PDF position in violation of the power-sharing arrangement worked out after Torrijos's death. The colonel's charges catalyzed an unprecedented nationwide outpouring of protest, strikes, and demonstrations that lasted for several months.

The opposition coalesced in the National Civic Crusade, a broad spectrum of business, labor, and community groups, which had significant support from the Catholic church. The opposition political parties also participated in the protests, but they respected the Civic Crusade's founders' intent that the protest rise above partisan politics in a popular, nonviolent insurrection. A public opinion survey showed that 75 percent of Panamanians wanted Noriega to relinquish power. Calling for a democratic government, the Civic Crusade insisted that Noriega relinquish his post as commander in chief of the PDF. Its leaders asked Panamanians to stop paying taxes and to boycott any establishment doing business with the government. These actions and the strikes jolted the economy, prompting a crisis of confidence that led to massive withdrawals from Panama's banks. Noriega was reportedly shocked at the outpouring of protest against him, but he was unyielding in his determination to stay in power and the civilian opposition simply did not have the muscle to force him out. Civic Crusade leaders had adopted the position that Noriega must go before any negotiations could take place, although they sought to reassure the PDF that they did not deny its legitimacy as an institution. During the summer of 1987, a group of Panamanian bankers drew up the "Bankers' Plan" with Noriega's representatives, which set a retirement date for the PDF chief. Noriega may have been toying with his opponents all along, but in any event, he backed off from discussions when he saw that the protest was ebbing for lack of U.S. support.

One reason for his intransigence was his confidence that the U.S. government, or at least certain sectors of it, would continue to back him. The Defense Department, the Central Intelligence Agency, and the Drug Enforcement Administration all had an interest in continuing cooperation with Noriega. In the critical months of mid-1987, the U.S. government reacted slowly, as it tried to gauge the magnitude of the crisis in Panama. Was Noriega becoming more of a liability than an asset? Washington halted U.S. aid after its embassy in Panama City was stoned and defaced by Noriega supporters who charged that U.S. diplomats were behind the unrest. The State Department called upon the Panamanian government to uphold the rule of law and show respect for democratic procedures, but "correct and formal" military-to-military and other bilateral U.S. relations continued.

The Reagan administration decided to try a low-key approach to the problem, and in December 1987, it sent Assistant Secretary of Defense Richard Armitage to Panama to explore quietly the conditions under which Noriega would step down from his post. The mission failed, despite an offer to drop the ongoing investigations of Noriega by U.S. Customs and other agencies charged with combating illegal drug traffic into the United States. When the Panamanian leader rejected this offer, the administration had no next step planned. Nor was the administration prepared when the federal indictments of Noriega were handed up by the federal grand jury in February 1988, although no government official who was knowledgeable about Panama should have been surprised by this development. At this point, the U.S. government had no choice but to escalate pressure on Noriega. Public concern about drugs was at an all-time high and the administration could not afford to be seen as coddling a dictator drug lord after U.S. grand juries had indicted him. Nevertheless, the anti-Noriega campaign ran into problems almost as soon as it was launched. Some government officials harbored misgivings about turning against a long-time ally. The resulting disunity within the administration complicated efforts to frame a coherent Panamanian policy.

Furthermore, the difficulty of dislodging Noriega was grossly underestimated by the officials in charge of formulating the anti-Noriega policy. On the heels of Noriega's indictment, Assistant Secretary of State for Latin America Elliott Abrams reportedly urged President Delvalle to dismiss Noriega as chief of the PDF. He did so on February 25, but the National Assembly was convened in emergency session hours later and dismissed Delvalle himself on the grounds that he had acted unconstitutionally in firing Noriega without the legislature's consent. On February 26, Education Minister Manuel Solis Palma was named acting president. Opposition politicians were annoyed at the United States for using Delvalle, Noriega's puppet, as its point man in its anti-Noriega campaign. In the end, the deposed president went into hiding, ending up in Miami, still recognized as president by the U.S. government.

Delvalle took the next step in the anti-Noriega campaign. His recognition as president of Panama by the United States permitted his lawyers to argue successfully in U.S. courts that Panamanian government assets in the United States should be placed under the control of Delvalle and his representatives. In early March 1988, the courts froze some $40 million in Panamanian government assets in U.S. banks and halted the U.S. operations of the government-owned airline, Air Panama. Delvalle also asked the United States to withhold canal revenues due Panama, but the administration was not yet ready to commit itself to all-out economic warfare against Noriega.

At this stage, the Reagan administration was still hoping that someone else would pull its irons out of the fire. In congressional testimony on March 10, State Department officials expressed the hope that PDF members would rebel against their leader. A coup, led by the chief of the Panamanian police, Col. Leonidas Macías, was attempted on March 16. One of the coup leaders, Maj. Fernando Quezada, later said he had asked for U.S. help, but none was forthcoming. Loyalist troops quickly put down the bumbled uprising, but it spurred the worst riots Panama had seen yet, prompting Noriega to call out combat troops to quash a general strike. Noriega arrested Macías and twelve of the fifty-four majors in the PDF. The purge and heightened surveillance ensured Noriega's control over the rest of the 15,000-strong force. Then, in a shrewd move, Noriega welcomed U.S. officials to Panama for talks. Two State Department officials relayed the administration's message that it would not seek Noriega's extradition if he went into exile (Spain had offered him asylum), although the indictments against him would not be dropped. Negotiations continued into April, but Noriega rejected any plan that would require him to leave the country. Several Latin American leaders had criticized the U.S. indictments of Noriega in view of the fact that Panama has no extradition agreement with the United States. Former Venezuelan president Carlos Andrés Pérez said that he and other leaders had been close to getting Noriega to agree to leave when the indictments were handed down. Yet, it was not clear at the time that Noriega thought that he would have to relinquish power.

ECONOMIC SANCTIONS AND NEGOTIATIONS

The Reagan administration next decided to impose selective economic sanctions on the Noriega regime, although their implementation was slow and uneven, and the sanctions themselves far from comprehensive. On March 31, the administration announced that it would put all monies it owed Panama into an escrow account in the United States under the control of President Delvalle, and it urged U.S. companies and individuals to follow suit. On April 8, President Reagan invoked the International Emergency Economic Powers Act, banning all U.S. individuals and organizations from making payments to the Noriega regime. The United States would now withhold canal toll revenues and payments for services of canal operations (about $80 million annually), as well as housing costs, taxes, and social security payments (the last were later resumed for canal employees). The administration also suspended Panama's preferential trade status, which allowed about 30 percent of its exports to the United States to enter duty-free.

The effect of the sanctions was diluted almost immediately when three hundred U.S. firms doing business in Panama protested the measures. By the end of April, the Treasury Department had begun making exceptions to the administration's order to enable these firms to continue operating in Panama. The sanctions' impact was also blunted by the fact that the important banking sector had already reacted to the Panamanian crisis. About three-quarters of the bank deposits in Panama had been made in off-shore banks. These funds were therefore readily transferable out of their Panama branches. By the time sanctions were imposed, the assets in banks in Panama had been drawn down to $20 billion (from a peak of $49 billion in 1982).

More important, however, was the limited nature of the sanctions themselves. The United States had refrained from imposing a total trade embargo to minimize the harm to Panamanian citizens and the economy; only transactions with the Panamanian government were prohibited. Although these sanctions would have cost the Noriega regime as much as $200 million annually, this would not have been fatal, since the United States was not Panama's only source of revenue. After the sanctions were imposed, Libya reportedly gave the regime $24 million in cash. The Panamanian government closed the banks to halt capital flight. It managed to continue meeting the government payroll, albeit with delays, by issuing script that could be used at supermarkets and other stores in exchange for goods. If the United States had taken more drastic economic measures, if it had imposed a total trade embargo, for instance, the impact would have been enormous, given the large U.S. stake in the Panamanian economy. And if comprehensive multilateral sanctions had been introduced, Panama's economy, which is heavily dependent on external trade and services, would have ground to a halt. In 1988, 45 percent of Panama's exports went to the United States (as compared to 68 percent in 1986), and 30 percent of its imports came from the United States. About $4 billion in merchandise passes annually through the Colon Free Zone, the second largest duty-free export center after Hong Kong, accounting for about 3 percent of Panama's GDP.[6] But such drastic economic warfare would probably have ruined one of the hemisphere's healthier economies. Panama's per capita GNP ($2,100 in 1987) is one of the highest in Latin America. If a total embargo had quickly led Noriega to resign, the damage might have been minimized. But Noriega appeared to be willing to gamble that the Panamanians would eventually blame the United States for their economic pain.

The U.S. rhetoric accompanying the economic sanctions fed expectations that they would have an immediate political effect. Assistant Secretary of State Abrams said on national television in March that Noriega was "hanging by his fingertips" and would be gone "in a matter of days." Two months later, Noriega was still in power, so the United States changed course again. Deputy Assistant Secretary of State Michael Kozak went to Panama to tell Noriega that the United States would drop the indictments against him in return for his departure from the country. When Noriega rejected the offer on May 25, Secretary of State George Shultz announced that "all offers are withdrawn from the table." The United States had played its trump card and lost.

It was becoming clear that General Noriega had a better grasp of how the United States calculated its interests than vice versa. There were in fact very few inducements that anyone could have offered the general that would have made exile attractive. He was not eager to leave the security of Panama and the protection of his PDF for the uncertainties of life abroad. Outside the country, he would be vulnerable to attack from almost any of his partners in his secret or illegal activities who might fear what he could divulge. Once out of power, he would no longer be useful to his partners but simply a great security risk. He was certainly aware of the Medellín drug cartel's ability to reach its targets anywhere, even behind the Iron Curtain.[7]

With its options dwindling, the United States considered covert military action. In the summer of 1988, President Reagan signed a finding for covert action authorizing the CIA to help former Colonel Eduardo Herrera Hassan foment a coup in the ranks of the PDF. When the plan was brought before the Senate Intelligence Committee, however, objections were raised because committee members feared that Noriega would be killed. The president was prohibited by law from ordering the assassination of foreign leaders.[8] In any event, the Panama issue receded in importance during the U.S. presidential campaign. The Panamanian opposition, irritated at having been excluded from the State Department's negotiations with Noriega, slipped into another period of quiescence. Arnulfo Arias died in August without anointing an heir, leaving the opposition without a clear leader for the upcoming elections.

THE ELECTIONS

The Bush administration was not eager to take on the problem that had frustrated every attempt of its predecessor to resolve, but it was forced to respond to Noriega's flouting of the results of the May 1989 elections. In the weeks preceding the vote, the administration expressed its concern that a fraud was being prepared in Panama, citing reports that opposition party members had been removed from the registration lists, that polling places had been moved to distant locations, and that fictional names had been added to the voter rolls. The Noriega regime also controlled all the media, except the television station run by the U.S. Southern Command. On the eve of the elections, it was revealed that President Bush had signed an intelligence finding in February authorizing $10 million in covert aid to the opposition for printing, transportation, and communications costs.[9] The opposition claimed that it had not received the money, but the net effect was to provide Noriega with a pretext for charging the United States with interference in Panama's elections.

In any case, the steps that Noriega had prepared to ensure his candidates' victory on May 7 proved to be insufficient. According to the results of a parallel count organized by the Catholic church and conducted by lay workers, the opposition outpolled the regime's candidates by a three-to-one margin. The pro-Noriega eight-party Coalition of National Liberation nonetheless claimed victory. COLINA's presidential candidate was Carlos Duque, a businessman and close Noriega associate; his running mates for first and second vice presidents were Ramón Siero, Noriega's brother-in-law, and Aquilino Boyd, former ambassador to the United States. The Alliance of Democratic Civilian Opposition (ADOC), the opposition coalition, ran Guillermo Endara, a little-known lawyer from Arnulfo Arias's party, for president. The Christian Democrat Ricardo Arias Calderón was also on the ticket, along with the Liberal Republican Nationalist Movement's Guillermo Ford.[10]

The official announcements of the vote counts were suspended, and the Noriega regime made no move to recognize the opposition's electoral victory, even though international observers, including former U.S. President Jimmy Carter, announced ADOC's apparent win and made public the governing regime's fraudulent activities. The opposition took to the streets, calling on the government to concede defeat. On May 10, the opposition leaders and some of their supporters were brutally attacked by members of Noriega's "Dignity Battalions," a paramilitary group that included members of the police. Hundreds were arrested. Later that day, the Panamanian electoral tribunal nullified the elections on the grounds that they had been invalidated by foreign interference.

On the following day, President Bush announced his decision to send 19,000 soldiers to Panama as reinforcements for the 10,000 U.S. troops stationed there. He ordered the evacuation of U.S. citizens from Panamanian soil and said that the United States would enforce its treaty rights to move its forces freely between its bases in Panama. The U.S. ambassador was recalled, and the economic sanctions remained in force. (Libya immediately offered the Panamanian regime $50 million more in cash and promised it an oil credit line of $100 million.)

The announced rationale for increasing the number of U.S. troops in Panama was to protect American lives. But a subsequent statement from Washington that the administration was not ruling out any of its options carried with it the threat of military action. The credibility of this threat was undercut, however, by the continuing resistance of U.S. military officials to this alternative. The chairman of the U.S. Joint Chiefs of Staff, Admiral William J. Crowe, Jr., had told the Senate Armed Services Committee a week before the Panamanian elections that the use of force could be "a messy, messy business."[11] Furthermore, it was known that the U.S. public was not inclined to support military operations abroad. The president had in any case signaled his desire to exhaust diplomatic remedies before resorting to more serious measures and to seek congressional and international support for U.S. policy. "The U.S.," the president said, "strongly supports, and will cooperate with initiatives taken by governments in this hemisphere to address this crisis through regional diplomacy and action in the Organization of American States."[12]

On May 17, the Organization of American States approved a resolution condemning the election abuses in Panama. It named a mediating commission to promote "formulas toward a national agreement that would ensure a transfer of power by democratic means and within the shortest amount of time, fully respecting the Panamanian people's sovereign will."[13] Not since June 1979, when the OAS had called for the "immediate and definitive replacement" of Nicaraguan dictator Anastasio Somoza, had it taken such a step. Even though the May 17 resolution was much weaker in its condemnation of Noriega than the earlier one had been of Somoza, it was still a significant initiative from an organization many had written off as moribund. The problem with this mediation effort was that the OAS brought no more inducements to the table than the United States had done in its 1988 negotiations with Noriega. Nor was it prepared to take punitive action (such as instituting multilateral economic sanctions) were Noriega to reject its involvement. The OAS action served to isolate Noriega, but he seemed unfazed by this diplomatic pressure.

The OAS team focused on gaining the regime's agreement to hold new elections rather than persuading Noriega to recognize the opposition's May 7 victory. On July 20, the OAS proposed that a provisional government take over on September 1 when the current presidential term would end and that this government hold new elections as soon as possible. But the Panamanian opposition was not happy with this proposal: "The Panamanian people have already decided on their destiny," said Endara.[14] In a characteristically adroit move, the Noriega camp put forward its own proposal for a provisional junta with opposition representation. The opposition, doubting that allowing Noriega to stay in power with a provisional junta would lead to elections any freer than those that had taken place in May, refused the offer. At this point, there was nothing left for the

OAS mediators to do. On September 1, Francisco Rodríguez was sworn in as Panama's new president. (Since he had annulled the May vote, Noriega decided it would be better not to impose Duque on the country.) Rodríguez had been selected by Panama's Council of State, which was composed of government and military officials, and had been comptroller general for the past seven years. The Bush administration refused to recognize the new president and announced that it would tighten the economic sanctions against Panama by adding more companies to the list of Panamanian entities with which U.S. firms and citizens were forbidden to do business.

THE CANAL AS A POLITICAL PAWN

At this juncture, the Bush administration decided to use the canal as leverage over Noriega, announcing that it would not accept any candidate proposed by the Noriega government to serve as administrator of the canal. According to the canal treaties, Panama was to nominate a Panamanian in 1989 to take over as administrator on January 1, 1990. The nominee was subject to the approval of the president and confirmation by the Senate. In June, the Senate had passed a nonbinding resolution (by a vote of 63–31) stating that it would not vote for a Noriega nominee even if the administration approved one. Earlier in the year, William Gianelli, a U.S. citizen, had resigned from his position as chairman of the Canal Commission's board of directors, saying that the canal was in danger of being closed down as a result of arbitrary and illegal actions by the Panamanian government.[15] Michael Rhode, the Canal Commission's secretary, testifying on May 18 before the Merchant Marine and Fisheries Subcommittee on the Panama Canal of the House of Representatives, said that he was beginning to worry about the state of the canal after the year 2000, that if Noriega continued to harass employees, the safety and efficiency of the canal's operation would be diminished. A Panamanian member of the commission, Luis Anderson, also resigned in May, protesting what he called the Panamanian government's violations of civil rights.

The president's announcement and his earlier decision to withhold canal revenues and fees provided Noriega with a propaganda ploy: Noriega told Panamanians that the only reason for the U.S. campaign against him was its desire to stop the transfer of the canal to Panamanian control. Gaining control of the canal was of paramount importance to Panamanians, regardless of their view of Noriega. On the other hand, many Panamanians believed that a Noriega-run canal would be simply another source of corruption and illicit activities.

It was widely believed that the United States had an interest in the continued smooth functioning of the canal. In military terms, the canal's importance had declined since World War II, particularly so since the Vietnam War, when most of the U.S. forces bound for Southeast Asia passed through it. Although U.S. aircraft carriers are too wide to use the canal, smaller naval vessels can and do pass through. In terms of commercial traffic, the canal is perhaps more significant, if not vital. In 1987, 10 percent of all U.S. seaborne trade passed through the canal (this constituted about 70 percent of total canal business). But the canal is far more important to Panama, by any measure, than it is to the United States. Total revenues from the canal amount to 8 percent of Panama's GDP, and it employs some eight thousand Panamanians. Yet the possibility remained that Noriega could contrive some threat to the canal that would work to his benefit. Economic cost/benefit calculations mattered less to him than political survival.

HOPING FOR A COUP

After the debacle of the May elections, President Bush encouraged Panamanians to take direct action against Noriega: "We share the Panamanian people's hope that the Panamanian Defense Forces will stand with them and fulfill their constitutional obligation to defend democracy."[16] Elsewhere, the president sought to reassure the Panamanian military that the United States' objection was to Noriega alone: "A professional Panamanian Defense Force can have an important role to play in Panama's democratic future."[17] Yet the likelihood that the PDF would remove Noriega was not great. He had easily thwarted the March 1988 coup attempt and could count on some two dozen loyal PDF officers to do his bidding in return for a share in the perquisites of power. These men were the nucleus of the general's extensive intelligence and security network. Even if some were to abandon him, the loyalty of the remaining group would have to be neutralized for a coup to succeed. There was no guarantee, furthermore, that any of these men who might take Noriega's place would be any better than he. Many Panamanians feared that the institutionalized corruption and the pervasive influence of the PDF guaranteed "another Noriega."

Nevertheless, on the morning of October 3, 1989, Maj. Moisés Giroldi, chief of security at the PDF headquarters in Panama City, led an uprising there aimed at forcing Noriega into retirement. Even though Noriega was reportedly a captive within his headquarters, he organized a successful counterattack, shot Giroldi, and put down the rebellion later the same day. The U.S. government at first denied that it had been involved but later acknowledged that it had played a limited role in the coup attempt.

Two days before the coup, Giroldi had met with CIA officials and requested that U.S. forces block two roads by which Noriega could bring in reinforcements. The United States complied with this request but took no further action to support the coup once it began to fail. The administration insists that no request for further U.S. aid came from Giroldi's forces, denying a report that rebel officers had asked the second-ranking U.S. military official in Panama to send a helicopter to take Noriega into custody.[18] It was reported that the rebels had earlier said that they did not want U.S. involvement to "taint" their "self-cleansing" action,[19] but they may have changed their minds once Noriega's well-trained Battalion 2000 turned up at the scene.

Brent Scowcroft, the U.S. national security adviser, later confirmed a report that President Bush had authorized the U.S. Southern Command to draw up a plan to apprehend the general covertly, but by that time the coup had already failed.[20] Many in Congress accused the administration of having lost a good opportunity to oust Noriega, but Bush officials insisted that their information had been too sketchy to act upon safely. They had been wary of Major Giroldi, since he was responsible for quashing the March 1988 coup attempt. The failure of the Giroldi coup was the last straw for many people in the United States watching policy failure after policy failure, even as U.S. officials continued predicting Noriega's imminent departure. It seemed that the Bush administration was banking on an unlikely contingency—that the Noriega problem would be solved by the Panamanians without direct U.S. help. Yet, as government officials pointed out to their critics, their freedom of action was limited by congressional strictures against covert operations. The administration was being particularly careful to steer clear of any actions that might result in Noriega's death.

DWINDLING OPTIONS

After the October coup attempt, Noriega began a systematic purge of the military, as well as of civilian officials whose loyalty was suspect. The harsh crackdown, and Noriega's defiant declaration of himself as Panama's "maximal ruler," suggested that no one in the PDF would be likely to revolt in the near future. And even though a successful PDF coup without U.S. help might have avoided political complications, the United States would have had little influence over Noriega's fate and the shape of the new government. The problem with returning to negotiating with Noriega was that there was still no clear incentive the United States—or Latin American leaders, for that matter—could offer to persuade Noriega to leave Panama. Indeed, the repeated public demands that he leave made it impossible for him to do so without appearing to be caving in to U.S. interventionist pressure. Yet were he to remain in the country under any guise, he would continue to wield de facto power.

The repeated public demands that Noriega leave also made Bush, who had long battled the "wimp" image, appear impotent. This perception of presidential weakness became as great a political problem as that of Noriega's rule. Full-scale sanctions or threats to abrogate the canal treaties were not promising options; they were far more likely to have turned Panamanians against the United States than to have induced Noriega's departure. Thus, U.S. options narrowed to a difficult choice between the use of force or coexistence with the general. Coexistence was not a long-term solution, however, and since it would mean turning over the canal operations to a Panamanian administrator in January 1990 with Noriega still pulling all the strings, this option may have been politically untenable even in the short run.

The U.S. military was fully capable of prevailing over the Panamanian military, although not without incurring casualties. Noriega had been fortifying the PDF and his Dignity Battalions with arms from abroad, but the PDF remained more a police force than an army. Few battalions were battle-ready and some were not even equipped for combat. The only real challenge was presented by crack special operations units trained by Israelis and Cubans. But the political obstacles to direct military action seemed insurmountable, except in the unlikely event of a Panamanian attack on U.S. citizens or the canal, and Noriega certainly knew how the United States would react to such a provocation. U.S. forces in Panama had increased their exercises and troop movements to assert U.S. treaty rights and in response to harassing actions by the Panamanians, and confrontations had occurred between U.S. and Panamanian military personnel since the crisis began, but these were in the nature of low-level spats.[21] This was essentially a game of chicken that neither side appeared to be interested in escalating.

The U.S. military was leery of any direct action by its forces, an attitude that had prevailed since the Vietnam debacle. In October 1989, Admiral Crowe, now retired from the Joint Chiefs of Staff, went public to reiterate his earlier opposition to "more vigorous" proposals for action as put forth by Assistant Secretary Abrams (Crowe thought Abrams's proposals were "naive"), and said that his position had been that he did not want to "put American lives at risk, unless the stakes clearly justified it."[22] Since the Pentagon had 13,000 soldiers based in Panama, its institutional inclination was to seek a modus vivendi with the host government and to avoid any initiatives that might threaten U.S. troops with serious retaliatory measures by Noriega's forces. Also, Defense Secretary Richard Cheney warned that if the

United States used military force in Panama, it would make the United States' relations with other Latin American countries more difficult.[23]

Congress, on the other hand, grew more supportive of the idea of covert U.S. action in Panama after the failure of the October coup. In late October, the House and Senate intelligence committees approved a $3-million covert plan to recruit disaffected PDF members and Panamanian exiles to rebel against Noriega. This plan was leaked to the press, although its details were not made public. The Bush administration also gained the intelligence committees' agreement to a reinterpretation of the 1976 law banning CIA participation in assassination plots. The ban against assassination remained in effect, but the agency was no longer barred from involvement in any operations that might result in violence.

George Bush had made it clear when he was running for president that he would not consider coexistence with Noriega. He broke with the Reagan administration over its May 1988 offer to drop the indictments against the dictator if he would relinquish power. (Bush's opponent, Michael Dukakis, had passed him by 10 percentage points in the voter polls when he attacked this overture.) As president, Bush had made his antidrug policy the subject of his first televised address to the nation, and he was not about to soft-pedal his stand on Noriega. In Colin Powell, the new chairman of the Joint Chiefs of Staff, and Maxwell Thurman, the commander of the Southern Command, he had two generals who, in stark contrast to their predecessors, would not try to dissuade him from considering military options.

The history of the previous two years had demonstrated that unless the United States closed the gap between the ends it wished to achieve in Panama and the means it was willing to employ, its policy would continue to fail. Given the president's reluctance to change the policy objective, and in view of congressional support for a more interventionist course, the Bush administration took off the shelf contingency plans for a military operation in Panama, which had been drawn up at the order of Gen. Fred Woerner, the former chief of the Southern Command. His successor, General Thurman, was more inclined than

Woerner had been to put them into action. Gen. Carl Stiner, a veteran of antiterrorist actions in the Middle East, was brought in to lead operations in the field. General Powell persuaded President Bush that a massive operation would be necessary to ensure the success of the mission and minimize casualties.

When a U.S. marine was killed on December 15 by Noriega's soldiers, the president had the pretext he needed to initiate military action. U.S. forces stationed in Panama on U.S. bases were supplemented by means of a massive airlift. There were 24,000 U.S. troops in Panama when the invasion got underway at 1:00 a.m. on December 20. Noriega's headquarters was bombarded; this action produced the heaviest casualties, as fire raced through the surrounding working-class neighborhood. Noriega's troops put up little resistance and began surrendering when their leader did not appear to be leading a defense effort. Some eight thousand armed irregulars, the Dignity Battalions, put up more of a fight, skirmishing with U.S. troops in the streets of Panama City, but, overall, General Powell's strategy of deploying massive force to intimidate potential resisters worked. Thousands of weapons were subsequently unearthed in raids on Noriega's hideouts, on the homes of his supporters, and on garrisons around the country, providing evidence that victory might have come at a much higher price if the United States had postponed the invasion until a later date when Noriega would have armed many more civilians.

Noriega, however, eluded the United States' grasp. When he took refuge in the Vatican Embassy on Christmas Eve, virtually all of his followers had given up the fight. Bush's gamble had paid off: only twenty-four U.S. troops died, and Panamanian casualties were in the low hundreds rather than in the thousands there might have been had the resistance been more sustained. Most surprising to journalists and other onlookers was the widespread welcome the Panamanians gave the U.S. troops. Although they mourned their casualties, many Panamanians said they believed U.S. intervention was the only way they could have been rid of Noriega. On January 3, after intense negotiations, Noriega was persuaded by his mistress and the papal nuncio, Sebastian Laboa, to give himself up. He was promptly flown to the United States to stand trial on drug-trafficking and money-laundering charges.

Even though the military operation was a success, and therefore generated relatively little criticism in the United States, it was a drastic and risky last-resort effort that pointed up the failure of U.S. and international diplomacy to ease Noriega out and democracy in. The legal justification for the U.S. action under international law was slim, the death of a single U.S. marine hardly warranting a full-scale invasion. It was simply an expedient way to end the ill-advised relationship with the dictator.

With one swift stroke, the United States had freed Panama of Noriega and his claque of corrupt officers, but the enormous challenge of building a functioning democratic system, essentially from the ground up, lay ahead. First, order had to be reestablished, an effective police force created, the new government shored up, the economy rebuilt, and steps taken to prevent the resumption of drug-trafficking and money-laundering activities. At the same time, the Bush administration had to reassure its Latin American allies that the Panama invasion was not a precursor to more aggressive policies elsewhere in the region.

In the days after the invasion, U.S. forces were engaged in two main tasks. The first of these was capturing documents and interrogating prisoners, most of whom were released. Those prisoners the new Panamanian government believed to have been involved in crimes were detained on the U.S. bases, where they would remain until the prison administrators were in place. Neither the captured documents nor the transcripts of the interrogations were made public, although the Panamanian government and Noriega's lawyers were given access to some of the 15,000 boxes of material that the U.S. military kept under its control.[24] Many observers—aware of the former dictator's zeal for collecting intelligence as well as the most sordid details of people's lives—were convinced that access was restricted because his files contained information that could severely embarrass—to say the least—U.S. officials and Panamanian citizens.

President Endara, in an interview with the author at the Presidencia in the early summer of 1990, said, "I'm sure there is information in there that I would not like to have, even about my worst enemy. I think these kinds of things should be destroyed." The process of sorting out these files and deciding which should be given to prosecutors in Panama promised to be a traumatic one since the web of corruption extended far beyond the PDF and a few Noriega cronies. Endara was happy to postpone this ordeal until after Noriega's trial in the United States. Yet Eusebio Marchosky, the judge in charge of recovering state funds— including overdrafts on the National Bank totaling nearly $1 billion—misappropriated by the Noriega regime, was one of many who complained because Panamanian justice would have to wait for U.S. justice to run its course.[25]

The second task of the U.S. forces in the invasion's aftermath was to help maintain order while the new government pulled together a new police force. The U.S. military police (MP) should have been put in place more rapidly to prevent the widespread looting that occurred in Panama City. But the MPs soon began patrolling with the former PDF members who were being inducted into the new Public Force. Panamanians naturally mistrusted the former PDF members, so the presence of the MPs was crucial; many were dismayed when the number of MPs was decreased in March. By June, only two hundred remained, and they were mostly stationed at police precincts for advice and backup. The rate of most violent crimes in Panama City did increase between March and June, but this was as much due to lack of equipment and fuel as to incompetence on the part of the police. Under a U.S. Department of Justice program, civilians were beginning to train the new police force, but it would take months before the success of the effort could be gauged.

First Vice President and Justice/Government Minister Ricardo Arias Calderón worked feverishly with U.S. assistance to put together the new Public Force. It was to be a smaller force than the old one, stripped of many of the functions that had given the members of the PDF the opportunity to intimidate citizens and enrich themselves. Unfortunately, the officer chosen to head the new force, Col. Roberto Armijo, had to be replaced when an examination of the records of the National Bank suggested that he had been involved in illegal activities.

The question also remained whether the rank and file of the new force would accept the principle of civilian control, a foreign concept in Panama. Many Panamanians criticized the decision to retain the majority of PDF members, arguing that corrupt military men could never be converted into "clean" policemen.

The appointment of Col. Eduardo Herrera to replace Armijo was a double-edged sword. His record was untainted by corruption, he had sought U.S. assistance in opposing Noriega, and he was committed to civilian authority. Yet his very strengths made him chafe at the severe limits imposed on the new force of discredited and discontented former military men. Even a "good" military officer found it difficult to fit into the new mold being created, and Herrera resigned in September. His replacement, Col. Fernando Quezada, also resigned after a nasty public spat with a newspaper publisher, Roberto Eisenmann, in which Quezada threatened to reveal slanderous information about Eisenmann from Noriega's files. A civilian adviser to Arias Calderón, Ebrahim Asvat, then became the director and, in short order, he cleared out the five lieutenant colonels remaining from the Noriega regime, as well as dozens of other officers. It was apparent by this point that the attempt to convert the PDF into a new force was not succeeding. Whether Arias Calderón will change course and move to train and install a completely new civilian police force remains to be seen.

Meanwhile, the party of President Guillermo Endara, a well-liked but little-known lawyer, received fewer votes in the March elections than the parties of his two vice presidents. Their parties therefore ended up with more seats in the legislature and more cabinet posts than his party. Differences among the three threaten to weaken the government, and Endara, with his conciliatory nature, may prove ill-suited for the tougher leadership tasks.

The most serious sign of trouble in the Endara government's first year was the growing realization that Panama's role as a drug-trafficking and laundering transit point did not end with Noriega's ouster. This is not surprising, given that Panama has attracted smugglers since the days of the Spanish Main, but it does open up questions about the achievements of the U.S.

invasion. In its September 1990 report, the State Department's International Narcotics Matters Bureau noted suspicions of a cocaine laboratory operating in Darién province, which borders Colombia. In 1984, Noriega had permitted Colombian drug-lords to locate a lab there in exchange for protection money— one of the charges on which he was indicted. While no evidence has surfaced of the current government's complicity in the suspected establishment of a new lab in the inaccessible jungles of Darién, its existence is at minimum a glaring sign of the government's inability to police its own territory. The State Department report went on to note that of forty policemen charged with investigating drug crimes, only thirteen even had weapons. Overall, the police were not much better equipped, either in terms of guns or transport. Eduardo Herrera had warned that the zeal to limit the new security forces' capabilities would lay the country open to increased trafficking, but many U.S. officials had dismissed this as a bid for more power. Now the United States is faced with the decision of whether it should assume direct responsibility for combating drug traffickers in Panama, and thus risk incurring an anti–U.S. nationalist backlash. On the other hand, it could encourage Panama to create a completely new police force to deal with the problem itself—with the knowledge, however, that as long as the enormously wealthy Colombian traffickers exist, Panama's police may be corrupted.

Full economic recovery from the invasion and the effects of three years of U.S. sanctions will take years, although the promise of significant U.S. aid initially produced signs of a return of public confidence, vital to Panama's banking and service economy. The Bush administration sent to Congress a proposal for a $1-billion package of direct aid, credits, and guarantees, and promised to lobby creditors to reschedule Panama's $4-billion debt on easy terms. But the aid request ran into trouble in Congress, which balked at its size at a time of severe budget constraints. Sen. Robert Dole proposed that foreign aid be reapportioned, taking some away from the traditional recipients, Israel and Egypt, to aid the emerging democracies in Central America and Eastern Europe. In the end, however, Congress approved a pared-down aid package for Panama of $420 million, plus $500 million in credits, which President Bush signed into law on Memorial Day weekend. This was welcome news for Panama's struggling government. But simply resuscitating Panama's economy will not solve its structural problems. Unemployment is running at between 30 and 35 percent, and thousands left homeless by the December intervention remain in refugee quarters. An estimated 44 percent of Panamanians are living below the poverty line. The government plan is to create an export-oriented free market economy. Yet without serious efforts to address the problems of poverty, lack of health care, and other such social issues, discontent with democracy could begin to grow. Many poor Panamanians now fondly recall the populist dictator Omar Torrijos, whose policies addressed their concerns and improved their lot.

Thus, months after intervening to rid Panama of General Noriega, the United States is beginning to understand the real burden it has assumed. Compared to the tasks of rebuilding Panama's economy, controlling the police force, and helping to root out the sources of institutionalized corruption, toppling the dictator is beginning to look like child's play.

7

CENTRAL AMERICA'S FUTURE: NEW DANGERS AND NEW OPPORTUNITIES

The dramatic realignment of political forces in Central America and the end of the Cold War dictate a shift in U.S. regional policy. Presented with an unprecedented opportunity to consolidate the trend toward democratization that began in the 1980s, the United States must shift its focus and resources from a policy based primarily on defending the region against security threats to one with an emphasis on promoting democratization and regional economic development. The war in the Middle East and the problems presented by the collapsing economies of the former Soviet bloc will sorely tempt U.S. policymakers to declare victory in Central America and turn their backs on the region. But this sort of "benign neglect" would put at risk the fragile gains won at great cost over the past decade.

Without sustained U.S. attention, the chance of a reversal in the region's improving fortunes is high. The continuing war in El Salvador threatens regional stability, as does the possibility of renewed turmoil in Nicaragua and Panama. Drug-trafficking, the still dominant role of the military everywhere except in Costa Rica, and the crippling poverty of the majority of Central Americans pose serious threats to the region's nascent democracies, even with communist expansionism on the wane. The gains of the 1980s will not be cemented unless fundamental economic and political reforms succeed. The American public seems to grasp this notion as it applies to Eastern Europe, but the decreased media attention being paid to Central America lulls many into thinking that the basic problems that have bedeviled the region have been solved. In fact, the indigenous threats to Central America's stability remain, even though the external threats are fading away.

The argument is frequently made that Central America is

not important enough to fundamental U.S. interests to merit serious attention. But given the region's geographic proximity, the United States will always be affected by problems there, whether by regional instability spurring massive emigration, or by weak governments allowing untrammeled drug-trafficking. Central Americans will remain in our backyard, and we in theirs. They will continue to look to the United States when their troubles grow too large for them to handle. And the United States will continue to be drawn into their crises, as it has been since long before the communist threat even existed.

The U.S. approach to coping with Central America's problems has historically been one of putting out fires. Yet, even those critics who today argue for benign neglect would agree that this has proved to be a costly policy. As in the past, the fires are bound to recur, and with them the attendant costs of firefighting. It would surely be a wiser investment to devote the necessary time and attention to preventing those fires in the first place. Even though the U.S. interests at stake are of a lower order than those involving the Middle East or the Soviet Union, the investment required is commensurately smaller. Moreover, the circumstances are more propitious than ever before for Washington to adopt a concerted, long-term policy to help Central Americans strengthen their political and judicial institutions and reduce the overweening power of their militaries, the corrupting influence of drug traffickers, and the widespread poverty that generates social unrest. For the first time, all of the countries in the region have democratically elected governments that are friendly to the United States and largely free of externally sponsored subversion. All are committed to market-oriented economic programs, and their centrist-conservative leaders are more mutually compatible—and capable of working together—than at any previous period in Central American history.

A STRATEGY FOR REGIONAL REFORM

The traditional U.S. crisis approach to Central America should be discarded in favor of a more methodical strategy for regional reform. To promote regional security, democratization, and development, the United States should:

- Give top priority to seeking diplomatic solutions to the remaining Cold War era security threats in El Salvador and Cuba

- Respond vigorously to the major security threat posed by drug-trafficking by increasing detection, enforcement, and eradication assistance that is strictly tied to the dismissal of local officials engaged in trafficking

- Support a general process of demilitarization that drastically reduces local military establishments (and U.S. aid to them) and replaces them with smaller, better-trained police forces under civilian leadership

- Require specific, verifiable progress in human rights, and improvement in local judicial systems, as a condition of continued economic aid

- Reduce trade barriers against Central American products and encourage nontraditional exports and regional economic integration

- Support more equitable development by funding basic needs programs in the areas of health, education, and housing

Conflict Resolution

Diplomatic negotiations proved to be the single most important factor in resolving the Nicaraguan civil war. The United States should take this lesson to heart by becoming a more active proponent of similar efforts to end both the Salvadoran and Guatemalan conflicts.

The Bush administration should initiate a diplomatic full-court press to end El Salvador's war, with the United Nations, which has already demonstrated its usefulness in resolving regional conflicts in Africa and the Middle East, as well as in Nicaragua, as the dominant player. Specifically, the United States should strongly endorse the current UN mediation effort in El Salvador, and work closely with the mediator to develop a proposal that addresses the concerns of both parties to the conflict. Washington should consult with the UN secretary general about how U.S. aid restrictions could best be employed to facilitate a settlement. (For example, it could agree to cut off aid to the Cristiani government if the secretary general determines that the Salvadoran government has rejected a reasonable peace proposal. The mediator should also be prepared to issue a public condemnation of the insurgents if they reject a reasonable peace proposal, and to seek UN sanctions against any country found to be supporting them militarily.) All of the Central American countries should undertake—with UN assistance and U.S. funding—measures for ending cross-border aid to insurgents not only in El Salvador, but in Guatemala and Honduras as well. The United States should also be prepared to support the deployment of UN peacekeeping forces to supervise demobilization and the implementation of a peace accord.

We know today that the Soviet Union was helpful in ending the Nicaraguan conflict by consulting with the United States and pressuring the Sandinistas into accepting an election-based solution. Although the Soviets have much less leverage over the Salvadoran guerrillas, Washington should continue to urge them to pressure Cuba—the FMLN's main external supporter—to stop training the guerrillas and to end arms transfers to the FMLN. Furthermore, Washington should seek to initiate direct talks with Havana on the subject of Cuban support for revolutionary movements, with the aim of securing Castro's commitment to end such support.

Drug-Trafficking

Situated between the principal producing and consuming centers of the illegal narcotics trade, all of Central America is being drawn into the maelstrom of violence and corruption generated by international drug-trafficking. Panama, Guatemala, and Honduras are the most seriously affected countries. Although Panama's top government officials are not collaborating with Colombian traffickers as Noriega did, the traffic through Panama continues. Over the past two years, the amount of cocaine transshipped through Guatemala has increased dramatically, as has opium production there. The United States has directed most of its aid toward detection, interdiction, and eradication programs in Mexico and the Andean countries of South America, with the result that traffickers have moved into Central America. Additional assistance is urgently required for such programs in Central America itself, in order to prevent this vulnerable region from falling completely under the traffickers' sway. Furthermore, Washington must insist that local officials (particularly in Panama and Guatemala) whom it knows to be in the traffickers' pay be removed from their posts.

Demilitarization

Central America's powerful armies remain the greatest menace to democratic institutions, as well as the biggest drain on scarce local resources. Gradual demilitarization, which could not be seriously contemplated while the region's civil conflicts raged, should now be made the top long-term U.S. policy goal for the region as a whole. Continuing the diplomatic initiatives spearheaded by former Costa Rican President Oscar Arias, the current Central American governments have taken a major step in this direction by beginning negotiations on a regional accord to reduce military forces in all of the countries in the region.

Washington should strongly support this process, and encourage the Central American governments to draw up blueprints for limiting the security forces in each country to under ten thousand policemen, with Costa Rica as a model. Panama is already moving in this direction, and Nicaragua has taken a bold first step, deciding to cut its huge forces by a third in 1990. Such actions demonstrate that the demilitarization of Central America is a realistic long-term goal. But cutting the size of forces is only one step in the process of dismantling military establishments that have long been the most powerful political institutions in most of these countries. Changing the military mentality by retraining or retiring military men and persuading them to accept a civilian-directed police force will be a far more difficult task.

The United States should prod Honduras and Guatemala to begin reductions immediately by phasing out its military assistance programs—as well as its own large (and now unnecessary) military presence in Honduras. There are no significant security threats in either Honduras or Guatemala that should prevent substantial reductions in the near future, although Honduras may insist on maintaining a border force until its traditional regional adversary, El Salvador, implements some reductions in its own military establishment. (Ongoing international mediation efforts should pave the way for a diplomatic resolution of their bilateral disputes, probably by mid-1991.) Reductions in El Salvador's forces will be contingent on an end to its civil war, but drastic cuts should be part of a final accord with the leftist guerrillas. In the interim, some continued U.S. military assistance is warranted, provided that the Salvadoran government demonstrates its willingness to accept a negotiated settlement (as outlined below).

Moving toward a largely demilitarized Central America does not preclude some continued U.S. security assistance—for training civilian police or to counter drug-trafficking, for example—but such aid should be administered under strict U.S. standards and with congressional oversight to minimize corruption and guard against human rights abuses by the forces receiving the assistance. Rotating police personnel and dismissing those linked to trafficking or abuses, as the Peruvian anti-drug police have done, are two specific policies that should be incorporated in all U.S. police assistance agreements—and applied.

Human Rights

The effective practice of making U.S. security assistance conditional on improvements in the human rights records of Central American governments has been repeatedly frustrated by vague standards and their inconsistent application—often due to security threats deemed overriding. But precisely because many of the old security threats to these governments have recently diminished, the United States can now exercise more vigorously the leverage that its assistance programs give it. Bluntly put, the United States can afford to cut off aid to any country that repeatedly and blatantly violates basic human rights. Demonstrating a willingness to cut aid by half (or more) will increase the effectiveness of the conditionality/certification process, which heretofore has been seen as a hollow threat that recipients could ignore with impunity. Exercising such leverage may not work in all cases (in Guatemala, for example), but that is no reason not to try. At a minimum, Washington will have disassociated itself from serious abuses (as it did in Guatemala in 1977 and again in December 1990), and can still hold out the incentive of renewed aid when the situation improves.

Reviving Growth

During the 1980s, per capita gross domestic production fell in all Central American countries, including Costa Rica. To revive growth, the Bush administration must continue to provide economic assistance to Central America, all of whose governments are making serious efforts to balance their budgets by increasing tax receipts, cutting spending, shedding inefficient state enterprises, and fighting inflation. Even so, U.S. budget pressures and the high costs of our recent intervention in the Middle East portend some shrinkage in aid for Central America. The Bush administration has proposed an Enterprise for the Americas Initiative to reduce trade barriers, encourage private investment, and reduce official debt—all steps that do not require large U.S. expenditures. Given their current, largely sound, economic policies and their extreme need, the countries of Central America should be offered maximum benefits under this initiative. Indeed, their debts to the U.S. government should be entirely forgiven (rather than simply reduced, as suggested in the initiative), since they represent only a small fraction of total Latin American debt.

Just as important, Washington should remove trade barriers promptly and expand the preferential treatment that Central America receives under the Caribbean Basin Initiative. The U.S. sugar quota system is an anachronism, and should be eliminated—despite the objections of inefficient domestic producers. The United States can favor Central America in talks on the multifiber agreement. U.S. producers should be encouraged to follow the lead of the Japanese and relocate operations to the region in order to take advantage of low labor costs. The development of new exports—such as citrus and processed foods—is the key to Central American economic recovery. Nontariff barriers on agricultural exports should also be ended, and Export-Import Bank financing credits should be made widely available to foster nontraditional export industries. The Inter-American Development Bank, to which the Bush administration has pledged matching funds, should give special preference to infrastructure projects. All of these measures require little or no capital outlay but are essential for the private sector and foreign investment to become the engines of economic growth and job creation in the region.

Alleviating Poverty

The current conservative governments in Central America are committed to free market policies. Yet they must also respond to the needs of their impoverished majorities if these countries are to become socially stable, with growing markets and climates hospitable to foreign investment. One of the tragedies of the past decade was that U.S. funds went largely to remedying balance-of-payments deficits rather than to productive development programs. The economic policies of the current Central American governments, the winding down of conflicts, and such U.S. incentives as those described above should make it possible to increase spending on health, education, and housing. Contrary to the arguments of some in Washington, such spending is perfectly consistent with an overall free market philosophy, and just as important as fiscal responsibility. The funding for social programs should come from decreasing the level of U.S. military assistance to the region. Yet instead of shifting funds, the United States has drawn down its overall level of assistance to Central America for fiscal year 1991. Total aid to El Salvador, Costa Rica, Nicaragua, Guatemala, and Honduras was cut back by $226.6 million from the previous year, and over the past two years aid has fallen 40 percent. Instead of moving to consolidate the gains by aggressively promoting economic and political development, Washington is turning its back on the region.[1] A reordering of the local governments' own spending priorities is also needed. Currently, these governments together spend $1 billion annually on their military budgets; and all Central American countries, even Costa Rica, decreased spending on health and education during the 1980s.[2] Now that the region's conflicts are ending, there is no excuse for such imbalances to continue.

ADDRESSING IMMEDIATE PROBLEMS IN INDIVIDUAL COUNTRIES

To promote the long-term regional goals outlined above, U.S. policy must also address the immediate problems facing individual countries, a subject to which we now turn.

Nicaragua

Economic recovery, demilitarization, and national reconciliation are the principal tasks facing Nicaragua's new government. The United States took two important steps in support of the first goal during 1990, by providing $300 million in aid and lifting the trade embargo imposed in 1985 against the Sandinista government. Despite this assistance, 1990 was a very difficult year for Nicaragua, as the painful effects of budget-cutting and anti-inflationary policies further reduced the living standards of a population already reeling from a decade of civil war and serious economic deprivation. The economic program announced by the Chamorro government was sound, but in the wake of Sandinista opposition and violent strikes, some of its important elements, such as reducing the state-owned sector, were gutted. (The Sandinistas took their confrontational stand even though they themselves had begun to implement austerity measures and rational economic policies when they were still in power.) Popular support for the government will begin to erode if tangible results are not seen during 1991. To help get Chamorro's reforms back on track, the United States should offer further economic aid to Nicaragua. War damages and lost productivity during the past decade amounted to several billion dollars, according to neutral observers. It is manifestly in the United States' interest that the Chamorro government succeed. If Washington does not do all that it can toward that end, the credibility of its commitment to furthering democracy, professed throughout the 1980s as the rationale for opposing the Sandinistas and funding the contras, will appear hollow indeed.

By late 1990, the Chamorro government appeared headed for a serious political crisis. It had alienated its rural and conservative backers to such an extent—because Chamorro had made so many concessions to the Sandinistas—that peasants, mayors, and ex-contras began to take over land and towns in protest. Washington must help Chamorro realize that she runs the risk of insurrection in the countryside if she does not address the demands of those who voted for her. If such a crisis does arise, Chamorro may not be able to rely on the Sandinista army and police to bolster her government. The only remedy is for Chamorro to assert herself and limit the power of the Sandinistas and the army. Army chief of staff Gen. Humberto Ortega has been steadily gathering power behind the scenes even as the army's size has been reduced. His formidable institutional power base is being augmented, not cut back. Over objections of her coalition's legislators, Chamorro proposed military spending of $78.6 million out of a total budget of $499 million, and has permitted Ortega to retain control of numerous companies that provide the army with additional income. Moreover, she had not moved to abrogate a Sandinista decree of early 1990 that transferred significant powers from the defense minister (now Chamorro) to the chief of staff. Although Chamorro's goal is to reconcile the Sandinistas and non-Sandinistas, she must realize that by making too many concessions to the former she has instead sowed the seeds for renewed civil war.

Two of the most difficult parts of the government's program to enact are the privatization of unproductive state companies and land, and the reduction of bloated government employment rolls. Assuming that the Chamorro government remains committed to these measures, the United States should help it withstand Sandinista efforts to stall the implementation of such reforms (and, as a result, of economic recovery). One way of doing this might be to earmark U.S. funds for purposes specifically outlined in the Chamorro program. Naturally, such steps must be carefully coordinated with the Nicaraguan government so as to provide no grounds for accusing the United States of forcing policies upon the Chamorro government.

Chamorro's predicament is further complicated by her decreasing support among Nicaraguan conservatives. Given the Sandinistas' strength in the unions and the military, Chamorro recognized the need to seek compromises with these sectors. Yet, by giving in to Sandinista pressures, she not only jeopardized her economic reforms but also alienated many of those who voted for her, and for change. As a result, her government has become increasingly isolated.

To shore up its support base, the government will have to draw the line in negotiating with the Sandinistas and respond to its own constituents' demands. Vice President Virgilio Godoy can no longer be shunned, and Chamorro must consult regularly with the coalition of parties that backed her candidacy. The executive branch now operates as a tight little circle without input from these parties. One step that would have gone far in repairing the growing split in the coalition is the annulment or repeal of many of the decrees passed during the Sandinistas' final days in power, decrees that permit the Sandinistas to siphon off government funds and that granted sweeping power to the military chief of staff. Chamorro should also support a vigorous investigation of the most serious charges against the Sandinistas for abuses of human rights and corruption while in office.

In addition, the Chamorro government should move quickly to fulfill its promises of providing land and financial aid to the demobilized contra forces. As of October 1990, it had not done so, with the result that many former rebels have attempted to take over Sandinista cooperatives. The Chamorro government, composed largely of middle- and upper-class Nicaraguans, is as remote from the peasantry from which the contras were drawn as the Sandinistas were. If it is to succeed, the government must reach out to the rural population.

At the June 1990 regional summit in Guatemala, President Chamorro announced that the army would be reduced from 96,000 regulars and reserves to 41,000 by the end of the year.

She later announced further reductions that would bring the number down to 28,000. These cuts should ease the pressure on the national budget, although Chamorro has pledged jobs and retraining assistance to demobilized soldiers. Even with the reductions, however, the army remains a Sandinista stronghold, as does the police force. It was therefore essential that the last-minute Sandinista Decree 490 and Law 75 be repealed or annulled in order to restore control of the army to the civilian defense minister, which she finally did partially in February 1991. The civilian government should assume an active, day-to-day role in decisions regarding military retirement, deployment, and spending. If Chamorro does not assert her authority over the security forces, she will not be able to count on them in a crisis. National reconciliation is crucial if Nicaragua is to heal its wounds after years of civil war, but this cannot occur without a simultaneous assertion of the authority of the elected government and of the rule of law. Addressing this problem of civilian control of the military is as crucial as economic recovery. So far, Chamorro has not made much progress toward either end. By opting for a tacit alliance with the Sandinistas, she may have jeopardized her prospects for success.

El Salvador

The events of the past decade have provided the outside world with concrete evidence that political reform is making headway in El Salvador, albeit at an excruciatingly slow pace. But the current peace negotiations provide an opportunity for the United States to exert pressure on both the Salvadoran government and the guerrillas to bring their terrible civil war to an end. Although small amounts ($5 million) of U.S. aid have been sequestered in previous years, Congress's sequestration of $85 million (50 percent) of U.S. military aid to El Salvador for FY 1991 in October 1990 was unprecedented. A cut of this magnitude was nonetheless necessary to send a clear message to El Salvador's recalcitrant right-wing hard-liners. The United States had never before exercised the leverage that its generous aid to El Salvador ($215 million in FY 1990, $4 billion since 1980) gave it. But with the end of the Cold War and the electoral defeat of the Sandinistas, the geopolitical rationale for indefinitely shoring up the Salvadoran government has nearly disappeared. Congress has sent a clear message to San Salvador that it is time to negotiate in earnest. Unfortunately, the guerrillas' execution of two U.S. military personnel, purchase of advanced anti-aircraft missiles from the Sandinista army, and renewed offensive in early 1991 led President Bush to authorize release of the sequestered aid.

There are *two* intransigent parties in El Salvador both of whom must be pressured into making certain concessions. In addition to making U.S. aid conditional, Washington should increase its efforts to persuade the Soviet Union and, if possible, Cuba, to renounce all support for the FMLN's armed struggle. The Bush administration should more actively support the peace proposal that is being developed by the UN mediator in the Salvadoran talks. This draft proposal contains the essential elements for a negotiated settlement: demobilization of the FMLN, in return for the reduction of the armed forces to their 1979 levels; the establishment of civilian control over the police; and the purge of those officers who have been credibly charged with the violation of human rights by an impartial commission. The implementation of all parts of this plan should be simultaneous. Both the Salvadoran government and the FMLN would find it hard to reject such a proposal without sacrificing their credibility.

The UN proposal constitutes a major breakthrough in negotiations, making peace a far more realistic possibility than is generally recognized. But to make peace in El Salvador a reality, President Cristiani will have to be uncharacteristically bold and take a stand in favor of this proposal as the only possible solution. Many believe that he is too beholden to hard-line members of his party, and that, were he to endorse such a settlement, he would be overthrown in a coup. His government has in fact proved to be far more moderate than outside observers originally expected, and he may yet demonstrate that he is a leader daring enough to face down those to his right—if he can be sure of staunch international support. Such support should be forthcoming from the United States. Washington should make it clear that if Cristiani supports the UN proposal, and the FMLN refuses to accept a reasonable offer, this would result in continued U.S. aid. But at the end of the day it will be up to El Salvador's elected leader to take the necessary risks to end a war that cripples all his other efforts.

Honduras

The major threat to Honduran democracy is its large and reputedly corrupt military. Since Honduras faces no significant internal or external threat to its security, the United States should lobby strongly for a dismantling of the Honduran military establishment. U.S. military assistance should be decreased and the large U.S. military presence there removed. The funds thus saved should be devoted to economic development programs geared to alleviating the country's extreme poverty. A formal assurance from the United States to assist Honduras militarily in case of attack by Nicaragua or El Salvador is sufficient defense against what is now a greatly reduced threat. Honduras will naturally balk at major reductions in its own armed forces until El Salvador can also commit itself to cuts as part of a Salvadoran peace accord, but the United States should strongly encourage Honduras to begin some force reductions now. The Honduran military is also in need of a thorough housecleaning to remove officers with links to drug-trafficking. According to the State Department's International Narcotics Matters Bureau, as of September 1990 Honduras was still dragging its feet in fulfilling its commitments to fighting the narcotics trade. Drug-sniffing dogs supplied by the United States, for example, were not even being used. Washington should link the provision of economic aid to improved Honduran cooperation in this area.

Despite the general revolutionary turmoil in the region over the past decade, Honduras—the third-poorest country in the Western Hemisphere after Nicaragua and Haiti—has, surprisingly, avoided becoming infected with the Marxist-Leninist virus. There is no significant indigenous political movement demanding radical change there, and the development of an armed insurgency appears unlikely. Civilians and officers holding political, economic, or military power have traditionally brokered their disputes peacefully. The military, governed by a council of senior officers, deposed its overweening chief in 1984; and in 1985, President Roberto Suazo Córdova, although reluctant to leave office, was persuaded by the military—and the United States—to give way to his democratically elected successor, José Azcona. Azcona, widely considered an ineffectual president, in turn passed the presidency to the more dynamic Rafael Leonardo Callejas in January 1990. Given the Honduran military's tendency to overreach its power, the retirement in late 1989 of the military chief, Héctor Antonio Regalado, was significant but not a solution to that institution's dominance. His bid to remain in power beyond his scheduled tenure was rejected by the Supreme Military Council, under pressure from the U.S. embassy in Tegucigalpa.

Yet the apparent calm in Honduras may be disrupted if several festering problems are not soon resolved. Honduran economic resources were severely strained by the presence of over eighty thousand Nicaraguan refugees, many of whom have not yet been repatriated. If Nicaragua's civil strife was to resume, Nicaraguans could come flooding back, with serious economic and social consequences for Honduras. Honduras also has a budding insurgency problem, primarily from the Chinchoneros. Indigenous conditions provide the breeding ground for what so far have been only tiny revolutionary cells. In 1989, a new group surfaced to claim responsibility for an explosion that wounded U.S. soldiers in the northern city of San Pedro Sula. About a thousand U.S. soldiers are stationed at the Palmerola airbase outside Tegucigalpa; thousands more have been assigned to temporary duty in Honduras over the last decade. Apart from participating in U.S. military exercises, they have constructed or upgraded roads, airbases, and other military facilities, and provided medical and dental services to Honduran citizens. But a U.S. presence of this size is overwhelming in such a small country and provides a visible target for subversive groups. The traditionally pacific Hondurans are a long way from turning to armed struggle in significant numbers, but they are growing frustrated with a government that not only appears to be paralyzed by mounting political and economic problems, but also dominated by a foreign power.

The most immediate challenge facing Honduras is its depressed and underdeveloped economy. The International Monetary Fund refused aid to the Azcona government, which had resisted the IMF's prescription for austerity measures and a devaluation of the currency. President Callejas has instituted austerity measures, devalued the currency, and initiated market reforms. Without a concerted effort to improve the lot of the impoverished majority of the population, however, the disaffected poor may gradually swell the ranks of various embryonic guerrilla groups. When Callejas announced his intention to implement an austerity program, the United States released $20 million of a $70-million economic aid package that had been approved but not disbursed while Azcona was in office. Yet, at the same time, the Bush administration asked Congress for only $60 million in economic aid to Honduras for FY 1990 ($10 million less than FY 1989) and military aid in the amount of $20.2 million (down from $40 million).

In the final analysis, however, the Honduran military's behavior will be the single most important determinant of the country's prospects for economic and political stability. Reports have circulated since 1987 that the CIA trained a Honduran military unit that was responsible for the abduction and torture of a number of citizens. Such practices, were they to become habitual, could lead to the birth of a truly radical opposition and the onset of guerrilla warfare. More ominous still are reports of the deep involvement of Honduran intelligence and navy officers in extensive drug-trafficking. The former chief of the armed forces, General Regalado, has been accused of participating in this and other illegal activities. In 1988, his half-brother was arrested in the Miami airport for smuggling cocaine. General José Bueso Rosa was accused of involvement in a 1984 drug-trafficking and assassination plot, and was tried and convicted for the latter. Washington turned a blind eye to such activities when it depended upon Honduran support for its contra policy; but it can no longer afford to do so, lest Honduras be taken over by a Panamanian-style narco-military alliance.

Guatemala

Compared to the other countries of the region, Guatemala has received limited attention from Washington. The problems of drug-trafficking and human rights abuses, however, have now reached such levels there as to dictate a new course of action. In September 1990, the State Department's International Narcotic Matters Bureau reported a dramatic increase in the amount of South American cocaine that was being routed through Guatemala (four tons monthly), and an astronomical surge in opium cultivation there (now thirteen tons annually). To this point, the United States has relied on the cooperation of Guatemalan military intelligence to fight trafficking. But because these are the very people suspected of involvement in human rights abuses, the United States should increase its own drug-fighting personnel there (there are now only three Drug Enforcement Administration, agents posted to Guatemala) and develop its own intelligence sources. In addition, Washington should bring evidence of drug-trafficking by public officials to the attention of the Guatemalan government and insist that the government take action. DEA sources in Guatemala say that it is the civilian population and civilian—rather than military—officials who have been most corrupted by the drug trade, but credible reports exist of military officers taking bribes to allow traffickers to cross Guatemala's borders. The United States must do everything possible to avoid a repetition of the Noriega affair. If it cannot convince the countries in the region to clean up their acts, it would be better to sever ties than to lend aid to those who profit from the drug trade. The only way to combat the immensely corrupting power of the international drug cartels is to set strict standards and abide by them.

The election of Marco Vinicio Cerezo Arévalo to the presidency in 1986 marked a successful transition to elected civilian rule after sixteen years of military dictatorship. Guatemala nonetheless remained extremely troubled. Factions within the military attempted two coups during Cerezo's tenure, and political violence increased steadily after 1987. After a rocky start, Cerezo was supported by the military hierarchy, particularly

Defense Minister Héctor Alejandro Gramajo Morales. In Guatemala, as in El Salvador, the armed forces chose to support constitutional government—and the Christian Democrat Cerezo—over upper-class interests in a bid to end their international isolation. It was because of Gramajo's support for the Cerezo government that the coup attempt of May 1988 failed. Unfortunately, the government chose not to bring the perpetrators to justice, relying on Gramajo to handle the problem. His brusque treatment of soldiers and denial of appointments or promotions to some of those who had tried to overthrow the government only served to fuel the fires of discontent, however. During a second attempted coup in May 1989, Gramajo's own house was surrounded by the tanks of the rebel soldiers. This time, right-wing civilians also participated, underlining the fact that the strength of the Right in Guatemala extends far beyond the military, much as it does in El Salvador. The government was not prepared to be lenient with the perpetrators the second time around, however, and Col. César Quinteros, the leader of the rebels, and five other officers were put on trial. Despite their lawyers' argument that the military code under which they were being prosecuted was unconstitutional, they were convicted.[3] (Their conviction was overturned on appeal in June 1990.)

In the weeks leading up to the 1989 coup attempt, President Cerezo was strongly criticized by many Guatemalans for creating an economic crisis, as well as for his extramarital affairs. (The Guatemalan press is largely conservative, and one of the major dailies is owned by Jorge Carpio Nicolle, a key rival politician.) Cerezo had antagonized the business class by pushing for tax reform and austerity measures, while disappointing many of his fellow Christian Democrats and others who had hoped he would attack the privileges of the wealthy more vigorously and push for land reform and other structural changes. The stagnant economy was further depressed in 1987 by a sharp fall in the price of coffee, the country's main export, although a modest economic upturn was registered in 1988–1989. A teachers' strike that he first tried to ignore grew and spawned protest marches that dragged on for months in 1989. Realistically, there was very little chance that the first civilian president could have engineered fundamental reforms after so many years of military rule, but he could have done more to begin the process. His primary task was simply to survive and pass on the presidential sash to a duly elected successor in 1991. During the campaign, Cerezo antagonized many people by blatantly pushing former Foreign Minister Alfonso Cabrera Hidalgo for their party's nomination over more popular candidates. He also placed government resources at Cabrera's disposal, compounding the charges of corruption that were already aimed at his administration. In May 1990, retired General Efraín Ríos Montt declared his candidacy for the presidency.

This bid put Guatemala's constitution to a severe test in the months preceding the November 1990 presidential elections. Ríos Montt, who ruled the country from 1982 to 1983 after ousting Gen. Angel Aníbal Guevara, challenged the constitutional ban on former coup leaders running for president, as well as the ban on leaders of religious sects becoming candidates. Although his candidacy was eventually barred by the courts, the general edged out the leading contender, conservative Carpio, in the public opinion polls. His popularity was due in large measure to his reputation for personal honesty and his tough law-and-order stand, as well as the widespread public disenchantment with the government's inability to control the country's spiraling violence. The harsh counterinsurgency policy he had instituted during his rule created fears among human rights activists that his return to power would only exacerbate Guatemala's problems. But the popular response to his comeback campaign in 1990 suggested that many Guatemalans remained in favor of military solutions to the country's problems. Yet his campaign was illegal. After he was declared ineligible, another evangelical, Jorge Serrano Elías, who had served in Ríos Montt's government, was the dark horse victor.

Guerrilla warfare was not much of a problem during Cerezo's term. The number of insurgents in Guatemala probably does not exceed 1,500. From the mid-1960s to the early 1980s, the Guatemalan military conducted a brutal counterinsurgency war against three guerrilla groups drawn from Indian, rural, and student bases. An estimated one hundred thousand people died in the violence. As a participant in the 1987 Central American peace accords, the Cerezo government formed a national reconciliation commission that held brief talks with the guerrillas in 1987–1988. The military objected to these contacts, however, and it was this, among other things, that prompted the 1988 coup attempt. Subsequently, government officials downplayed the importance of the rebel threat, but after Cerezo's country retreat was attacked in early 1990, the government agreed to reinstitute the dialogue with the guerrillas. The commission reached a preliminary agreement with the rebels in April 1990, but continuing violence on both sides frustrated efforts to end the insurgency.

The army maintains its de facto rule in the countryside, where the population is largely of pure Indian extraction. More than any other Central American country, Guatemala remains starkly divided between Spanish-descended Ladinos and Indians, who are themselves divided into distinct cultural groups. (There are twenty different Indian languages.) After the guerrillas began organizing the Indians in the 1970s, the Ladino army responded with fierce repressive measures against these "backward" peoples, rounding them up and forcing them to live in villages where they were taught Spanish and "reeducated." The military claims these *polos de desarrollo*, as the villages were called, no longer exist but have been replaced by "reconstructed villages" run by the civilian government.[4] The government says the Indians are free to leave the villages if they wish, but outsiders' access to many of these settlements is still strictly controlled by the military.

Over the past decade, Guatemala's human rights problems have not received as much attention as El Salvador's because the U.S. government was not heavily involved in bankrolling the country's military. In 1977, the Guatemalan military government announced that it would no longer accept U.S. aid, preempting an almost certain cutoff by the Carter administration due to reports of massive human rights abuses. In 1979, Amnesty International estimated that between fifty and sixty thousand people had been killed in political violence in Guatemala during the 1970s. After the cutoff in U.S. military aid, Israel replaced the United States as the country's military supplier and the violence reescalated. The Reagan administration renewed military sales to the government of General Ríos Montt in 1983, citing a decline in government-perpetrated human rights abuses, but Congress suspended the sales the following year.[5] After Ríos Montt was ousted, the incidence of abuses shot up again.[6]

Once Cerezo took office, the Reagan administration began sending a small amount of nonlethal military aid to Guatemala, and in June 1989, the House of Representatives approved the Bush administration's request to sell M-16 rifles and ammunition to Guatemala in FY 1990. But budgetary considerations forced a reduction in U.S. military aid to Guatemala from $9 million in FY 1989 to $2.9 million in FY 1990. Economic aid was also cut from $80 million to $56.5 million.

Human rights abuses did not end with the advent of civilian government. According to Amnesty International, between Cerezo's 1986 accession to the presidency and January 1989, there were two hundred cases of unresolved disappearances "in which the available evidence suggests official complicity."[7] Cerezo acknowledged that some 1,700 people disappeared in 1988 but claimed that most cases had been resolved and that, in any event, over half were of a nonpolitical nature. Yet there is little doubt that terrorist tactics were employed by some persons in positions of power. In 1988, a judge investigating police complicity in the so-called death van murders was himself kidnapped and the investigation was subsequently dropped. In the previous year, a journalist who had started a weekly newspaper critical of the government was briefly abducted, his home was burglarized, and the paper's offices were bombed; he ceased publication and later left the country. The Right has also threatened reformists such as Father Andres Girón, who leads peasant takeovers of fallow or underutilized land; the Cerezo government was sufficiently concerned for the safety of the controversial priest to provide him with bodyguards.

According to Americas Watch, political violence ratcheted up another notch between August 1989 and January 1990, beginning with the abduction and murder of several university students and teachers. Repression of unionists and human rights monitors has increased, and Salvadoran leftists who fled the violence in their own country have also been targeted in Guatemala, including the prominent political leader Héctor Oquelí Colindres. There is no evidence that Cerezo was directly involved in such abuses, but he failed to investigate and prosecute members of the government security forces alleged to have been involved in these crimes. When, in mid-1990, U.S. Ambassador Thomas Stroock publicly denounced the Guatemalan government's failure to curb the violence, Cerezo questioned whether these comments were authorized by Washington. The State Department recalled the ambassador to show its displeasure with Cerezo and U.S. officials hinted that all aid would be terminated if Guatemala's record did not improve.

The June 1990 torture and murder of Michael DeVine, a U.S. citizen living in Guatemala, prompted the U.S. government to act, with Stroock leading the charge. Five soldiers were detained, but not charged, for DeVine's murder, and no higher officials were arrested. In December 1990, the Bush administration cut off its $2.9-million military assistance program for FY 1991—a clear message to the incoming government that it had to act forcefully against human rights abuses by the military.

In Guatemala, as in El Salvador, stability and democratization depend upon the acceptance of civilian authority and democratic norms by the military. External pressures can help spur the process, but in the final analysis it is the Guatemalan mentality that must change. At this stage, the military and the large civilian right-wing sector are far behind their Salvadoran counterparts in accepting the need for change. In part, this is because they believe they have won their war against the guerrillas, and that this vindicates their methods. The violence of the "Guatemalan solution" touched all sectors of society, but even so, many defend the brutally repressive measures of the military as warranted and efficacious. And because the extreme Right is too fragmented to win power through elections, its members will continue to conspire with like-minded military officers against those who seek to reform their society.

Costa Rica

The opposition of former President Oscar Arias to the Reagan administration's contra policy created frictions in U.S.–Costa Rican relations during the 1980s. Relations with the new president, Rafael Angel Calderón, have been much closer. U.S. support for a sweeping reduction of Costa Rican debt to private foreign creditors has boosted the country's prospects for renewed economic growth. But to assist Costa Rica further, the debt owed to the U.S. government should be entirely written off, especially since Calderón is pursuing IMF-approved policies.

In 1989, Costa Rica celebrated the one-hundredth anniversary of its establishment as a constitutional democracy—an impressive milestone for any country, and all the more so in this case, given the turmoil in the region. Costa Rica's political good fortune can be attributed in part to the abolition of the national army by the 1949 constitution, as well as to a relatively equitable distribution of land and wealth. Costa Rica faced some difficult years in the 1980s, although its problems pale by comparison with those of its neighbors. The fairly developed agro-economy was affected by declining prices for its primary commodity exports of coffee, beef, bananas, and sugar. President Arias imposed austerity measures that, while reviving the economy by 1988, made him unpopular at home. Although Costa Ricans took pride in the international acclaim for Arias's leading role in the Central American peace process, they were not happy with what they considered to be his disregard of domestic problems.

In October 1989, the Arias government concluded a major debt reduction agreement with Costa Rica's foreign commercial creditors. The Brady Plan, an initiative of the U.S. secretary of the treasury, which called on lenders to reduce the debt of those countries that adopted belt-tightening measures and market-oriented reforms, prodded banks to be more forthcoming in negotiations. The agreement permits Costa Rica to buy back over $1 billion of its $1.8 billion in commercial debt at an 80 percent discount. Although the country's total foreign debt is $4.5 billion, the projected annual savings of $100 million in debt service will greatly help its balance-of-payments problems.

Funding for the buyback and for payment of back interest was pledged by the United States, international institutions, and Japan, which has shown increasing willingness to aid Latin American countries, expanding on its previous, primarily commercial, transactions with the region. Budget pressures resulted in a reduction of U.S. aid to Costa Rica for FY 1990 to $63.5 million, down from $90 million in 1989.

The debt deal pushed Arias's approval rating to 80 percent, but it did not rescue the political fortunes of his National Liberation party, which was founded by the late José Figueres Ferrer. The constitution barred Arias from seeking a second four-year term, and the PLN's candidate, Carlos Manuel Castillo Morales, was narrowly defeated on February 4, 1990, by the Social Christian Unity candidate Calderón, whom Arias had bested in the 1986 elections.

During the 1980s, most Costa Ricans were fearful of the spillover effects of the successful Sandinista revolution, but they were also concerned that the United States' contra policy would only bring them additional troubles. Their primary interest in the Arias regional peace plan was the hope that it would stem the influx of Nicaraguans into their country. The presence of over a hundred thousand Nicaraguans placed great strains on Costa Rica's economy, and the contras' presence threatened to bring down on the nearly defenseless country the military power of the Sandinistas. Arias forced the contras living in Costa Rica to renounce their armed struggle or leave, and sought to maneuver the Sandinistas into adopting his definition of democracy. His view was that security agreements merely limiting troop levels, arms, and subversive activities were insufficient, that only democratization could bring stability to the region. In this, Arias agreed with the Reagan administration's goals, although he steadfastly opposed its policies.

President Calderón is ideologically more conservative than Arias, whose party is affiliated with the Socialist International. His election extended a trend that began with the election of Cristiani in El Salvador and Callejas in Honduras—both conservatives. With Chamorro's win in Nicaragua, it also increases the chances for the emergence in the years ahead of a regional consensus on how best to promote further democratization, what security measures (including the reduction of the region's standing armies) to adopt, and how to coordinate market-oriented economic policies. At the June 1990 regional summit, the five presidents pledged to pursue regional economic integration and market liberalization.

Panama

The United States was extremely fortunate that its military invasion of Panama was concluded as rapidly as it was, with Noriega's surrender, and with casualties in the hundreds instead of thousands. The majority of Panamanians had come to believe that only U.S. military intervention could remove the dictator they reviled, a view that dampened legitimate international criticism of the invasion. But the long-term costs of the intervention, as well as the damage Noriega wrought with U.S. backing, will take far longer to repair. Whatever help (the record is still open to debate) Noriega provided in promoting U.S. interests in Central America, it did not warrant Washington's egregious oversight of the danger he posed—to Panamanian *and* U.S. interests.

Having engaged militarily to bring about Noriega's demise, it is now incumbent upon the United States to work actively to remedy the conditions in Panama that fostered his antidemocratic rule. There is a distressing consensus apparent in Washington that says that U.S. responsibility for Panama's future ended with Noriega's ouster. This shortsightedness ignores a history of weak civilian rule, evidence of continuing corruption and drug-trafficking, as well as sources of discontent that could bring back to power another Torrijos if we are lucky, or another Noriega if we are not. Leaving Panama to pull itself up by its bootstraps is an unwise policy during this crucial phase of economic recovery and institution-building.

Although few Latin Americans publicly supported the U.S. invasion of Panama in December 1989, the damage to regional relations was surprisingly small. Yet there was considerable unease generated by the fact that the United States' intervention had been galvanized by his involvement in drug-trafficking. Those governments with a hefty drug trade within their borders now had reason to worry that the United States might take military action in their territory without their consent. Immediately after the invasion of Panama, the United States blundered by sending an aircraft carrier to Colombia's coast to track drug shipments leaving the country. The Colombians protested, which is not surprising, given their special ties to Panama—once part of Colombia until it seceded, with the aid and encouragement of the United States, in 1903. Indeed, the most serious cost of the U.S. intervention is likely to be to Washington's antidrug war. The plan to step up the U.S. military's role in fighting drug-trafficking will meet with unyielding resistance from Latin governments. It would have run up against their long-held anti-interventionist stand in any event, but the massive display of U.S. force in Panama will bolster such resistance even further for years to come.

The cost to Panama, aside from the considerable physical damage done, was more subtle. Panama is a weak state without a strong national identity. While polls showed that 90 percent of Panamanians supported the U.S. action, the invasion may have also promoted the growth of latent—and virulently anti–U.S.— nationalism. The new Endara government may have encouraged this trend, first by urging U.S. troops to round up thousands of Noriega supporters and then by trashing the image of Omar Torrijos, the populist dictator whose regime fostered Noriega's rise. Torrijos was perhaps Panama's only true nationalist symbol, yet the Endara government focused only on the fact that he was not a democratically elected leader instead of trying to embrace the popular aspects of his legacy. Just days after the invasion, the Endara government tore down the Torrijos bust at the international airport and proceeded to shut down other Torrijos institutions. Furthermore, even though the Endara government was legitimately elected (in March 1989), its image was damaged by the fact that the United States helped to install it in office.

Most Panamanians were, however, willing to give the new government a chance to prove its bona fides. Building up a nonmilitaristic feeling of national pride in Panama will be made easier to the extent that the Endara government proves effective and able to implement a recovery plan that distributes the benefits of economic progress to Panama's poor. Panamanians overwhelmingly supported Endara as an alternative to Noriega. But if they do not see the new government as working to solve their basic problems, many are likely to grow disenchanted with democracy, since this is the first democratically elected government in twenty-two years. Indeed, a poll taken in November 1990 showed that Endara's approval rating had dropped from 80 percent in early 1990 to under 40 percent. The civilian opposition leadership is in disarray, and it is quite possible that a military *caudillo* could rise up again to reclaim the populist legacy of Torrijos.

With nearly half of the population living in poverty, the Endara government faces a serious test in promoting economic development. But it has a far better chance of passing that test than its other Central American neighbors. Panama's economic base is far more developed, and therefore better able to support redistributive policies and offer opportunities that are wholly compatible with a free market economy. Beyond fulfilling its 1990–1991 commitment of $420 million in aid, the United States should provide additional help for health, education, and housing programs.

There is the danger that the Endara government, which is composed of members of the upper and middle classes, will not perceive the vital nature of this challenge from below. In January 1990, Endara proclaimed that building new housing for the poor left homeless by the invasion would be his top priority. Yet six months later, not one of these people had moved into a new home. Those fortunate enough to be able to prove their refugee status were living in tiny cubicles set up in the hangars of a former U.S. airbase. Panamanians are a patient, flexible people, but they will sooner or later react violently if the government does not address their needs—and against a U.S. presence that they perceive to be exacerbating the situation.

In the event, the departure of Noriega and his top cronies does not ensure an end to military domination and illegal drug activities in Panama. Noriega may have perverted the country's institutions, but he alone was not responsible for the corruption so prevalent within the Panamanian military establishment, as well as in the civilian government. Moreover, Panama's bankers were—and are—understandably reluctant to impose restrictions on the secret banking activities that made the country a global financial center, although they have agreed to report transactions of more than $10,000, as U.S. banks now do. The Panamanian free trade zone, a source of legitimate profits, has been the center of smuggling activities as well. The ease with which dummy companies could be set up and ships registered and the fact that the dollar is the country's legal tender—all facets of Panama's economic success—also facilitated corruption. The United States has pushed, with good reason, for the new government to implement further modifications in Panama's business and banking practices in order to root out corruption. But, during the whole of 1990, the Endara government balked at signing a bilateral mutual legal assistance treaty, which the United States seeks to bolster efforts in prosecuting money-laundering activities and drug-trafficking in its own courts. The treaty would also allow the United States to provide information to Panamanian authorities and help them prosecute violators of their local laws more aggressively. The Panamanians understandably fear that the treaty would drive away legitimate business, so it is imperative that Washington address their concerns and defuse what is threatening to become a major rallying point for anti–U.S. sentiment.

Although combating corruption requires, above all, the emergence of a new mindset on the part of the Panamanian business class, the United States must use the leverage its aid dollars give it. To send a clear signal of its seriousness of purpose, the United States should insist that Panama prosecute those persons implicated—by evidence contained in documents seized by U.S. forces in December 1989—in illegal activities. Failing this, it should pursue indictments against them in the United States.

Another problem that cannot be underestimated, given Panama's long record of weak civilian rule, is the potential for another military coup. The revolving-door aspect of the directorship of the Public Force—which has had four directors in eight months—was a warning sign. Vice President Ricardo Arias

Calderón, the official in charge of constructing this new security force, decided to incorporate in it former members of Noriega's PDF on the theory that they could be converted into honest policemen. But old habits die hard, and the new Panamanian government should instead train an entirely new civilian force as rapidly as possible.

A second warning sign was the rebellion, on December 4–5, 1990, by Panamanian police and former members of Noriega's military force. Although its leader, former Public Force Director (and Torrijos favorite) Eduardo Herrera Hassan, said he was only trying to get the Endara government to address the low salaries and demoralized condition of the force, the rebellion severely shook the fragile Panamanian government, which called upon U.S. troops to put it down. This was necessary since the government could not be certain of the loyalty of its own police; but the sight of U.S. soldiers disarming Panamanian policemen promised to stir anti–U.S. feelings even further, while undermining the public's confidence in Endara.[8]

The continuing problem of militarism in Panama is made more complex by the fact that the military institution created by Torrijos (and inherited by Noriega) was the repository of widespread nationalistic and populist feelings among the Panamanian masses. Today, those same men fill the ranks of the police force. Along with disgruntled former officers, who now sit on the sidelines, these lower-class and dark-skinned Panamanians share the grievances of the poor majority from whose ranks they were drawn. They were taught by Torrijos and Noriega that the military has the responsibility and the right to govern.

The supreme challenge for the upper-class, light-skinned Endara government, therefore, is to quash the military threat to civilian rule and, *at the same time*, address the demands of the Panamanian working class. Over the longer term, this sector of the population may coalesce into a civilian political opposition party, but if the current government does not attempt to become a government for all Panamanians, it runs the very real risk that many discontented citizens will turn toward a new *Torrijista* military alternative.

To guard against such an eventuality, the mandate and power of the Public Force should be strictly limited. While some observers have argued for a police force and border guard on the lines of Costa Rica's security forces, Arias Calderón and others have correctly countered that Panama's defense responsibilities are greater than Costa Rica's. Two well-equipped mobile units with true military capabilities and antiterrorism training are needed to defend the Panama Canal, for example. In addition, so long as neighboring Colombia continues to be the region's drug-trafficking center, a number of police units equipped with fast boats and sophisticated weapons will be necessary as well. Nevertheless, a strict constitutional prohibition against a fullscale standing army would guard against any efforts to duplicate Noriega's expansion of security forces beyond these legitimate needs. In addition, civilian oversight, coupled with a U.S. willingness to blow the whistle on any signs of corruption or empire-building within the Panamanian police, will remain essential.[9]

In the furor caused by the U.S. attempts to get rid of Noriega by brute force, the question of why Washington had promoted his rise to power in the first place was inadequately addressed. In recruiting him as an intelligence asset, the United States obviously chose to overlook his long record of objectionable activities.[10] Washington should have learned from this experience never to overlook the serious misdeeds of its clients abroad, least of all for the sake of intelligence activities of dubious value. Noriega was, in the final analysis, not worth the trouble he caused the United States, not to mention Panama.

Most Panamanians were quite happy to have Noriega taken off their hands. Moreover, U.S. officials have expressed confidence that he will be convicted in the United States, given the number of witnesses who have come forward. But if he is acquitted, he could conceivably launch some new effort to destabilize the Panamanian government. This threat is not likely to succeed, however, and Noriega would most certainly be arrested were he to return to Panama. Even if large numbers of Panamanians grow disaffected with the current government there, they are unlikely to turn to Noriega as their standard-bearer, since he has been thoroughly discredited.

The U.S. government authorized $420 million in aid to the new Panamanian government, with the tacit understanding that it would not supplement that package in 1991. While the 1990 aid was deemed adequate by a number of economists for bringing Panama's economy back to its 1987 level, it should be noted that nearly a third went toward clearing the arrears on Panama's debt to international financial organizations. This was necessary in order to help restart these institutions' lending processes, which will in turn relieve the United States of some of the burden in assisting Panama's economic recovery. Nevertheless, Washington should be prepared to offer additional aid in 1991. Such a commitment would also help resolve an ongoing dispute over whether the United States owes Panama reparations for war damages. Congress authorized such a solution in the aftermath of the U.S. intervention in Grenada, and it should now act quickly in the Panamanian case before this issue drives a wedge between the two governments and becomes yet another rallying point for anti–U.S. spokesmen. The United States should also push the Panama Canal Commission toward reaching an early decision on structural changes that are required to make the canal a competitive means of transport in the next century, and agree to share in the costs of their implementation. Finally, Washington should prod the Endara government to attack the country's fundamental structural problems, including poverty, unemployment, corruption in high places, and drug-trafficking.

Partly due to other more pressing foreign policy concerns, there is a strong tendency developing in Washington toward adopting an attitude of complacency about Panama. U.S. Ambassador Deane Hinton, an experienced diplomat, recently said that his main concern was that Panama would remain dependent upon the United States. "We have to break these mental habits . . . including the U.S. tendency to think it knows best," he said.[11] But simply ending Panama's dependence cannot be our only goal. For when the United States took it upon itself to oust Noriega, it also incurred an obligation to get Panama off to the best start possible on the road to democracy.

EXTERNAL INFLUENCES: THE SOVIET
UNION AND CUBA

Unprecedented opportunities exist today for U.S. policymakers to turn Soviet, and even Cuban, influence in Central America away from antagonistic objectives toward a coordinated search for peace and stability in the region. U.S.–Soviet cooperation greatly aided the resolution of the Nicaraguan conflict, and can now prove to be an equally important factor in bringing the Salvadoran civil war to an end. This constructive cooperation was the result of the Bush administration's willingness to trade the contra policy for an election-based solution in Nicaragua, as well as the Soviet Union's willingness to put pressure on the Sandinistas to accept such a solution. Moscow urged Managua to hold elections and implement market reforms in the faltering Nicaraguan economy, and also restricted arms shipments to the Sandinistas.

President Bush had encouraged the Soviet Union to use the leverage provided by its military aid to Nicaragua—estimated by the CIA at $515 million in 1988 alone. In May 1989, Soviet leader Mikhail Gorbachev sent a letter to Bush, stating that the Soviet Union had halted arms shipments to Nicaragua at the end of 1988. Accepting the administration's linkage of the overall superpower relationship to Central American issues, Gorbachev said: "I agree that productive Soviet–U.S. engagement on regional questions will lead to a growing potential of goodwill in Soviet–U.S. relations."[12]

During a visit to Nicaragua in October 1989, Soviet Foreign Minister Eduard Shevardnadze clarified the terms of this military aid cutoff. The Soviet Union would send only replacement materiel to Nicaragua until the February 1990 elections took place. Although this was not the complete cutoff the United States had sought, the Soviet gesture was nonetheless a clear signal to Nicaragua of the Soviet preference for a diplomatic, rather than a military, solution to the Nicaraguan conflict.[13] In turn, the Bush administration assured the Soviets that the United States would respect the outcome of free and fair elections, even if this meant recognizing a Sandinista victory.

Such U.S.–Soviet cooperation was made possible by a new U.S. desire to negotiate over Central American issues. The Bush administration has indicated a greater willingness than its immediate predecessor to treat the Soviets as an indispensable party to any lasting peace in the region, and to link Soviet behavior there to the overall U.S.–Soviet relationship. "Soviet behavior toward Cuba and Central America," said Secretary of State Baker in November 1989, on the eve of the Malta Summit, "remains the biggest obstacle to a full, across-the-board improvement in relations between the U.S. and the Soviet Union."[14] Reagan officials had repeatedly stated that negotiating an end to Soviet bloc military involvement in Central America would legitimize the Soviet presence there. In mid-1989, former Honduran Foreign Minister Carlos López Contreras characterized this attitude with an apt analogy: "There is a thief in your house; you have three options. To call the police, to confront him yourself, or let him do what he wants. The U.S. has chosen not to deal with him, so he is doing as he likes in the Central American house."[15]

On the Soviet side, shifting national and global policy priorities accounted for the Soviet Union's scaling-back of its involvement in Central America. Political turmoil and economic woes at home and problems on its borders forced the Soviet government to concentrate its attention on what it now perceived to be its vital interests. By declaring its preference for the peaceful resolution of regional conflicts over its support of armed national liberation movements, Moscow opened up the possibility of a cooperative U.S.–Soviet approach to Central American problems. At the same time, the Bush administration contributed to this budding rapprochement by setting out a clear, yet circumscribed, redefinition of U.S. security interests in the region. Unlike Reagan's policymakers, who believed that leftist revolutionaries in Central America automatically posed a direct threat to the security of the United States, the Bush administration and its principal advisers on Latin America see no such direct threat, but rather a threat to the regional states themselves. In his landmark speech given before the Soviet parliament on February 10, 1990, Secretary Baker made this position clear: "We don't see Cuba as a threat to the United States. For that matter we don't see Nicaragua as a major threat. But both are major threats to the democratically elected leaders around them."[16] This statement opened the way for resolving the remaining security problems in Central America through diplomatic avenues.

Unfortunately, efforts to extend this new U.S.–Soviet cooperation beyond Nicaragua have not borne fruit so far. Despite both superpowers' endorsement of the 1987 Central American peace plan—specifically its call for an end to cross-border aid to insurgents—the Sandinistas were found to have sent in November 1989 SA-7 antiaircraft missiles of Soviet design and North Korean manufacture to the Salvadoran rebels. Subsequently, reports of continuing shipments made as recently as October 1990 were confirmed, after Sandinista soldiers were arrested for selling advanced missiles to the Salvadoran guerrillas.[17]

Three steps should be undertaken in an attempt to limit the arms flows that fuel insurgencies in El Salvador and elsewhere in the region. The first would be to revive, with U.S.–Soviet support, the Central American plan—spelled out in 1987—for UN monitoring of international borders. A UN force might not be able to halt arms transfers completely, but it would at least provide a deterrent and a credible, neutral source of public information about such activity.

Second, in its discussions with the Soviets, the Bush administration should impose the same type of linkage on the Salvadoran issue that it did regarding Nicaragua. Of course, since the Kremlin has far less direct leverage on the Salvadoran guerrillas than it did on the Sandinistas, the real pressure point must be Havana, for Cuba continues to be the main benefactor of the region's leftist revolutionaries. It supplies training, advice, and materiel, passing on military hardware it receives from the Soviet Union, as well as ammunition and light arms of its own manufacture. Should it choose to exercise it, the Soviet Union does have substantial leverage there, by dint of its $5-billion annual subsidy to Fidel Castro. The United States should request, for example, that the continuation of Soviet deliveries of oil to Cuba be linked to a Cuban commitment to cease arms transfers.

While Gorbachev did not publicly ask Castro to cease providing this type of aid, as many expected him to do, during his

April 1989 visit to Havana, the Soviet leader did express his own opposition to the "export of revolution." Soviet pressure on the Cuban leader has increased since then. Seeing the handwriting on the wall, Castro subsequently warned his countrymen not to expect Soviet aid to Cuba to continue with the same "clockwork efficiency" as before. And, indeed, Fidel Castro is not immune to cost-benefit calculations as Cuba's economic condition grows ever more precarious. The threat of a halt in Soviet oil deliveries would most likely produce results, even if the Kremlin is unlikely to sever completely its assistance program to Cuba.[18] In a May 30, 1990, interview with the author, the Soviet foreign ministry official in charge of Latin America pointed to storm clouds on the Cuban horizon. The Soviet parliament, said Yuri Pavlov, is going to determine the future of aid to Cuba, and sentiment in that body is increasingly opposed to such aid, given the Soviet Union's own serious economic problems. Thus, Soviet aid and trade commitments for 1991 are slightly lower, but the Soviets may not be able even to fulfill them. In 1990 there was already a 20 percent shortfall in Soviet oil deliveries to Cuba.

On several previous occasions, Castro has demonstrated his willingness to defy the Soviet Union despite his regime's dependence on the Kremlin's assistance programs. Therefore, the United States should not simply count on Soviet pressure to produce all of the desired changes in Cuban policy toward Central America. Consequently, a third component of U.S. strategy should be to offer to open direct multilateral talks with Cuba that would include the Soviets and Central Americans. That Castro's determination to promote revolution abroad is not entirely open-ended was demonstrated in Angola; he opted to pull out Cuba's fifty thousand troops when the U.S.–brokered agreement between South Africa and Angola offered him a way to do so gracefully. Cuba was offered a place at the negotiating table, and Castro could claim that the accord that was reached secured Cuba's primary objectives: South African withdrawal from Angola and Namibia, along with the recognition of the latter's independence. This accord left the Angolan conflict open to eventual resolution by the indigenous parties to the civil war.

The Angolan settlement may serve as a useful model for addressing Cuba's role in Central America, even though its involvement there has been quite different. Cuba has no massive military force stationed in the region, but has perhaps a greater commitment to assisting fellow Latin revolutionaries with training and arms. In October 1989, for example, Cuba's foreign minister, Isidoro Malmierca Peoli, stated that Cuba would not end its aid to the FMLN until the United States cut off its own aid to the Salvadoran government: "We need a collective agreement to stop such aid."[19] At the same time, he and other Cuban officials have also called for a ban on U.S. and Cuban military aid to the entire region. This said, a willingness on the part of the United States to include Cuba in formal negotiations on Central American issues might produce a modification of Castro's position, just as it did in the Angolan case. Washington can, and should, seek to engage Havana in such discussions without having to address—or solve—the larger issue of U.S.–Cuban relations.[20]

Many observers staunchly oppose direct U.S.–Cuban talks because they assume that in light of recent developments in Eastern Europe Castro's own downfall will not be long in coming. Yet despite all the strains in the Cuban economy, at present there are no clear signs that Castro is losing control. Waiting for his fall postpones the clear benefits to the region to be gained from an end to Cuban subversion in Central America.

MULTILATERAL DIPLOMACY AND DEVELOPMENT

The 1980s have been one of the bleakest decades in recent Central American history. But at the decade's end promising changes have occurred, primarily as a result of concerted diplomatic initiatives. There is no single blueprint for resolving all of the region's conflicts, but a variety of useful mechanisms and strategies are available. In the Nicaraguan case, it was the *combination* of multilateral efforts that assured success: Central American diplomatic activity, U.S.–Soviet cooperation, the United Nations, and the Organization of American States all played different but very important roles. Naturally, conflicts of this sort cannot be solved by international goodwill alone. The military pressure exerted by the contra resistance in Nicaragua and the battlefield stalemate in El Salvador contributed heavily in making these two wars "ripe" for resolution. In El Salvador's case, it is to be hoped that both sides have by now come to realize that further bloodshed will not produce a distinct advantage to one side or the other.

During the past few years, the United Nations has been called upon with increasing frequency to help settle regional conflicts—a hopeful sign that its peacemaking and peacekeeping resources will be drawn upon more consistently in the future. For one thing, the UN's election-monitoring capabilities are unmatched in their efficiency and impartiality. The Organization of American States, much maligned for most of its history, also played an important role in the efforts to resolve the Nicaraguan and Panamanian crises. The contras believed that the UN forces favored the Sandinistas. The OAS Commission for International Verification acted as a counterweight in this instance. Having gained the contras' trust, the commission played a key role in their repatriation and demobilization. And even though the OAS failed in its attempt to negotiate Noriega's departure from Panama, by acting on the mandate of its charter to support democracy, it set an important precedent for future multilateral intervention of a positive sort. It could supplant the United States in its traditional role as the policeman of Central America.

Perhaps most important, the Central American presidents have initiated a process of regional consultation that increases their ability to manage their own affairs. Taking into account similar South American initiatives as well, it appears that Latin America as a whole may finally be developing the cohesion and determination necessary for the region to find solutions on its own, without waiting for the United States to solve its problems. All of these diplomatic initiatives suggest that the traditional taboo against *any* measures smacking of "foreign" intervention may be dissipating in favor of a generally accepted definition of democracy and willingness to strike bargains that require each country to abandon a portion of its national autonomy for the greater good of the entire region.

Multilateral approaches will be equally important to Central America's economic future. The development of free trade and regional integration are the only ways by which these small countries will be able to become self-sufficient and, eventually, no longer dependent upon large infusions of foreign aid. Unfortunately, of late the United States has been reducing its outright economic aid, while talking about the promotion of trade, private investment, and economic integration—none of which requires large cash outlays from Washington—as the path toward economic development. Yet this is not the time for the United States to be niggardly with its resources, if it wishes to see Central America on a permanently stable footing.

An extensive literature exists arguing that the only cure for the region's endemic instability is economic development. While this may be true, the 1980s also demonstrated that real development cannot take place *until* civil wars end. Two-thirds of U.S. aid to El Salvador, for example, has been in the form of economic assistance, but the civil war has destroyed the country's infrastructure, spurred capital flight, and prevented people from working. Most of the $4.4 billion the United States provided to El Salvador has gone to balance the country's current accounts budget and toward rebuilding only a fraction of its infrastructure. But in several other Central American countries there is now an opportunity to begin serious efforts at reconstruction and development. What is badly needed is an overall plan for regional development, backed by U.S. funds and technical assistance. The International Commission on Central American Recovery and Development (ICCARD), a latter-day version of the Kissinger Commission, was created by legislation sponsored by Sen. Terry Sanford in 1987. The commission's report, released in 1989, recommended a massive rebuilding effort along the lines of the Marshall Plan. The time to implement it has arrived.

The report rightly emphasizes the fact that just as important as outright aid would be such nongrant measures as preferential trade arrangements. Trade, private investment, and regional integration are crucial to future Central American economic development, and they require assistance in planning and coordination even more than cash outlays. Given the free market orientation of all the region's current governments, reviving the defunct Central American common market of the 1960s is now once again a realistic possibility.

President Bush's Enterprise for the Americas Initiative, announced in June 1990, sets out a sensible vision for all of Latin America to follow: to renew economic growth through free trade and private investment. The two prerequisites for realizing such a vision—the reduction of Latin America's huge debt burden and domestic economic policy reforms—have already begun to be implemented. But to ensure that the region is not left behind in the move toward a hemispheric free market trading bloc, the U.S. government should forgive the accumulated debt of Central American governments and also press other official lenders to do likewise. Washington should, in addition, promptly extend the preferential U.S. trade terms and the investment incentives of the Caribbean Basin Initiative to all Central American countries (as it has already done for Nicaragua). As the Bush administration begins to negotiate its bilateral free trade agreement with Mexico, it should make a special effort to ensure that Central America is not adversely affected by any of its provisions—and, if possible, that it benefits by them. Mexico and Venezuela are leading the way by offering concessional terms for oil to Central America.

The most farsighted development plans, including the one outlined in the ICCARD report, recognize that Central America must diversify its production base if it is to achieve a high, sustained growth rate capable of providing enough jobs for an expanding working-age population. The region's economies are still far too heavily dependent on a few export commodities, and drops in world prices for coffee, bananas, cotton, and sugar always hit them extremely hard.[21] Some efforts at diversification have begun in the agricultural sector, as well as in the processing of primary products and light manufacturing. El Salvador, in particular, with its high population density, needs to promote industrial development.

In recent years, Japan (along with other Asian countries) has displayed increasing interest in the economies of Latin America. Although so far its primary investments have been in Mexico,

Brazil, and Panama, Japan—along with Taiwan—is a growing source of aid and investment for Central America as well. It would indeed make sense for Washington to coordinate its own assistance programs with Tokyo and thereby construct a long-term development strategy that relies on trade, investment, and integration as the primary engines of regional growth. This is not a prescription for "bailing out" Central America but rather for putting the region solidly on the path to development by the turn of the century, under the leadership of the private sector.

Will Washington be able to muster the attention and resources necessary to cement the progress already made in Central America? The dramatic turnabout in the region's political configuration has created greater opportunities for democratic and economic development than have existed in the region for two decades. Yet the hard-won gains recently achieved could be easily reversed as U.S. attention becomes diverted elsewhere. Assistant Secretary of State for Inter-American Affairs Bernard Aronson had it right when he said that "the historic U.S. failure in Latin America has not been interventionism but, rather, neglect."[22]

APPENDIX I: ESQUIPULAS ACCORD

Central American Peace Plan, August 7, 1987

PROCEDURE FOR ESTABLISHING A STABLE AND
LASTING PEACE IN CENTRAL AMERICA

The Governments of the Republics of Costa Rica, El Salvador, Guatemala, Honduras, and Nicaragua, having undertaken to achieve the objectives and develop the principles established in the United Nations Charter, the Charter of the Organization of American States, the Document of Objectives, the Caraballeda Message for Peace, Security, and Democracy in Central America, the Guatemala Declaration, the Punta del Este Communique, the Panama Message, the Esquipulas Declaration, and the draft Contadora Act for Peace and Cooperation in Central America of June 6, 1986, have agreed upon the following procedure for establishing a stable and lasting peace in Central America.

1. National Reconciliation

(a) Dialogue—to carry out urgently, in those cases in which deep divisions have occurred within a society, actions of national reconciliation to allow the people to participate, with full guarantees, in authentic political processes of a democratic nature, on the basis of justice, freedom, and democracy, and, for that purpose, to establish mechanisms for dialogue with opposition groups, in accordance with the law.

To that end, the respective governments shall initiate dialogue with all domestic political opposition groups that have laid down their arms and with those that have accepted the amnesty.

(b) Amnesty—in each Central American country, except in those where the International Evaluation and Follow-up Committee determines that it is not necessary, decrees of amnesty shall be issued, which shall establish all the provisions to guarantee the inviolability of life, freedom in all its forms, property, and the security of the persons to whom such decrees apply. Simultaneously with the issue of the amnesty decrees, the irregular forces in the respective country shall release any persons they may be holding.

(c) National Reconciliation Committee—in order to verify the fulfillment of the commitments undertaken by the five Central American governments upon signing this document with regard to amnesty, cease-fire, democratization, and free elections, a National Reconcilia-

174

tion Committee shall be created. Its function shall be to determine whether the process of national reconciliation is actually under way, and whether there is absolute respect for all the civil and political rights of Central American citizens guaranteed herein.

The National Reconciliation Committee shall be composed of one regular delegate and one alternate from the Executive Branch and one regular member and one alternate suggested by the Episcopal Conference and selected by the government from a slate of three Bishops to be submitted within 15 days of receipt of the formal invitation. This invitation shall be extended by the governments within 5 working days of the signing of this document. The same nomination procedure shall be used to select one regular member and one alternate from the legally registered opposition political parties. The three-person slate shall be submitted in the same time period as mentioned above. Each Central American government shall also select to serve on the committee one outstanding citizen who is not part of the government and does not belong to the government party, as well as one alternate. Copies of the agreements or decrees creating each National Committee shall be transmitted immediately to the other Central American governments.

2. Urging a Cessation of Hostilities

The governments vehemently urge that a cessation of hostilities be arranged in those states in the area currently experiencing the action of irregular or insurgent groups. The governments of such states undertake to carry out all actions necessary to achieve an effective cease-fire within a constitutional framework.

3. Democratization

The governments undertake to provide the impetus for an authentic democratic process, both pluralistic and participatory, which entails the promotion of social justice, respect for human rights, sovereignty, territorial integrity of the states, and the right of all nations to choose, freely and without any outside interference whatsoever, their economic, political, and social system. Furthermore, the governments shall adopt in a verifiable manner measures conducive to the establishment and, where appropriate, improvement of democratic, representative, and pluralistic systems that will guarantee the organization of political parties and effective participation by the people in the decision-making process and ensure that the various currents of opinion have free access to fair and regular elections based on the full observance of citizens' rights. To ensure good faith in the development of this process of democratization, it shall be understood that:

(a) There must be complete freedom for television, radio, and the press, which shall encompass the freedom for all ideological groups to open and maintain in operation communications media, and the freedom to operate such media without prior censorship.

(b) There shall be complete pluralism of political parties. In this respect, political groups shall have broad access to the communications media and full enjoyment of the rights of association and the ability to hold public demonstrations in the unrestricted exercise of the right to publicize their ideas orally, in writing, and on television, as well as freedom of mobility for the members of the political parties in their campaign activities.

(c) Similarly, the Central American governments that are maintaining in effect a state of siege or emergency shall abolish it and bring about the rule of law in which all constitutional guarantees are in effect.

4. Free Elections

Once the conditions inherent in any democracy have been created, free, pluralistic, and fair elections shall be held.

As a joint gesture of the Central American states toward reconciliation and lasting peace for their peoples, elections shall be held for the Central American Parliament, which was proposed in the Esquipulas Declaration of May 25, 1986.

To that end, the Presidents have expressed their wish to move forward with the organization of the Parliament. The Preparatory Committee of the Central American Parliament shall therefore conclude its deliberations and deliver the respective draft treaty to the Central American Presidents within 150 days.

These elections shall be held simultaneously in all the countries of Central America during the first 6 months of 1988 on a date to be agreed upon in due course by the presidents of these states. They shall be subject to monitoring by the appropriate electoral bodies, and the respective governments agree to extend an invitation to the Organization of American States and to the United Nations, as well as to governments of third states, to send observers to attest to the fact that the electoral procedures have been governed by the strictest rules of equal access for all political parties to the communications media, as well as extensive opportunities for holding public demonstrations and engaging in any other type of campaign propaganda.

In order that the elections for membership in the Central American Parliament may be held within the time period indicated in this section, the treaty establishing that body shall be submitted for approval or ratification in the five countries.

As soon as elections for membership in the Central American Parliament have been held, equally free and democratic elections shall be held in each country, with international observers and the same guarantees and within the established intervals and the timetables to be proposed under the present political constitutions, to select the people's representatives in the municipalities, congresses, and legislative assemblies, as well as the Presidents of the Republics.

5. Cessation of Aid to Irregular Forces and Insurgent Movements

The governments of the five Central American states shall request governments in the region or those outside it that are providing, either overtly or covertly, military, logistic, financial or propagandistic aid or assistance in the form of troops, weapons, munitions, and equipment to irregular forces or insurgent movements to cease such aid as an essential requirement for achieving a stable and lasting peace in the region.

The foregoing does not include assistance used for repatriation, or, if that does not occur, relocation, and assistance needed to accomplish the reintegration into normal life of those persons who have belonged to the above-mentioned groups or forces. Similarly, the irregular forces and insurgent groups active in Central America shall be asked to refrain from receiving such aid for the sake of a genuine Latin Americanist spirit. These requests shall be made in fulfillment of the provisions of the Document of Objectives as regards elimination of the traffic in weapons within the region or from outside sources to persons, organizations, or groups attempting to destabilize the Central American governments.

6. Non-use of Territory to Attack Other States

The five countries signing this document reiterate their commitment to prevent the use of their own territory and to neither furnish nor allow logistical military support for persons, organizations, or groups seeking to destabilize the governments of the Central American countries.

7. Negotiations on Security, Verification, Control, and Limitation of Weapons

The governments of the five Central American states, with participation by the Contadora Group in the exercise of its function as mediator, shall proceed with negotiations on the points on which agreement is pending in matters of security, verification, and control under the draft Contadora Act for Peace and Cooperation in Central America.

These negotiations shall also cover measures for the disarmament of those irregular forces that are willing to accept the amnesty decrees.

8. Refugees and Displaced Persons

The Central American governments undertake to address, with a sense of urgency [the problem of] the flow of refugees and displaced persons caused by the regional crisis, by means of protection and assistance, especially with regard to health, education, employment, and security and, furthermore, to facilitate their repatriation, resettlement, or relocation, provided that it is of a voluntary nature and takes the form of individual cases.

They also undertake to arrange for aid from the international community for the Central American refugees and displaced persons, whether such assistance is direct under bilateral or multilateral agreements or obtained through the United Nations High Commissioner for Refugees (UNHCR) or other organizations and agencies.

9. Cooperation, Democracy, and Freedom for Peace and Development

In the climate of freedom guaranteed by democracy, the Central American countries shall adopt such agreements as will permit them to accelerate their development in order to achieve societies that are more egalitarian and free from misery.

The consolidation of democracy entails the creation of an economy of well-being and economic and social democracy. In order to attain those objectives, the governments shall jointly seek special economic assistance from the international community.

10. International Verification and Follow-up

(a) International Verification and Follow-up Committee. An International Verification and Follow-up Committee shall be created, composed of the Secretaries General of the Organization of American States and the United Nations, or their representatives, as well as by the foreign ministers of Central America, the Contadora Group, and the Support Group. The functions of this committee shall be to verify and follow up on the fulfillment of the commitments contained herein.

(b) Support and Facilities for Mechanisms of Reconciliation and of Verification and Follow-up. In order to reinforce the efforts of the International Verification and Follow-up Committee, the governments of the five Central American states shall issue statements of support for its work. All nations interested in promoting the cause of freedom, democracy, and peace in Central America may adhere to these statements.

The five governments shall provide all necessary facilities for the proper conduct of the verification and follow-up functions of the National Reconciliation Committee in each country and of the International Verification and Follow-up Committee.

11. Timetable for Implementing the Commitments

Within 15 days of the signing of this document, the Central American foreign ministers shall meet as an Executive Committee to regulate and promote the agreements contained herein and to make their application feasible. They shall also organize the working committees so that, as from this date, the processes leading to the fulfillment of the commitments entered into within the intervals stipulated may begin through consultations, negotiations, and any other mechanisms deemed necessary.

When 90 days have elapsed from the date of the signature of this document, the commitments with regard to amnesty, cease-fire, democratization, cessation of aid to irregular forces or insurgent movements, and the non-use of territory to attack other states, as defined in this document, shall simultaneously begin to govern publicly.

When 120 days have elapsed from the date of the signature of this document, the International Verification and Follow-up Committee shall analyze the progress made in the fulfillment of the agreements provided for herein.

When 150 days have elapsed, the five Central American Presidents shall meet and receive a report from the International Verification and Follow-up Committee and shall make pertinent decisions.

FINAL PROVISIONS

The points included in this document form a harmonious and indivisible whole. Signing it entails the obligation, accepted in good faith, to comply simultaneously and within the established time limits with the provisions agreed upon.

The Presidents of the five Central American states, with the political will to respond to our people's yearnings for peace, hereby sign this document in Guatemala City on August 7, 1987.

Oscar Arias Sanchez
President, Republic of Costa Rica

Vinicio Cerezo Arevalo
President, Republic of Guatemala

Jose Napoleon Duarte
President, Republic of El Salvador

Jose Azcona Hoyo
President, Republic of Honduras

Daniel Ortega Saavedra
President, Republic of Nicaragua

JOINT DECLARATION AT SAN JOSE (ALAJUELA), COSTA RICA, JANUARY 16, 1988

The Presidents have received the findings of the report of the International Commission for Verification and Follow-up, prepared in accordance with item 11 of Esquipulas II, with the reservations some have indicated.

The Presidents acknowledge the endeavor and the enormous work done by the Commission, which it thanks for its dedication and effort in contributing to the fulfillment of the Esquipulas II agreement.

The Presidents entrust the Executive Commission with the task of examining the general report when it has been received and to make any pertinent recommendations.

The Presidents confirm the historic value and the importance of Esquipulas, the concept and spirit of which they recognize and renew today as vital to the achievement of democratization and peace in the region.

Inasmuch as the commitments of Esquipulas II have not been entirely fulfilled, they [the Presidents] undertake to fulfill unconditional and unilateral obligations for which total and mandatory compliance is required of the governments. Among these obligations are dialogue, talks for the coordination of a cease-fire, general amnesty and, above all, democratization, which shall include the lifting of the state of emergency, total freedom of the press, political pluralism, and termination of the use of special courts. The aforementioned commitments yet to be fulfilled by the governments shall immediately be fulfilled publicly and openly.

Fulfillment of the agreements of the Esquipulas II document involves commitments, observance of which by the governments is subject to essential and specific verification, especially for the suspension of aid to irregular groups, the non-use of territory to support same, and genuine freedom of electoral processes, which shall be verified by the National Reconciliation Commission, with special emphasis on the elections for the Central American Parliament—all of this "as an indispensable element for the achievement of a stable and lasting peace in the region."

The principal functions of the Executive Commission, the members of which are the Ministers of Foreign Relations of the Central American States, shall be verification, control, and follow-up of the commitments contained in the Guatemala Accord and in this declaration. To that end, it shall seek the cooperation of regional or extraregional States or organizations of recognized impartiality and technical capacity that have manifested a desire to assist in the peace process in Central America.

In addition, the fulfillment of Esquipulas II involves the follow-up of those obligations that encompass an already established strategy, such as the regulation of arms levels and security and disarmament agreements.

We should like to express our appreciation to the international community for the political and financial support it has pledged with a view to promoting regional projects directed toward attaining economic and social development in Central America, as an objective directly related to achieving, preserving, and strengthening peace. Because the primary causes of this conflict are economic and social, it is not possible to achieve peace without development.

The Presidents, conscious of their historic responsibility to their peoples, reaffirm their desire for fulfillment in the manner expressed, which they view as irrevocable and inalterable, pledging to fulfill the remaining, unmet obligations unhesitatingly and unequivocally, aware that their peoples and the international community will judge their compliance with obligations undertaken in good faith.

APPENDIX II: COSTA DEL SOL ACCORD

Joint Declaration of the Central American Presidents Adopted in Costa del Sol, El Salvador, February 14, 1989

The Presidents of El Salvador, Guatemala, Honduras, Nicaragua and Costa Rica, met in the Department of La Paz, Republic of El Salvador, on February 13 and 14, 1989. They analyzed the status of the Central American peace process and adopted the necessary decisions to make it effective, with the understanding that the commitments undertaken in Esquipulas II and the Alajuela Declaration are a harmonious and indivisible whole.

The Presidents of Costa Rica, El Salvador, Guatemala and Honduras heard the Constitutional President of Nicaragua, Daniel Ortega Saavedra, express his readiness to carry out a process of democratization and National Reconciliation in his country, within the framework of the Esquipulas II Accords and through the following measures, among others:

First, electoral legislation and laws regulating the expression of thought, information and the area of public opinion shall be reformed so as to guarantee the broadest organization and political activity of the parties. Then an initial four-month period shall begin for the preparation, organization and mobilization of the parties. It shall be immediately followed by a six-month period of political activity, which shall culminate in elections for President, Vice-President, representatives to the National Assembly, for the municipalities, and the Central American Parliament.

The elections shall be held no later than February 25, 1989, unless the government and the opposition political parties mutually agree to hold them on another date.

The Government of Nicaragua shall form the Supreme Electoral Council with the balanced representation of the opposition political parties. To this effect the Presidents call upon the political parties of Nicaragua to participate in the electoral process.

International observers shall be invited to participate, particularly delegates for the Secretaries General of the United Nations and the Organization of American States. They shall be present in all the election districts during the two aforementioned stages in order to verify the rectitude of the process.

By revising and amending the Media Law, the Government of

Nicaragua shall guarantee the free operation of the communications media. It shall guarantee all political parties equal access to broadcast time and scheduling on state-run television and radio stations. The Government of Nicaragua shall authorize all the broadcast media to equip themselves either domestically or from abroad, at their discretion, with all the materials, tools and equipment necessary to fully perform their work.

According to the proposal by the President of Nicaragua and at the initiative of the President of Honduras, the Central American Presidents undertake to draw up within 90 days a joint plan for the demobilization and voluntary repatriation to Nicaragua or relocation to other countries of the members of the Nicaraguan resistance and their families. They shall request technical assistance for this purpose from the specialized agencies of the United Nations.

In order to help create conditions for the demobilization and voluntary relocation or repatriation of Nicaraguans who may have been involved directly or indirectly in armed activities and who are in Honduran territory, the Government of Nicaragua has decided to proceed to release prisoners according to the classification made by the Inter-American Human Rights Commission.

Such plan must also include assistance for the demobilization of all persons who were or are involved in armed activity in the countries of the region, when they voluntarily request it.

In order to comply with the commitments to verify security, the Executive Commission shall be instructed to immediately organize technical meetings aimed at establishing the most appropriate and efficient mechanism for verification, pursuant to the talks held in New York with the Secretary General of the United Nations.

The Presidents reaffirmed the authority of the National Reconciliation Commissions to continue to perform the specific tasks of verification in the areas indicated in the Guatemala Procedure and the Alajuela Declaration. They are to report regularly to the Executive Commission on the results of their work.

The Central American Presidents firmly repeated the request contained in Number 5 of the Esquipulas II Accord: That all governments inside and outside the region who either covertly or overtly aid the irregular forces or insurrectional movements of the area, immediately halt such aid, with the exception of humanitarian aid that may contribute to the objectives of this document.

The Presidents urge all sectors, particularly the insurrectional movements and irregular forces operating in the area, to join the Constitutional political processes in each country. To this end they call upon all sectors in El Salvador to participate in the upcoming elections.

The Presidents reiterated the importance of the Central American Parliament. It is a forum in which the peoples of the area, through their freely and directly elected representatives, shall discuss and make appropriate recommendations for the political, economic, social and cultural problems of Central America.

The Presidents made an urgent appeal to the international community to support the Central American nations' process of socioeconomic recovery, in the short- and medium-term. The seriousness of the foreign debt problem makes the need to resume intra-regional trade levels a fundamental element for strengthening the process of integration.

They made a very special request for support from the European Community to implement the program to restructure, reactivate and strengthen the economic integration process of the Central American isthmus, officially presented in Guatemala this January.

By the same token, they welcomed the report of the International Commission for the Recovery and Development of Central America. It constitutes a significant contribution to the consolidation of democracy and creation of a system of well-being and economic and social justice in the region.

The Presidents remain committed to primarily seek direct, negotiated solutions to overcome the conflicts that have arisen from the Central American crisis.

The Presidents agreed to create a Central American Commission on the Environment and Development. It is to be a regional cooperation mechanism for the optimal, rational use of the area's natural resources, to guard against pollution, and to reinstate an ecological balance. At its next meeting the Executive Commission shall form said Commission and immediately convene it in order to draw up a draft agreement to regulate its character and functions.

The Presidents also expressed their firm support for the International Conference on Central American Refugees (CIREFCA) to be held in Guatemala in May of this year. This meeting shall help find solutions to the flood of refugees and displaced persons created by the regional crisis.

They agreed to promote a regional cooperation agreement for the eradication of illegal drug trafficking. To this end the executive Commission shall draw up a draft agreement that shall be submitted to the governments involved.

They also expressed the will of their governments to support the initiative for the formulation of a Convention on the Rights of the Child in the United Nations.

The Presidents agreed to meet in the Republic of Honduras on a date to be set later.

The Presidents of Guatemala, Honduras, Nicaragua and Costa Rica thank the people and Government of El Salvador, especially their

President, Jose Napoleon Duarte, for their hospitality which facilitated the appropriate environment for holding this meeting.
La Paz Department, El Salvador, February 14, 1989.

Oscar Arias Sanchez
President, Republic of Costa Rica

Jose Napoleon Duarte
President, Republic of El Salvador

Vinicio Cerezo
President, Republic of Guatemala

Jose Azcona Hoyo
President, Republic of Honduras

Daniel Ortega Saavedra
President, Republic of Nicaragua

APPENDIX III: TELA ACCORD

Tela, Honduras, August 7, 1989

The Central American Presidents, meeting in the port city of Tela in the Republic of Honduras on August 5, 6 and 7, 1989,

Taking into consideration and recognizing the important work undertaken by the Executive Commission at its Ninth Meeting and by the Technical Working Group, whose efforts allowed this meeting to take place, and

Considering that, in order to achieve a firm and lasting peace and ensure implementation of the commitments assumed by the Presidents in the Declarations of Accords successively made at Alajuela and Costa del Sol, it is necessary to comply with the steps agreed upon in Esquipulas II,

AGREE:

1. To ratify their conviction to promote all measures aimed towards compliance with numerals 5 and 6 of the Esquipulas Accord in order to prevent the use of one's national territory to destabilize the Governments of the Central American countries. In keeping with the above, they subscribed the document containing the Joint Plan for the Demobilization and Voluntary Repatriation and Relocation in Nicaragua or Third Countries of the Members of the Nicaraguan Resistance and Their Families, and on assistance for the demobilization of all persons involved in armed activities in the countries of the region, when they voluntarily request such assistance.

2. To promote direct and mutually agreed resolutions to those disputes that may arise between various Central American countries. The Presidents of Guatemala, El Salvador and Costa Rica thereby lent their moral support to and endorsed the Agreement between Honduras and Nicaragua regarding the case before the International Court of Justice in The Hague.

3. To ratify the appeal to armed groups in the region that still persist in the use of force, particularly the FMLN, to abandon such actions. Towards this end, they have approved Article III on assistance for the Voluntary Demobilization of the FMLN. In Article III, the FMLN is vehemently called upon to put an immediate and effective end to hostilities, in order to engage in a dialogue which will lead to a

cessation of the armed struggle and to incorporation of the members of the FMLN into the institutional and democratic life of the country.

4. The Presidents recognize the efforts of the Government of Guatemala to strengthen its process of national reconciliation through extensive and permanent dialogue in which the National Reconciliation Commission occupies a leading role. They likewise express their desire that this dialogue will serve to consolidate the democratic, pluralist and participatory process and, in accordance with numeral 1 of the Esquipulas Procedure and domestic legislation, reiterate an appeal to armed groups to abandon those activities which contradict the spirit of this accord and join in institutional political life by taking part in the process of national reconciliation.

5. In light of the fact that Honduras and Nicaragua have arrived at an agreement which includes the withdrawal by Honduras of its reservation regarding the enactment of the said Plan and the reiteration of the Honduran request to send an international peace force to Honduran territory, the Central American Presidents agree to request the United Nations to adopt the necessary measures for establishing the verification mechanism for security matters.

6. To ratify the call made by the Executive Commission at its Ninth Meeting that the Central American Commission on Environment and Development hold its First Meeting in Guatemala City on August 30 and 31, 1989 so that work be undertaken to prepare the draft convention governing its nature and functions.

7. To reiterate the importance of the Central American Parliament as a forum in which the peoples of the area will discuss and formulate recommendations on the political, economic, social and cultural problems of Central America. It is essential that the treaty establishing the Central American Parliament should enter into force as rapidly as possible.

8. To forcefully condemn drug trafficking and abuse. The Central American Presidents commit themselves to promulgate laws and adopt drastic measures to prevent our countries from becoming bases for drug traffickers. To achieve these goals, regional and international cooperation will be sought, agreements will be signed with countries affected by such illicit trafficking, and steps will be taken to permit effective control of drug trafficking.

9. The Central American Presidents agree to entrust the Executive Commission with the task of discussing and approving the document concerning political verification, which will be ratified by the Presidents at their next meeting.

Two years after the signing of the Esquipulas II Peace Plan, the Presidents of Costa Rica, El Salvador, Guatemala, Honduras and Nicaragua reiterate their resolve to comply fully with all the commitments and agreements stipulated in the Guatemala Procedure and the

Alajuela and Costa del Sol Declarations, particularly those pertaining to the strengthening of the processes of national reconciliation and the perfecting of the democratic processes, for which strict compliance with the agreements reached is fundamental.

The Central American Presidents agree to meet again before the end of the year in the Republic of Nicaragua.

The Central American Presidents thank the people and Government of Honduras, and in particular President Jose Azcona Hoyo, for the hospitality extended to them.

Tela, Honduras, August 7, 1989.

Oscar Arias Sanchez
President, Republic of Costa Rica

Alfredo Cristiani Burkard
President, Republic of El Salvador

Vinicio Cerezo Arevalo
President, Republic of Guatemala

Jose Azcona Hoyo
President, Republic of Honduras

Daniel Ortega Saavedra
President, Republic of Nicaragua

Joint Plan for the Demobilization and Voluntary Repatriation or Relocation in Nicaragua and Third Countries of the Members of the Nicaraguan Resistance and their Families, Together with Assistance for the Demobilization of All Those Involved in Armed Activities in the Countries of the Region, When Such Persons Voluntarily Request this Assistance. (August 7, 1989)

The Presidents of Costa Rica, El Salvador, Guatemala, Honduras and Nicaragua,

Honoring their historic pledge to achieve a firm and lasting peace in Central America,

Bearing in mind the Guatemala Procedure signed on August 7, 1987, and the Declarations of Alajuela and Costa del Sol,

Considering Resolution 637 adopted unanimously by the Security Council of the United Nations on July 27, 1989,

Seeking to advance the objectives of the Central American Peace Process and as a steady manifestation of their commitment to the full rule of international law,

Have agreed to this *Joint Plan for the Demobilization and Voluntary Repatriation or Relocation of the Members of the Nicaraguan Resistance and Their Families,* together with assistance for the demobilization of all persons involved in armed activities, when they may voluntarily request such assistance.

CHAPTER I

The Demobilization and Voluntary Repatriation or Relocation in Nicaragua and Third Countries of the Members of the Nicaraguan Resistance and Their Families.

Introduction

This chapter is aimed at implementing the agreement by the Presidents regarding this subject, taking into account inter alia:

1. The report of the Secretary General of the Organization of American States.

2. The National Political Agreement between the Government of Nicaragua and the 21 political parties of the country, where a call is made for the Central American Presidents to reach important political agreements regarding the democratic process so that the Plan for the Demobilization and Voluntary Repatriation and Relocation may be approved.

This chapter defines the mechanisms and methodology for the demobilization and voluntary repatriation or relocation of the members of the Nicaraguan Resistance, together with the material conditions and guarantees that persons covered shall enjoy under this Plan. This Plan will be implemented in collaboration with international organizations. The Plan also applies to the voluntary repatriation or relocation of the families of the members of the Nicaraguan Resistance and to Nicaraguan refugees, without prejudice to existing accords concerning this matter.

The Government of Nicaragua has demonstrated, in accordance with the Esquipulas Procedure and the Declaration of Costa del Sol, its readiness to strengthen the processes of national reconciliation and democratization, and thereby encourage a willingness on the part of the Nicaraguan Resistance to be repatriated. For this purpose we have decided to sign the present Plan that will attempt to make repatriation the general rule, with relocation in third countries the exception.

The five Central American Governments renew their pledge to prevent the use of their territory by persons, organizations or groups to destabilize other states in the region and to cease all types of aid to armed groups, with the exception of humanitarian aid that serves the purposes that the Presidents have outlined in this Plan.

Mechanism

1. For the execution and fulfillment of this plan an International Commission of Support and Verification will be established, to be known as the CIAV, in which the Secretary General of the United

Nations and the Secretary General of the Organization of American States will be invited to join. The Secretaries General may participate through their representatives.

2. Within 30 days of the signing of this Accord, the International Commission of Support and Verification (CIAV) shall be formed. The five Central American Presidents call upon the Nicaraguan Resistance to accept the implementation of this Plan within 90 days from the date of the formation of the CIAV. During these 90 days the Nicaraguan Government and the CIAV will maintain direct contacts with the Nicaraguan Resistance to promote their return to the country and integration into the political process. Upon completion, the CIAV will issue a report on compliance with this Plan to be submitted to the Central American Presidents.

3. The CIAV will be responsible for all activities that make possible the demobilization and voluntary repatriation or relocation, including the reception in final destinations, and the setting up of repatriates. In addition, the CIAV will ensure that necessary conditions for the full incorporation into public life are maintained for the repatriates and will undertake the follow-up and control that these processes require.

4. The CIAV will undertake its activities with the collaboration of the Central American Governments and will seek support from specialized international organizations with experience in the region, and others that it considers necessary and that shall be officially invited by the Governments.

The support of the specialized international organizations shall have among its objectives to facilitate the execution of the Plan. For this purpose, the specialized organizations shall collaborate with the CIAV in monitoring the full exercise of fundamental rights and freedoms of the repatriates, as well as the monitoring of the efforts to promote their economic well-being.

5. Once established, the CIAV will immediately:

(A) Consult and make the necessary agreements to facilitate the implementation of this Plan with the authorities of the Government of Nicaragua, the other Governments of Central America, the Nicaraguan Resistance, and officials of humanitarian organizations, as the case may require.

(B) Visit the camps of the Nicaraguan Resistance and of the refugees for the purpose of:

(i) Making known the scope and benefits of this plan.

(ii) Ascertaining the human and material resources in the camps.

(iii) Organizing the distribution of humanitarian aid.

(C) Assume responsibility, to the extent possible, for the distribution of foodstuffs, medical attention, clothing and other basic necessities in the Resistance camps, through the bodies and organizations that are aiding in this process; and

(D) Make arrangements with third countries to receive and provide the necessary assistance to those persons who do not wish to be repatriated.

6. The CIAV will provide every Nicaraguan adhering to this Plan with a certificate and will implement a voluntary repatriation programme for those wishing to return to Nicaragua. Exit and entry will take place at border posts determined and prepared by joint agreement of the Governments concerned. At those posts, the Government of Nicaragua will, in the presence of CIAV representatives, extend the necessary documentation to guarantee the full exercise of their civil rights.

At the same time, work will be undertaken on the resettlement in third countries of those not opting for repatriation under the present Plan. For that purpose, the Government of Nicaragua will, in cooperation with the CIAV, facilitate the issuing of passports to those who request them.

The five Central American Presidents call upon the international community to provide financial assistance for the present Demobilization Plan.

Procedures

7. Once installed, the CIAV will establish the procedures for reception, under the Plan for the Demobilization and Voluntary Repatriation or Relocation in Nicaragua and Third Countries, of the arms, equipment and munitions of the members of the Nicaraguan Resistance, which will remain in the custody of the CIAV pending a decision by the five Presidents regarding their destination.

8. The CIAV will verify the dismantling of the camps left by the Nicaraguan Resistance and refugees.

9. The repatriated persons will, circumstances permitting, be taken directly by the CIAV to their place of definitive settlement, which, whenever possible, will be their place of origin, or to a site chosen by mutual agreement between the Government of Nicaragua and the CIAV. Temporary residence areas may be established in Nicaragua for these purposes. These areas will remain under the control and supervision of the CIAV while definitive locations are being determined.

Land will be allotted and economic and technical assistance will be provided for repatriates who wish to pursue agro-industries, in conformity with the possibilities of the Government of Nicaragua and the experience of specialized international agencies, and in accordance with the amount of funds obtained for this purpose.

10. In collaboration with the Government of Nicaragua, the CIAV will establish reception centers capable of providing basic services, first

aid, family counselling, economic assistance, transportation to settlement areas, and other social services.

11. As an additional measure to provide the necessary guarantees for repatriates, the CIAV will establish from the outset monitoring offices so that persons may, where necessary, report any non-compliance with the guarantees originally offered for their repatriation. These offices will be maintained as long as the CIAV, in consultation with the Central American Governments, deems necessary.

Staff from these offices will periodically visit repatriates to verify compliance and will prepare reports on the implementation of this Plan. The reports will be sent by the CIAV to the five Central American Presidents.

12. Situations not provided for in this Chapter will be resolved by the CIAV in consultation with the Central American Governments and institutions, or persons concerned.

CHAPTER II

Assistance for the Demobilization of All Persons Involved in Armed Action in the Countries of the Region, When Such Persons Voluntarily Request This Assistance

This chapter is aimed at assisting the demobilization of all persons involved in armed activities in the countries of the region when they voluntarily request such assistance. The demobilization of these persons should be done in a manner consistent with the procedures of Esquipulas II and domestic legislation, and relevant agencies of the country in question.

In order to guarantee such assistance, the CIAV may be officially invited by the Central American Governments.

CHAPTER III

Assistance for the Voluntary Demobilization of the Members of the FMLN

As established under the Guatemala Procedure and the Alajuela and Costa del Sol Declarations, and in order to help bring about a cessation of the armed operations suffered by the Republic of El Salvador, the Governments of Costa Rica, Guatemala, Honduras and Nicaragua reiterate their firm conviction for the need of an immediate and effective cessation of hostilities in that sister country. Consequently, they emphatically urge the Farabundo Marti National Liberation Front (FMLN) to carry out a constructive dialogue for the purpose of securing a just and lasting peace. The aforesaid Governments likewise urge the Government of El Salvador to agree to incorporate the members of the FMLN into the normal life of the country, with full guarantees and in the spirit of numeral 2 of the Guatemala Procedure.

The Government of El Salvador undertakes to ensure unrestricted respect for its commitments regarding national reconciliation and to continue strengthening the process of pluralist, participatory and representative democratization already under way whereby social justice and full respect for the human rights and fundamental freedoms of Salvadorans may be promoted.

Once the FMLN, as a result of dialogue, has agreed to abandon armed struggle and to join the democratic and institutional life of the country, steps will be taken for the demobilization of the members of the FMLN in accordance with procedure established in Chapter I of this Plan, as applicable and with such modifications as the case may require, and to facilitate their demobilization.

Notwithstanding the aforesaid, members of the FMLN who may at any time voluntarily decide to lay down their arms and join in the political and civic life of El Salvador, shall receive the benefits of this Plan. For this purpose, the Government of El Salvador will, through the CIAV and appropriate national and international bodies, call on such persons to avail themselves of the benefits herein established, using all suitable means available.

Agreed and signed in the port city of Tela, Republic of Honduras, on the seventh day of August nineteen hundred and eighty-nine.

Oscar Arias Sanchez
President, Republic of Costa Rica

Alfredo Cristiani Burkard
President, Republic of El Salvador

Vinicio Cerezo Arevalo
President, Republic of Guatemala

Jose Azcona Hoyo
President, Republic of Honduras

Daniel Ortega Saavedra
President, Republic of Nicaragua

NOTES

CHAPTER 2

1. For the political landscape of Nicaragua during this era, and the parochial, familial characteristics that continue to thrive in the underbrush of Sandinista dominance, see Shirley Christian, *Nicaragua: Revolution in the Family* (New York: Random House, 1985); and Arturo Cruz, Jr., *Memoirs of a Counter-Revolutionary: Life with the Contras, the Sandinistas, and the CIA* (New York: Doubleday & Co., 1989).
2. Interview with the author, Managua, Nicaragua, July 10, 1989.
3. Xabier Gorostiaga, former planning minister in the Sandinista government, interview with the author, Managua, Nicaragua, July 8, 1989.
4. Peter Passell, "For Sandinistas, Newest Enemy Is Economy," *New York Times*, July 6, 1989, A6.
5. Quoted in James Chace, "Dithering in Nicaragua," *New York Review of Books* (August 17, 1989): 46.
6. Interview with the author, Managua, Nicaragua, July 10, 1989.
7. Interview with the author, Managua, Nicaragua, July 11, 1989.
8. Ibid.
9. See Julia Preston's excellent articles on the Sandinista's ten years in power in *Washington Post*, July 2 and 3, 1989.
10. Ramírez justified the nondemocratic nature of the Sandinista party's internal workings as necessary to maintain national unity in the fight against the United States. Interview with the author, Casa de Gobierno, Managua, Nicaragua, July 10, 1989.
11. Interview with the author, archbishop's office, Managua, Nicaragua, September 27, 1986. The Nicaraguan bishops had called for negotiations to end the war between the Sandinistas and the contras since 1984.
12. Alejandro Bendaña, interview with the author, Managua, Nicaragua, July 10, 1989.
13. Gordon McCormick, Edward Gonzalez, Brian Jenkins, and David Ronfeldt, *Nicaraguan Security Policy: Trends and Projections* (Santa Monica: Rand Corporation, 1988), vi, 48. This analysis of Soviet efforts to upgrade Nicaraguan ports and airbases predicted the gradual development of Soviet-Nicaraguan military ties "likely to resemble current Soviet access arrangements with such states as Syria, Libya and Angola" (p. 50).
14. First estimate in Roy Gutman, *Banana Diplomacy: The Making of American Foreign Policy in Nicaragua, 1981–1987* (New York: Simon and Schuster, 1988), 304; second estimate in U.S. Department of State, *Nicaraguan Biographies: A Resource Book, Special Report No. 174* (January 1988), 6, 49.
15. The Coordinadora Democratica Nicaragüense (Democratic Coordinator), founded in 1981, included the Social Christian Nicaraguan party; the Liberal Constitutionalist party; the Social Democratic party; the Conservative party (Mario Rappaccioli and Miriam Arguello wings); COSEP (Superior Council of Private Enterprise); CUS (Council of United Trade Unions,

which was founded in 1972 and is an AFL-CIO affiliate); and CTN (Nicaraguan Workers' Congress). The Independent Liberal party (PLI) also planned activities with the Democratic Coordinator.

16. Gutman, *Banana Diplomacy*, 242–43.

17. After an agreement to postpone the elections until February 1985 was reached in Rio de Janeiro with Comandante Bayardo Arce Castaño, the Sandinistas said no postponement was possible (Gutman, *Banana Diplomacy*, 247–53).

18. The 1984 elections resulted in 61 seats for the Sandinistas; 14 for the Democratic Conservative party (PCD); 9 for the unwilling Independent Liberal party (PLI); 6 for the Popular Social Christian party (PPSC); 2 apiece for the Marxist-Leninist Popular Action Movement and the Communist and Socialist parties, all three of which were critical of the Sandinistas as insufficiently leftist.

19. The battles are described by some of the participants in their memoirs: Constantine C. Menges, *Inside the National Security Council: The True Story of the Making and Unmaking of Reagan's Foreign Policy* (New York: Simon and Schuster, 1988); Michael Ledeen, *Perilous Statecraft: An Insider's Account of the Iran-Contra Affair* (New York: Charles Scribner's Sons, 1988); and Frank McNeil, *War and Peace in Central America: Reality and Illusion* (New York: Charles Scribner's Sons, 1988).

20. Interviews with U.S. officials, U.S. embassy, San Salvador, El Salvador, 1986–1988. Other arms traffic went by air, including from Papalonal and Sandino airports in Nicaragua in the early 1980s, as well as through Honduras. In 1989, two Salvadorans were apprehended in Cedros, fifty kilometers north of the Honduran capital of Tegucigalpa with sixty AK-47s presumably destined for the FMLN.

21. For an in-depth picture of "Suicida," see Christopher Dickey, *With the Contras: A Reporter in the Wilds of Nicaragua* (New York: Simon and Schuster, 1985).

22. Arturo J. Cruz, *Nicaragua's Continuing Struggle* (New York: Freedom House, 1988).

23. Interview with the author, Tegucigalpa, Honduras, June 21, 1989.

24. Julia Preston, "Contra Leader Quits; U.S. Policy Seen at Issue," *Washington Post*, March 31, 1989, A27.

25. Gutman, *Banana Diplomacy*, 297.

CHAPTER 3

1. The United States had also made two attempts at direct negotiation with Nicaragua, even though the Reagan administration's focus was on the military rather than the diplomatic track. In 1981, Assistant Secretary of State for Latin America Thomas Enders tried to secure the Sandinistas' agreement not to export their revolution to neighboring countries. In 1984, U.S. and Nicaraguan diplomats held a series of meetings in Manzanillo, Mexico. In the first effort, the talks focused on U.S. security concerns. The Reagan administration was divided, however, over the desirability of carrying on any negotiations that would leave the regime in

power. In the 1984 talks, internal liberalization of Nicaragua was part of the U.S. agenda, but the Sandinistas were not inclined to negotiate on this subject.

2. Interview with the author, Tegucigalpa, Honduras, June 24, 1989.
3. Interviews with the author, Yamales, Honduras, June 25, 1989.
4. Interview with the author, Estado Mayor camp near Yamales, Honduras, June 24, 1989. Franklyn was the *nom de guerre* of Israel Galeano, who had been a farmer in the northern province of Jinotega before joining the contras in 1981.
5. Interview with the author, Yamales, Honduras, June 25, 1989.
6. Helen Dewar, "Arias Said to Favor Contra Aid Till February," *Washington Post,* August 30, 1989, A37.
7. Mark Uhlig, "Nicaraguans Register in Huge Numbers," *New York Times,* October 23, 1989, 3.
8. Interview with the author, Managua, Nicaragua, August 20, 1986.
9. Ibid.
10. The poll, conducted for *La Cronica* by the Manolo Morales Foundation, sampled opinion in all departmental (provincial) capitals and 63 of the country's 140 municipalities; 2,800 people were surveyed. Reported by Radio Catolica and reprinted in Foreign Broadcast Information Service, Latin American Daily Report (hereafter, FBIS-LAT) 89-080, April 27, 1989, 18.
11. Christopher Marquis and Martin McReynolds, "For Nicaraguan Voters, There's a Poll for Every Taste," *Miami Herald,* January 30, 1990, 1.
12. Interview with the author, FSLN campaign headquarters, Managua, Nicaragua, February 7, 1990.
13. Interview with the author, Foreign Ministry, Managua, Nicaragua, February 6, 1990.
14. Alexander Baryshev (deputy editor of *Latinskaya Amerika,* journal of the USSR Academy of Sciences), *Miami Herald,* March 11, 1990, op-ed page.
15. Telephone interview with the author, March 28, 1990.
16. Interview with the author, UNO headquarters, Managua, Nicaragua, February 28, 1990.

CHAPTER 4

1. For those U.S. critics who argue that the change in El Salvador has been all but imperceptible, and the cost—in lives and treasure—too high, a historical comparison may serve as a useful corrective. Although brutality, injustice, and inequality are certainly widespread in El Salvador today, when our own Civil War broke out in 1861 one of seven Americans was a slave; it would take a full century before blacks would gain full civil rights. Up to this point, 1.5 percent of El Salvador's population has died as a result of its civil war; the U.S. Civil War killed 2 percent of this country's population. There is no guarantee that El Salvador will become a bona fide democracy overnight: but, then again, no other country has done so in the past.

2. Max G. Manwaring and Courtney Prisk, eds., *El Salvador at War: An Oral History of the Conflict from the 1979 Insurrection to the Present* (Washington, D.C.: National Defense University Press, 1988), 43.
3. José Napoleón Duarte, *Duarte: My Story* (New York: G. P. Putnam, 1986), 134.
4. Both quotations in Robert S. Leiken and Barry Rubin, eds., *The Central American Crisis Reader* (New York: Summit Books, 1987), 392, 380.
5. See, in particular, Christopher Dickey, "The Truth about the Death Squads," *New Republic* (December 26, 1983): 16–21; and Raymond Bonner, *Weakness and Deceit: U.S. Policy and El Salvador* (New York: Times Books, 1984).
6. Manwaring and Prisk, *El Salvador at War*, 148.
7. Interview with the author, Estado Mayor, San Salvador, El Salvador, September 19, 1986.
8. Interview with the author, Casa Presidencial, San Salvador, El Salvador, September 16, 1986.
9. Interview with the author, September 19, 1986.
10. Interview with the author, San Salvador, El Salvador, September 16, 1986.
11. Remarks made at a meeting of journalists and academics, Columbia University, February 28, 1989. Walker also made this point on U.S. national television ("The McNeil–Lehrer Report") in the fall of 1988, shortly after becoming ambassador.
12. The Lawyers Committee for Human Rights, *Underwriting Injustice: AID and El Salvador's Judicial Reform Program* (April 1989), 44. This report describes the current status of many recent and earlier cases, as well as the state of the reform program.
13. Interview with the author, San Salvador, El Salvador, August 26, 1987. That no insurrectionary threat has arisen has also accounted for the relatively low level of abuses attributed to the Right.
14. Interview with the author, Council on Foreign Relations, New York City, March 16, 1988.
15. *Documento Final del Debate Nacional 1988*, La Arquidiócesis de San Salvador (San Salvador, El Salvador, September 1988), 99. The Jesuit University of Central America conducted the poll. 22.5 percent of respondents answered the FMLN, 17.7 percent said the FMLN *and* the military, and 10.8 percent said the military.
16. Interview with the author, ARENA executive campaign headquarters, San Salvador, El Salvador, September 30, 1988.
17. Ibid.
18. Salvadoran news broadcast (text printed in FBIS-LAT), July 26, 1989, 24.
19. Lindsey Gruson, "He's a Rightist (No Doubt About It)," *New York Times*, August 11, 1989, A4.
20. *El Diario de Hoy*, July 3, 1989, 21.
21. An article in NACLA, *Report on the Americas* (August 1989) warned activists in the United States that their expectations of an ARENA bloodbath were off the mark.
22. Interview with the author, CEL offices, San Salvador, El Salvador, June 27, 1989.
23. Ibid.

24. Interview with the author, September 30, 1988.
25. Ibid.
26. Interview with the author, Casa Presidencial, San Salvador, El Salvador, July 1, 1989.
27. Ibid.
28. Interview with the author, September 30, 1988.
29. U.S. Department of State, "El Salvador: The Battle for Democracy," November 1988.

CHAPTER 5

1. James LeMoyne, "El Salvador's Forgotten War," *Foreign Affairs* 68, no. 3 (Summer 1989): 114.
2. The FMLN has one of the most elaborate, well-defined structures of any guerrilla movement. Its diversity has also given rise to serious internal conflicts. Listed below are each army's top comandante; each army's representative(s) on the Political-Diplomatic Commission, which serves as the FMLN's liaison to the world; and each army's popular organization (of workers, teachers, peasants), which forms its popular base inside El Salvador. While the FMLN has developed ties with other mass organizations, the groups listed here are an integral part of the FMLN's structure.

    ERP (People's Revolutionary Army). The ERP is the largest army. Top Comandante: Joaquín Villalobos. CPD Representatives: Ana Guadalupe Martínez and Comandante Luisa (Mercedes del Carmen Letona). Washington office: Guadalupe González. Popular Organization: LP-28 (28 of September Popular Leagues).

    FPL (Popular Liberation Forces). The FPL is the second largest army. Top Comandante: Leonel González (Salvador Sánchez Ceren). CPD Representative: Salvador Samayoa. Popular Organization: BPR (Popular Revolutionary Bloc), which is the umbrella organization for FECCAS (campesinos), ANDES (teachers), UR-19 (Revolutionary University Students—July 19), and UTC (rural workers).

    FARN (Armed Forces of National Resistance). Top Comandante: Fermán Cienfuegos (Eduardo Sancho). CPD Representative: Rubén Rojas. Washington office: Salvador Sanabria. Popular Organization: FAPU (United Popular Action Front).

    FAL (Armed Forces of Liberation). Top Comandante: Shafik Handal. CPD Representative: Miguel Saenz. Popular Organization: National Democratic Union (UDN). This is the legal front for the outlawed Communist party, of which Handal is the secretary general.

    PRTC (Central American Revolutionary Workers' Party). The PRTC is the smallest of the five armies, with 400 troops. Top Comandante: Roberto Roca (Francisco Jovel). CPD Representatives: Mario López and Nidia Díaz (María Concepción de Valladares). Popular Organization: MLP (Popular Liberation Movement).

3. The primary components of the FDR are the MNR (National Revolutionary Movement), led by Guillermo Ungo, who ran for president in 1989; and the MPSC (Popular Social Christian Movement) led by Rubén Zamora.

Their representatives on the Political-Diplomatic Commission were the late Hector Oquelí (MNR) and Hector Silva (MPSC). Most members of the MNR and MPSC have returned to live in El Salvador. Ungo died in February 1991.

4. The FPL's current leader, Leonel González, aged forty-four, was formerly a rural grammar school teacher. In addition to its Communist party origins, the FPL has a strong Jesuit orientation; its CPD member, Salvador Samayoa, was a professor of philosophy at the Jesuit University of Central America before joining the 1979 junta government as education minister. FARN commander Fermán Cienfuegos, a forty-four-year-old former art history teacher from a middle-class professional family of San Salvador, cited the influence of liberation theology on his decision to become a guerrilla. "Ana María" (Melida Anaya Montes) came from the ANDES teachers movement, an FPL-affiliated group, before joining the armed struggle. Comandante Luisa of the ERP, now thirty-five years old, also organized teachers before joining the armed struggle at age nineteen. Villalobos's common-law wife, she directed the rebel "Radio Venceremos" inside El Salvador until late 1988.

5. The FARN-ERP split of 1975 was rooted in differences over strategy, namely, what FARN criticized as the ERP's "militaristic" tendency versus FARN's "political" objectives of incorporating the widest variety of groups in the armed struggle. In May 1975, the ERP executed the leader of this latter tendency, Roque Dalton García ("Julio"), for political deviance, although it accused the poet-revolutionary, who was sometimes compared to Che Guevara, of being a CIA agent. FMLN documents reprinted in Robert S. Leiken and Barry Rubin, eds., *The Central American Crisis Reader*, 354–70.

6. According to the widow of FARN leader Ernesto Jovel, Villalobos and Ana Guadalupe Martínez tried to assassinate Jovel in 1976, accusing him of being a renegade and a schismatic. In 1980, the ERP joined the rebel front, but this prompted FARN to leave the alliance. In September 1980, Jovel died in an airplane accident, after which FARN, led by Fermán Cienfuegos, rejoined the front. Jovel's wife said that there had been competition between her husband and Cienfuegos, who was in favor of the rebel groups' uniting. See "¿Por que Asesinaron Al Comandante Miguel Castellanos?" *Analisis*, Ano II (March–April 1989).

7. Kenneth Freed, "Bad Times for Salvador Coffee Growers," *Los Angeles Times*, February 21, 1989, 1, 17.

8. Douglas Farah, "Salvadoran Rebels See Wider War," *Washington Post*, February 26, 1989, A34.

9. Interview with the author, Estado Mayor, San Salvador, El Salvador, June 30, 1989.

10. A. J. Bacevich, James D. Hallums, Richard H. White, and Thomas F. Young, *American Military Policy in Small Wars: The Case of El Salvador* (New York: Pergamon-Brassey's, 1988), vi. Lieutenant Colonel Hallums served in 1983 as a U.S. trainer assigned to the Salvadoran army general staff.

11. Douglas Farah, "El Salvador's Mayors Quit in Droves," *Washington Post*, January 8, 1989, A27. This figure includes fifty who had died in the war. Most of the resignations of mayors have been in ERP zones; the FPL has

reportedly downplayed this tactic, preferring to win over adherents by organizing youths into baseball teams and other social activities.

12. Meeting with FMLN leaders at Cocoyóc, Mexico, July 23, 1989. See note 21 of this chapter for a full description of the meeting.

13. Interview with the author, office of CEL (Lempa River Hydroelectric Executive Commission), San Salvador, El Salvador, June 27, 1989.

14. A deserter from the Nicaraguan military, Sergio Alejandro Gutiérrez López, reportedly helped arrange shipments to the FMLN from the Nicaraguan port of Corinto to El Salvador. According to him, Nicaraguan Interior Ministry officials crewed the boat that shipped arms to FMLN. U.S. officials said Gutiérrez had been chief of Naval Intelligence at Corinto Naval Base. Former U.S. officials in El Salvador also said there were radio intercepts over the past three years of communications between arms-bearing ships and rebels in El Salvador. Other Nicaraguan deserters have said that the FMLN received M-16s from Vietnam via Cuba and Nicaragua. A high Defense Ministry aide who left Nicaragua, Roger Miranda Bengoechea, claimed that the Sandinistas were training Salvadorans. (James LeMoyne, "Salvador Rebels: Where Do They Get the Arms?" *New York Times,* November 24, 1988, 1.)

15. In interviews, the Salvadoran defense minister and U.S. officials emphasized that the find demonstrated the Soviet-bloc connection, because such large quantities were generally unavailable on the black market. Their intelligence showed that the arms and ammunition had come in trucks originating in Costa Rica and transiting Nicaragua. But the size of the cache also indicates that, wherever they come from, the FMLN is able to acquire significant quantities of arms and get them inside El Salvador without detection. Salvadoran officials also reported the capture in 1988 of Russian hand grenades, Chinese rocket-propelled grenades, Russian Dragonov sniper rifle scopes, and Hungarian pistols. Most recently, two Salvadorans were captured in July 1989 in Honduras smuggling sixty AK-47s, allegedly destined for the FMLN.

16. Interview with the author, Casa Presidencial, San Salvador, El Salvador, July 1, 1989. The United Nations Development Program offered a grant of $30 million to El Salvador for refugee resettlement, and the Duarte government had proposed a project, which the Cristiani government reviewed. It decided that it wanted the displaced to be settled in the west and south of the country, away from the conflict zones.

17. He defected from the FPL army in April 1985 and, with other former guerrillas, formed a think tank, the Center for the Study of the National Reality (CEREN), in El Salvador. He had recently given numerous interviews detailing his past. He joined the armed struggle in 1973 and went underground in 1977, receiving training in Cuba and Vietnam.

18. He had been the head of *Estudios Centroamericanos (ECA)* magazine of the Jesuit University of Central America in the 1950s and frequently published articles elaborating anticommunist and conservative doctrine.

19. Miguel Angel Salaverria, ambassador-designate to the United States, in an interview with the author, San Salvador, El Salvador, June 26, 1989.

20. Cienfuegos's admission of responsibility in the Chacon case was also inadvertent, and somewhat equivocal: asked if it was a mistake, the comandante

nodded, but then Samayoa looked quizzically at him and Cienfuegos said, "We have not officially acknowledged this" (meeting with FMLN leaders at Cocoyóc, Mexico, July 22, 1989; see note 21 in this chapter).

21. Meeting with FMLN leaders, July 22, 1989. The July 21–24 meeting, organized by the Washington-based International Center for Development Policy, was held at the Hacienda Cocoyóc, Mexico. The author attended. The FMLN delegation was composed of Samayoa, Cienfuegos, Mercedes del Carmen Letona, Dr. Miguel Saenz, Rubén Rojas, Guadalupe González, Francisco Altschul, and Salvador Sanabria. This discussion is recounted extensively because the published literature on FMLN tactics, and FMLN thinking about its tactics, is sparse. Assassination is a particularly controversial tactic, and as information about the FMLN's use of it has gradually come to light, the rebels' international image has suffered. The focus on this issue here is justified because it is a little-known aspect of the war. It is not my intent to minimize the violence of the Salvadoran Right, but there is an extensive literature on this subject, including ten years of reports by a variety of human rights groups and the writings of many reporters, among them those cited in Chapter 4, note 4.

22. Meeting with FMLN leaders, Cocoyóc, Mexico, July 22, 1989.

23. Interview with the author, Cocoyóc, Mexico, July 23, 1989.

24. Meeting with FMLN leaders, Cocoyóc, Mexico, July 22, 1989.

25. Ibid., July 24, 1989.

26. The proposed legislation was reprinted in *La Prensa Grafica*, July 2, 1989, 3, 29.

27. Interview with the author, New York City, May 5, 1989.

28. Comments made at a meeting at the Council on Foreign Relations and in an interview with the author, New York City, April 27, 1989.

29. Interview with the author, New York City, October 12, 1989.

30. Interview with the author, Cocoyóc, Mexico, July 23, 1989.

31. "Strategic Appraisal" was published in full in the April 1988 issue of *Analisis* (journal of the New University of San Salvador), and is quoted in James LeMoyne, "El Salvador's Forgotten War," 116.

32. The article appeared in the Salvadoran journal *ECA*, published by the Jesuit University. It argued for the necessity of the military struggle against the current system. An abridged version of the article appeared in *Foreign Policy*, no. 74 (Spring 1989), 103–22.

33. Interview with the author, New York City, May 5, 1989.

34. Marjorie Miller, "Rebels Start New Offensive: Diplomacy," *Los Angeles Times*, November 17, 1988, 1, 13.

35. Interviews with the author, New York City, May 5, and Cocoyóc, Mexico, July 23, 1989.

36. Interview with the author, Estado Mayor, San Salvador, El Salvador, June 30, 1989.

37. The article appeared in the August–September 1989 issue of *ECA*.

CHAPTER 6

1. The 1977 treaties provided for the immediate transfer of the Canal Zone to Panamanian sovereignty and the closing of the U.S.–run (military)

School of the Americas. The chief executive of canal operations, the administrator, was to be a Panamanian national beginning in January 1990. Until December 31, 1999, the canal operations were to be overseen by the Panama Canal Commission, with a U.S. citizen as chairman of its board of directors and with a U.S. majority among its members. The United States was to maintain jurisdiction over its military bases until 1999. The treaties allowed the possibility of further negotiations on some U.S. military base rights or on maintaining some other presence after that date. In any case, the United States was guaranteed the permanent right to use military force to defend the canal—unilaterally if necessary—from threats and the right to move freely from base to base until the year 2000.

2. The economy slowed in the 1980s, burdened by a foreign public debt of $3.97 billion, one of the largest per capita debts in the world.

3. The Torrijos government first helped send weapons to the Sandinistas, cementing a relationship that continues today; subsequently it reportedly began shipping weapons to the Salvadoran guerrillas, whose multimillion-dollar ransoms from kidnappings in the 1970s were parked in bank accounts in Panama.

4. See Frederick Kempe, *Divorcing the Dictator: America's Bungled Affair with Noreiga* (New York: G. P. Putnam's Sons, 1990).

5. The subcommittee's hearings were held on February 8–11, April 4–6, and July 12–14, 1988. The Senate Permanent Committee on Investigations also held hearings on January 28, 1988.

6. U.S. direct investment in Panama totaled $4.5 billion in 1986, the third largest U.S. investment in Latin America. Japan is Panama's largest foreign investor. Its investment of $8 billion in Panama is second only to its investment in the United States. Japan did not follow the U.S. lead in imposing sanctions.

7. Medellín cartel hit men shot former Colombian justice minister Enrique Parejo González, who had been sent to Hungary as ambassador, in January 1987.

8. William Scott Malone, "How Not to Depose a Dictator," *Washington Post Weekly*, May 1–7, 1989, 23. The CIA had given Herrera assistance in setting up a clandestine radio station in Panama, which was funded by the Panamanian escrow accounts.

9. Carla Anne Robbins, "Taking Aim at Noriega," *U.S. News and World Report*, May 1, 1989, 40–41.

10. ADOC emphasized that the vote was a referendum on Noriega more than a vote for these three candidates. Although *Arnulfistas* had been considered most numerous, church exit polls showed Arias Calderón with 37 percent of the vote and Ford with 20 percent; Endara trailed both of his running mates with 11 percent (Eva Loser, "The 1989 Panamanian Elections, Post Election Report," CSIS Latin American Election Study Series, May 18, 1989, 12).

11. Quoted in George C. Wilson, "Bush Turns to Gunboat Diplomacy," *Washington Post*, May 12, 1989, A27.

12. A number of Latin American leaders praised Bush for his measured remarks and his support for regional diplomacy. This was in contrast to their criticism of the Reagan administration for having undercut the

1987 negotiating efforts of Venezuelan Carlos Andrés Pérez and former Costa Rican President Daniel Oduber, among others, to secure Noriega's departure.

13. FBIS-LAT-89-095, May 18, 1989, 3. The resolution passed with 20 votes, 7 abstentions, and with only Nicaragua and Panama voting against it.

14. FBIS-LAT-89-144, July 21, 1989, 3.

15. In June 1989, the commission elected Robert Page, assistant secretary of defense for civil works, to take Gianelli's place.

16. Transcript of a press conference, *Washington Post*, May 12, 1989, A26.

17. Bernard Trainor, "Bush's Latin Gamble: Hoping Panamanian Armed Forces Will Oust Noriega," *New York Times*, May 17, 1989, A3.

18. According to one report, the rebels asked the number-two U.S. military official in Panama, Maj. Gen. Marc Cisneros, to promise not to extradite Noriega to the United States for trial. The request and the condition were relayed to Washington, but no answer arrived before the coup was put down (Frederick Kempe, "How the Inexperience of American Officials Helped Doom Coup," *Wall Street Journal*, October 6, 1989, 1, 4).

19. Ibid.

20. Lt. Gen. Brent Scowcroft, "This Week with David Brinkley," ABC News, October 8, 1989.

21. In May, a Defense Department official, Deputy Assistant Secretary Richard Brown, reported to Congress that there had been 1,200 violations of the canal treaties by Panama in the previous fifteen months, citing its harassment of U.S. military personnel and their dependents. The most serious incident took place on August 9, after two U.S. soldiers were detained by Panamanian police; the United States closed off access to Fort Amador, one of the military bases, and detained the Panamanian soldiers there who shared guard duty with U.S. soldiers. The base was surrounded by U.S. armored personnel carriers and other deployments were made elsewhere. The crisis was resolved with an exchange of detainees, as in other incidents, but the U.S. reaction was of unprecedented magnitude.

22. Admiral William J. Crowe, Jr., letter to the *New York Times*, October 16, 1989, in response to a *New York Times* op-ed essay by Elliott Abrams, October 5, 1989.

23. Richard Cheney, "Face the Nation," CBS News, October 8, 1989.

24. The legal justification for restricting access was to prevent Noriega's lawyers from charging that documents helpful to his defense had been destroyed.

25. Maj. Gen. Marc Cisneros expressed another opinion, only half in jest: "The documents are war booty. They're ours 'til we're done with them."

CHAPTER 7

1. Fiscal year aid for El Salvador is $260 million, the lowest level since 1982. Aid to Honduras dropped 35 percent to $107.2 million. Aid to Costa Rica fell 66 percent to $33.4 million. Aid to Nicaragua was cut back 47 percent to $161 million. And Panama received nothing, since its FY 1990 aid was intended as a two-year package.

2. Panama's new government increased health and education spending only slightly, despite the U.S. $420-million aid package. Between 35 and 62 percent of the population is illiterate in Nicaragua, El Salvador, Honduras, and Guatemala. Yet these countries spend an average of $6,000 a year on each soldier, and only $78 per person on education.

3. *Prensa Libre,* June 20, 1989, 2.

4. Interview with two Guatemalan officers in the army's public information office, Guatemala City, June 20, 1989.

5. In a February 1988 report, centrist legislator Oliverio García Rodas, vice president of the congressional human rights commission, confirms "the reduction of criminality that occurred during the government of Efraín Ríos Montt." One way this was achieved, García Rodas notes, was the requirement that police officers leave their weapons in the police barracks when they went off duty. Yet, "it is indisputable," he wrote, "that one of the major causes of violence in Guatemala, and of violations of human rights in Guatemala, was precisely the security forces of the government." Mimeograph report, given to the author during an interview with García Rodas, Guatemala City, June 20, 1989.

6. Interview with García Rodas, who showed the author statistics he had compiled for the congressional human rights commission.

7. *Mexico and Central America Report* (London: Latin American Newsletters Ltd.), August 17, 1989, 4.

8. Thus, it was no coincidence that the December military rebellion occurred on the same days as a protest march and strike organized by state-sector employees—also a repository of *Torrijista* sentiment.

9. A dangerous indication that this willingness was lacking surfaced in 1990. As incredible as it may seem after the ordeal both countries had just been through with Noriega, both U.S. and Panamanian officials failed to move against the head of the new Technical Judicial Police, the force designated to combat narcotics crimes, including trafficking. Officials had information that strongly suggested he was in the pay of traffickers. Yet, as of the end of 1990, no action had been taken to dismiss this nascent Noriega, who had in fact been deputy chief of Noriega's feared investigative police. The United States has provided $12 million to help fund a police academy and for programs to recruit and train an entirely new civilian security force—a laudable example of the kind of long-range effort that is needed—but more U.S. and Panamanian resources must be devoted to such tasks. The United States should help the Panamanian government monitor new recruits, and also remain alert to any threatening activity by former Noriega associates.

10. See Kempe, *Divorcing the Dictator,* especially chapters 2, 4, 5, 7, 11, 12, 13, and 17.

11. Interview with the author, June 23, 1990.

12. Don Oberdorfer, "Gorbachev Vows Halt of Arms to Managua," *Washington Post,* May 16, 1989, 1, 17.

13. When the Soviets sent helicopters to Nicaragua in December 1989, they agreed to recall the shipment after the Bush administration protested. Although the helicopters were later shipped, the Soviet Union had reached

a general agreement with the United States to refrain from exacerbating regional tensions.

14. John M. Goshko, "Baker Accuses Soviets of Abetting Salvadoran Strife," *Washington Post*, November 14, 1989, A32.
15. Interview with a U.S. State Department official, Washington, D.C., June 1989.
16. Thomas Friedman, "Baker Braves the Gantlet in the Moscow Parliament," *New York Times*, February 11, 1990, 20.
17. Also, in August 1990, a van entering Honduras from the Nicaraguan border was found to contain mortars, explosives, and plans for attacks on two Salvadoran military installations. And, in December, the Salvadoran rebels, after shooting down a Salvadoran army plane, acknowledged they had even more sophisticated antiaircraft missiles.
18. The Soviet Union has decided in principle to require payment in hard currency for its goods other than oil, beginning in 1991.
19. Interview with the author, Council on Foreign Relations, New York City.
20. It is possible that Castro might not accept a U.S. offer to talk about Central America without some concessions regarding bilateral relations or U.S. aid. But making such major concessions at this time would create a firestorm of controversy within the domestic Cuban American lobby. Nor are such steps warranted, given the broad range of objections the United States has to Castro's government. The proposal here is simply to try to gain the cooperation of all participants in finding a way out of the Salvadoran war, as occurred in Angola/Namibia. Cuba might well accept an offer to talk about Central America with no strings attached, since this would grant Cuba quasi-formal recognition as a main actor in the region.
21. The collapse of the international coffee-pricing agreement in 1989 further reduced projected revenues of the small Central American producers. While the U.S. government was blamed by many Central Americans for not lobbying more forcefully for an agreement, it was Brazil, the world's largest producer, that stood in the way of efforts to revive the accord.
22. Interview with the author, Department of State, January 22, 1990.

SELECTED BIBLIOGRAPHY

Acevedo, Carlos. "La Propuesta de paz mas viáble del FMLN." *Estudios Centroamericanos* 44 (January/February 1989): 53–78. (Bimonthly publication of the University of Central America José Simeon Cañas, San Salvador, El Salvador.)

Allman, T.D. *Unmanifest Destiny: Mayhem and Illusion in American Foreign Policy—From the Monroe Doctrine to Reagan's War in El Salvador.* New York: Dial Press, 1984.

Americas Watch. *Carnage Again: Preliminary Report on Violations of the Laws of War by Both Sides in the November 1989 Offensive in El Salvador.* New York: November 24, 1989.

———. *The Civilian Toll, 1986–1987.* Ninth Supplement to the Report on Human Rights in El Salvador. New York: August 30, 1987.

———. *Draining the Sea.* (On El Salvador.) New York: March 1985.

———. *Human Rights in Guatemala During President Cerezo's First Year.* New York: February 1987.

———. *Human Rights in Honduras: Central America's Sideshow.* New York: May 1987.

———. *Human Rights in Nicaragua, 1985–1986.* New York: March 1986.

———. *Human Rights in Nicaragua, August 1987–August 1988.* New York: August 1988.

———. *Human Rights in Panama.* New York: April 1988.

———. *Nightmare Revisited 1987–88.* Tenth Supplement to the Report on Human Rights in El Salvador. New York: September 1988.

———. *Settling Into Routine: Human Rights Abuses in Duarte's Second Year.* New York: May 1986.

———. *Violations of the Laws of War by Both Sides in Nicaragua 1981–1985.* New York: March 1985.

Americas Watch Committee and the American Civil Liberties Union. *As Bad as Ever: A Report on Human Rights in El Salvador.* New York: January 31, 1984.

Americas Watch and Lawyers Committee on Human Rights. *Free Fire: A Report on Human Rights in El Salvador.* New York: August 1984.

Armstrong, Robert and Janet Shenk. *El Salvador: The Face of Revolution.* Boston: South End Press, 1982.

Bacevich, A.J.; J.D. Hallums; R.H. White; and T.F. Young. *American Military Policy in Small Wars: The Case of El Salvador.* Special Report 1988. A Publication of the Institute for Foreign Policy Analysis. New York: Pergamon-Brassey's, 1988.

Baloyra, Enrique. *El Salvador in Transition.* Chapel Hill, N.C.: University of North Carolina Press, 1982.

Berryman, Phillip. *Inside Central America.* New York: Pantheon, 1985.

Blachman, Morris J.; William M. LeoGrande; and Kenneth E. Sharpe; eds. *Confronting Revolution: Security Through Diplomacy in Central America.* New York: Pantheon Books, 1986.

Bonner, Raymond. *Weakness and Deceit: U.S. Policy and El Salvador.* New York: Times Books, 1984.

Bruck, Connie. "How Noriega Got Away." *The American Lawyer* (July/August 1988): 34–42.

Cabezas, Omar. *Fire from the Mountain.* New York: Crown Publishers, 1985.

Cayetano Carpio, Salvador. *Secuestro Capucha.* San José, Costa Rica: EDUCA, 1979.

Centro de Documentación de Honduras. "Militarismo en Honduras: El Reinado de Gustavo Alvarez, 1982–84." *Serie: Cronologias,* no. 2. Tegucigalpa, Honduras: August 1985.

Chace, James. "Dithering in Nicaragua." *The New York Review of Books,* August 17, 1989, pp. 46–51.

———. *Endless War: How We Got Involved in Central America and What Can Be Done.* New York: Vintage Books, 1984.

———. "Nicaragua: The End of the Affair?" *The New York Review of Books,* October 8, 1987, pp. 24–34.

Chamorro Cardenal, Jaime. *La Prensa: The Republic of Paper.* New York: Freedom House, 1988.

Christian, Shirley. *Nicaragua: Revolution in the Family.* New York: Random House, 1985.

Committee of Sante Fe. *Sante Fe II: A Strategy for Latin America in the Nineties.* Washington, D.C.: August 13, 1988.

Council of Freely-Elected Heads of Government. *Observing Nicaragua's Elections, 1989–1990.* Special Report No. 1. Atlanta, Georgia: Carter Center of Emory University, 1990.

Cruz, Arturo J. *Nicaragua's Continuing Struggle.* New York: Freedom House, 1988.

Cruz, Arturo, Jr. *Memoirs of a Counter-Revolutionary: Life with the Contras, the Sandinistas, and the CIA.* New York: Doubleday & Co., 1989.

Dickey, Christopher. *With the Contras: A Reporter in the Wilds of Nicaragua.* New York: Simon and Schuster, 1985.

―――. "The Truth About the Death Squads." *The New Republic,* December 26, 1983, pp. 16–21.

Diederich, Bernard. *Somoza and the Legacy of the U.S. Involvement in Central America.* New York: Dutton, 1981.

Dinges, John. *Our Man in Panama: How General Noriega Used the United States—And Made Millions in Drugs and Arms.* New York: Random House, 1990.

Duarte, José Napoleón with Diana Page. *Duarte: My Story.* New York: G.P. Putnam's Sons, 1986.

Edelman, Marc and Joanne Kenen, eds. *The Costa Rica Reader.* New York: Grove Weidenfeld, 1989.

Ellacuría, Ignacio. "Una nueva fase en el proceso salvadoreño." *Estudios Centroamericanos* (ECA) 44 (March/April 1989). (Journal of the cultural extension of the University of Central America José Simeon Cañas.)

Estudios Centroamericanos (ECA). Bimonthly journal of the University of Central America José Simeon Cañas, San Salvador; El Salvador. Publishes in-depth analyses as well as all important documents and statistics of the government, political parties, and FMLN.

Fagan, Richard. *Forging Peace: The Challenge of Central America.* New York: Basil Blackwell and Policy Alternatives for the Caribbean and Central America, 1987.

Falcoff, Mark and Robert Royal, eds. *Crisis and Opportunity: U.S. Policy in Central America and the Caribbean.* Washington, D.C.: Ethics and Public Policy Center, 1984.

Fernández, Guido. *El Desafío de la Paz en CentroAmerica.* San José, Costa Rica: Editorial Costa Rica, 1989.

Figueres, José; D. Oduber; R. Carazo; and Javier Solís. "Special Report on Costa Rica: Reflections on U.S. Policy." *World Policy Journal* 3, no. 2 (Spring 1986): 301–30.

Fontaine, Roger. *Panama: After Noriega.* Washington, D.C.: Council for Inter-American Security, 1990.

Fried, Jonathan L.; M.E. Gettleman; D.T. Levenson; and N. Peckenham; eds. *Guatemala in Rebellion: Unfinished History.* New York: Grove Press, 1983.

Galvin, Gen. John R. "Challenge & Response: On the Southern Flank Three Decades Later." *Military Review* (August 1986): 5–14.

Gettleman, Marvin E.; P. Lacefield; L. Menashe; D. Mermelstein; R. Radosh; eds. *El Salvador: Central America in the New Cold War.* New York: Grove Press, 1981.

Gilbert, Dennis. *Sandinistas: The Party and the Revolution.* New York: Basil Blackwell, 1988.

Gorostiaga, Xabier, ed. "Informe Especial: La Disputa por el poder." *Pensamiento Propio* 7, no. 67 (January/February 1990): 14–27. (Monthly journal published by the Coordinadora Regional de Investigaciónes Económicas y Sociales, Managua, Nicaragua.)

Greene, Graham. *Getting to Know the General: The Story of an Involvement.* London: Lester & Orpen Dennys, 1984.

Gutman, Roy. *Banana Diplomacy: The Making of American Policy in Nicaragua, 1981–1987.* New York: Simon and Schuster, 1988.

Immerman, Richard H. *The CIA in Guatemala: The Foreign Policy of Intervention.* Austin: University of Texas, 1982.

International Commission for Central American Recovery and Development. *Poverty, Conflict, and Hope: A Turning Point in Central America.* Durham, N.C.: Duke University Press, 1989.

Jorden, William J. *Panama Odyssey.* Austin: University of Texas, 1984.

Kagan, Robert. "Losing in Latin America." *Commentary* 86, no. 5 (November 1988): 45–51.

Kempe, Frederick. *Divorcing the Dictator: America's Bungled Affair with Noriega.* New York: G.P. Putnam's Sons, 1990.

Kinzer, Stephen. *Blood of Brothers: Life and War in Nicaragua.* New York: G.P. Putnam's Sons, 1991.

Kissinger, Henry et al. *Report of the National Bipartisan Commission on Central America.* Washington, D.C.: Government Printing Office, 1984.

Kornbluh, Peter. *Nicaragua: The Price of Intervention*. Washington, D.C.: Institute for Policy Studies, 1987.

Koster, R.M. and Guillermo Sánchez. *In the Time of Tyrants, Panama: 1968–1990*. New York: W.W. Norton & Co., 1990.

Krauss, Clifford. *Inside Central America: Its People, Politics, and History*. New York: Summit Books, 1991.

Krauthammer, Charles. "The Poverty of Realism." *The New Republic*, February 17, 1986, pp. 14–22.

———. "Morality and the Reagan Doctrine." *The New Republic*, September 8, 1986, pp. 17–24.

LaFeber, Walter. *Inevitable Revolutions: The United States in Central America*. New York: W.W. Norton & Co., 1984.

Lake, Anthony. *Somoza Falling*. Boston: Houghton Mifflin Co., 1989.

Lawyers Committee for Human Rights. *From the Ashes: A Report on Justice in El Salvador*. New York: 1987.

———. *Underwriting Injustice: AID and El Salvador's Judicial Reform Program*. New York: April 1989.

Ledeen, Michael A. *Perilous Statecraft: An Insider's Account of the Iran-Contra Affair*. New York: Charles Scribner's Sons, 1988.

Leiken, Robert S. "Nicaragua's Untold Stories." *The New Republic*, October 8, 1984, pp. 16–23.

———. "The Nicaraguan Tangle." *The New York Review of Books*, December 5, 1985, pp. 55–64.

———. "The Battle for Nicaragua." *The New York Review of Books*, March 13, 1986, pp. 3–52.

———, ed. *Central America: Anatomy of Conflict*. New York: Pergamon, 1984.

Leiken, Robert S. and Barry Rubin, eds. *The Central American Crisis Reader*. New York: Summit Books, 1987.

LeMoyne, James. "El Salvador's Forgotten War." *Foreign Affairs* 68, no. 3 (Summer 1989): 105–25.

Lernoux, Penny. *Cry of the People*. New York: Doubleday & Co., 1980.

McCormick, Gordon; E. Gonzalez; B. Jenkins; and D. Ronfeldt. *Nicaraguan Security Policy: Trends and Projections*. Santa Monica, Ca.: Rand National Defense Research Institute, January 1988.

McNeil, Frank. *War and Peace in Central America: Reality and Illusion.* New York: Charles Scribner's Sons, 1988.

Manwaring, Max G. and Courtney Prisk, eds. *El Salvador at War: An Oral History of the Conflict from the 1979 Insurrection to the Present.* Washington, D.C.: National Defense University Press, 1988.

————. "A Need for Strategic Perspective: Insights from El Salvador." Washington, D.C.: Booz Allen & Hamilton Inc., March 1989. (Unpublished.)

Massing, Michael. "Who are the Sandinistas?" *The New York Review of Books,* May 12, 1988, pp. 51–59.

Menchú, Rigoberta. *I, Rigoberta Menchú: An Indian Woman in Guatemala.* New York: Verso Press, 1984.

Menges, Constantine C. *Inside the National Security Council: The True Story of the Making and Unmaking of Reagan's Foreign Policy.* New York: Simon and Schuster, 1988.

Miles, Sara and Bob Ostertag. "D'Aubuisson's New Arena." *NACLA Report on the Americas* 23, no. 2 (July 1989): 14–39. (Bimonthly publication of the North American Congress on Latin America, New York.)

Miles, Sara; B. Ostertag; L. Cabral; and F. Jovel. "The NACLA Report: FMLN New Thinking." *NACLA Report on the Americas* 23, no. 3 (September 1989): 15–38.

Millett, Richard. "Looking Beyond Noriega." *Foreign Policy,* no. 71 (Summer 1988): 46–63.

Muravchik, Joshua. *News Coverage of the Sandinista Revolution.* Washington, D.C.: American Enterprise Institute for Public Policy Research, 1988.

Nicaraguan Resistance Educational Foundation. *White Paper on Breakdown of Negotiations.* Washington, D.C.: July 1988.

Nolan, David. *FSLN: The Ideology of the Sandinistas and the Nicaraguan Revolution.* Coral Gables, Florida: Institute of Interamerican Studies, University of Miami, 1984.

Pastor, Robert A. *Condemned to Repetition: The United States and Nicaragua.* Princeton, N.J.: Princeton University Press, 1987.

Preston, Julia. "The Battle for San Salvador." *The New York Review of Books,* February 1, 1990, pp. 6–12.

————. "What Duarte Won." *The New York Review of Books,* August 15, 1985, pp. 30–35.

Purcell, Susan Kaufman. "Demystifying Contadora." *Foreign Affairs* 64, no. 1 (Fall 1985): 74–95.

Ramírez, Sergio. *El Alba de Oro: La Historia Viva de Nicaragua.* Mexico: Siglo XXI, 1983.

————. *Las Armas del Futuro.* Managua: Editorial Nueva Nicaragua, 1987.

Radu, Michael and Vladimir Tismaneanu. *Latin American Revolutionaries: Groups, Goals, Methods.* New York: Pergamon-Brassey's, 1990.

Reding, Andrew. "Special Report on Costa Rica: Democratic Model in Jeopardy." *World Policy Journal* 3, no. 2 (Spring 1986): 331–45.

Robinson, Linda. *Congress and U.S. Policy Toward Nicaragua in 1987.* CRS Report for Congress. Washington, D.C.: Congressional Research Service, Library of Congress, March 2, 1989.

Ropp, Steve C. *Panamanian Politics: From Guarded Nation to National Guard.* New York: Praeger Publishers, 1982.

Sánchez Borbón, Guillermo. "Panama Fallen Among Thieves." *Harper's Magazine,* December 1987, pp. 57–67.

Sanders, Sol W. *The Costa Rican Laboratory.* A Twentieth Century Fund Paper. New York: Priority Press Publications, 1986.

Schlesinger, Stephen and Stephen Kinzer. *Bitter Fruit: The Untold Story of the American Coup in Guatemala.* New York: Doubleday & Co., 1982.

Servicio Informativo Centroamericano. Unidad de Información. Proyecto CSUCAPAX. San José, Costa Rica. (Weekly fax information service of Costa Rica's Central America University.)

Sheehan, Edward R.F. *Agony in the Garden: A Stranger in Central America.* Boston: Houghton Mifflin Co., 1989.

Tinoco, Víctor Hugo. *Conflicto y Paz: El Proceso Negociador Centroamericano.* Mexico City: Editorial Mestiza, 1989.

United States. Department of State. *"Revolution Beyond our Borders": Sandinista Intervention in Central America.* Special Report No. 132. Washington, D.C.: 1985.

United States. Foreign Broadcast Information Service. *Daily Report: Latin America.* Various issues. (U.S. government publication that compiles information obtained from foreign radio and television broadcasts, news agency transmissions, newspapers, books, and periodicals.)

U.S. Congress. Arms Control and Foreign Policy Caucus. *1987 Briefing Book on Central America: A Reference Guide on Issues Before the 100th*

214 □ INTERVENTION OR NEGLECT

Congress and Political, Military and Economic Data of the Region. 100th Cong. 1st sess. 1987.

U.S. Congress. House. *Interim Report of the Speaker's Task Force on El Salvador.* April 30, 1990. (Mimeo.)

U.S. Congress. House. Committee on Foreign Affairs. Subcommittee on Western Hemisphere Affairs. *Recent Events Concerning the Arias Peace Proposal.* Hearing and markup. 100th Cong. 1st sess. On H. Con. Res. 146, July 9, 15, 28, 1987.

———. *U.S. Policy Options with Respect to Nicaragua and Aid to the Contras.* Hearing, 100th Cong. 1st sess. January 28 and February 5, 1987.

U.S. Congress. House Select Committee to Investigate Covert Arms Transactions with Iran and Senate Select Committee on Secret Military Assistance to Iran and the Nicaraguan Opposition. *Report of the Congressional Committees Investigating the Iran-Contra Affair, with Supplemental, Minority, and Additional Views.* H. Rept. 100–433, S. Rept. 100–216. 100th. Cong. 1st sess. 1987.

Vaky, Viron P. "Positive Containment in Nicaragua." *Foreign Policy,* no. 68 (Fall 1987): 42–58.

Valenta, Jiri and Esperanza Durán, eds. *Conflict in Nicaragua: A Multidimensional Perspective.* Boston: Allen and Unwin, 1987.

Villalobos, Joaquín. "A Democratic Revolution for El Salvador." *Foreign Policy,* no. 74 (Spring 1989): 103–22.

———. "Perspectives de victoria y proyecto revolucionario." *Estudios Centroamericanos* 44 (January/February 1989): 11–52.

Wiarda, Howard J., ed. *Rift and Revolution: The Central America Imbroglio.* Washington, D.C.: American Enterprise Institute for Public Policy Research, 1984.

Walker, Thomas W. *Nicaragua: The Land of Sandino.* Second Edition. Boulder, Co.: Westview Press, 1986.

———, ed. *Reagan Versus the Sandinistas: The Undeclared War on Nicaragua.* Boulder, Co.: Westview Press, 1987.

Woodward, Bob. *Veil: The Secret Wars of the CIA, 1981–1987.* New York: Pocket Books, 1988.

INDEX

ABOUT THE AUTHOR

Linda Robinson has been the Latin American correspondent for *U.S. News & World Report* since December 1989. Her articles on Central America and Panama have appeared in *Foreign Affairs,* where she was associate editor and senior editor from 1983 to 1989, as well in the *New York Times, Newsday, Los Angeles Times, Dallas Times Herald, Commonweal, Freedom at Issue, Dialogue,* and the Congressional Research Service. Ms. Robinson has also appeared on CNN, the McLoughlin Show, and other radio and television shows to discuss Latin American events and issues.

The Council on Foreign Relations publishes authoritative and timely books on international affairs and American foreign policy. Designed for the interested citizen and specialist alike, the Council's rich assortment of studies covers topics ranging from economics to regional conflict to East-West relations. If you would like more information, please write:

Council on Foreign Relations Press
58 East 68th Street
New York, NY 10021
Telephone: (212) 734-0400
Fax: (212) 861-1789 or 861-1849

5023